The Structure of
School Improvement

Bruce R. Joyce
Richard H. Hersh
Michael McKibbin

Longman
New York & London

DEDICATION

to P.K. and Seamus
Bruce Joyce

to Alison
Richard Hersh

to Carl, Dorothy, and Tana
Michael McKibbin

The Structure of School Improvement

Longman Inc., 95 Church Street, White Plains, N.Y. 10601
Associated companies, branches, and representatives
throughout the world.

Developmental Editor: Lane Akers
Editorial and Design Supervisor: Frances Althaus
Production Supervisor: Ferne Kawahara
Manufacturing Supervisor: Marion Hess
Composition: Jay's Publisher's Services

Library of Congress Cataloging in Publication Data

Joyce, Bruce R.
  The structure of school improvement

  Bibliography: p.
  1. Educational innovations. 2. Curriculum planning.
3. Teachers—Selection and appointment. 4. Educational
technology. I. McKibbin, Michael. II. Title.
LB1027.J647 1983   371   82-17931
ISBN 0-582-28092-3

Manufactured in the United States of America
Printing: 9 8 7 6 5 4 3   Year: 91 90 89 88 87 86

Contents

The improvement of schools takes place in a social context that both impels the improvement of education and complicates the process. We open with the current theoretical and empirical bases for establishing a process of school improvement as a part of the regular business of educational life. Our strategy depends on the development of an organization that we will call the Responsible Parties to scrutinize the health of each school and oversee its improvement. The Responsible Parties examine the program of the school and make decisions about how to refine it so as to make it more effective, renovate particular curriculum areas, and, eventually, redesign the entire educational program.

Deals with the social forces that promote improvement and retard it. Calls for the establishment of a school committee to oversee the health of the schools and to make the continuous minor improvements that get the educational process under control, build strong staff development programs that enable teachers to implement new curricular and instructional processes, and make major curricular and instructional changes when those are deemed necessary.

A brief case study of a school. This case will be analyzed throughout the next several chapters as we discuss the nature of effective schools, the history of school improvement, and the means of establishing school improvement as a normal part of educational life.

Stage Two: Renovation. Curriculum areas are systematically analyzed and steps taken to strengthen them. Staff development is embedded into the operation of the school. This stage establishes the school improvement process as routine.

Stage Three: Redesign. Changes in the society and the development of educational technologies are considered by the Responsible Parties as they reflect on the overall mission of the school and the development of educational designs for the future.

We analyze the tasks involved in making each one of these stages come to pass.

PART III   STAGE ONE. REFINING THE SCHOOL

In this stage a school improvement committee is established, the health of the school is scrutinized, using information about effective teaching in schools, and plans are made and carried out to refine the program.

7   The Social Dimension of Quality Education

What is taught and how it is taught are critical to the success of schools, but many of the qualities that make a difference reside in the social climate of the school as a whole. What has sometimes been called the "hidden curriculum" is really a major part of the educational experience of children. The social climate of the Cameo School is analyzed in terms of the social dimensions that lead to effective education.

8   First Steps in Instructional Improvement

The Responsible Parties analyze the educational program of another school and take steps to improve the basic skills areas of reading and arithmetic. They select and implement a curriculum that will increase the engagement of the students in activities appropriate to their ability and achievement levels and make provisions for individual differences in learning style. The process of school improvement is beginning to be established and through a scenario, we visit a school that is passing from Stage One to Stage Two.

PART IV   STAGE TWO. RENOVATING THE SCHOOL

Staff development is established, the faculty is built into a problem-solving unit, the curriculum areas are systematically studied and improved.

9   Effective Staff Training for School Improvement

Research on training has given us principles for operating effective programs that enable teachers to transfer new content and skills into their teaching. We analyze this research and present a paradigm for organizing effective staff development.

The growth states of teachers are critical to the education of children. A great deal of energy devoted to staff development needs to be directed toward ways of helping teachers maintain a lively state of growth and weld the faculty into a problem-solving unit.

The Responsible Parties examine curriculum areas and make decisions to improve them: Scenarios.

Our purpose is to enable schools to become congenial settings for sensible initiatives from within and without. A major national initiative, popularly called "mainstreaming," provides resources to schools to enable students with special needs to be educated under the least restrictive conditions possible. We present case studies of several schools as they struggle to respond. The cases illustrate the problems that occur when an initiative arrives in schools where the process of improvement is not well established.

Once the process of school improvement has been established and the school meets basic effectiveness criteria and can improve its curriculum areas at will, the Responsible Parties are ready to examine the missions and means of the school, consider the possibilities in current technology and examine social change. A number of very powerful options are available which involve changes more radical than specific improvements in the social system and the curriculum areas.

Scenarios are presented of schools where teachers and resources are organized to make maximum use of the teacher and provide students with the most contemporary learning technologies. We examine the social climate necessary to weld students, teachers, and resources and to generate a meaningful personal education using the best in our technical options.

Foreword

The Structure of School Improvement comes at a propitious time. Change is in the air. No single event galvanizes us into school reform as did the launching of Sputnik in 1957. But the conditions are similarly ripe. We are reconsidering the role of schools in advancing high technology, improving the economy, and helping us understand the rapidly changing global circumstances of which the United States is an interdependent part.

Therein lies danger as well as opportunity. In the 1960s, too, we came to believe that education in schools could and would solve all our problems: urban decay, joblessness, violence, and even war among nations. Disillusionment quickly followed the Elementary and Secondary Education Act of 1965, which brought the federal government into unprecedented direct participation in the reforms thought needed. It was widely believed that new ideas and money could accomplish what was envisioned. Few of the innovations proposed found their way through school and classroom doors, however.

The postmortem of that exciting but less than satisfactory period provides us with useful lessons to guide a fresh round of intensive efforts to make schools more effective. Those analyses combine with studies of institutional change in fields such as urban planning, architecture, the health sciences, management, social work, and education to create a substantial literature on the subject of school improvement. The trouble is that most of it is a well-kept secret and scarcely known by educators and improvement-minded legislators and citizens. Recent findings on the nature of effective schools are, however, becoming much better known.

The prevailing mode of seeking to effect change has been and is to legislate and mandate. We tend to be impatient with notions about involving those to be affected, dealing with schools as cultures and ecologies, and all those processes of identifying problems, planning, discussing alternatives and the like recommended by serious students of individual, group, and institutional change. Let's get on with it, we say.

ix

If effective schools have good principals, then legislate requirements for good principals. Are we doomed always to repeat the mistakes of the past?

We are entering, I am convinced, another era of markedly raised expectations for schools (this time, perhaps, with more realistic expectations regarding what schools can and cannot accomplish). We have available a backlog of useful ideas regarding the substance of improvement and a similarly useful set of concepts about the processes of implementation. But prevailing models and principles of improvement are outworn; they belong to a bygone era. It is in addressing the gap between the present condition of schools and what we could and should have that *The Structure of School Improvement* promises to make a significant contribution.

There are books, articles, and case studies on effective schools. Similarly, there are books, articles, and case studies on the dynamics of planned change. There are scarcely any that succeed in addressing both substance and process simultaneously. *The Structure of School Improvement* comes as close as any book I know.

Perhaps the book's most useful contribution is that it establishes early and reiterates frequently a fundamental, unifying concept: school improvement occurs when the process is established as part of the regular business of educational life. This principle is worlds apart from prevailing notions. It means, for example, that instead of seeking to install innovations, a school develops the capability to innovate. In effect, it becomes self-renewing. Joyce and his colleagues refer to this condition as *homeostasis of improvement*.

As the authors say several times, neither their conception of the process to be established nor any of the alternative practices proposed is new. They cite a long list of published works to which they give credit. Their primary contribution is one of synthesis. But it goes beyond synthesis and comes close—perhaps as close as is desirable—to providing a technology of change.

Their book is in the progressive, humanistic tradition, although perhaps centrist with respect to the soft/tender–hard/tough dichotomy formulated at the turn of the century by William James. The practical problem with this tradition is its near-avoidance of a procedural technology. William Heard Kilpatrick enthralled a Saturday-morning audience of 600 teachers with images of children inquiring into phenomena but on Monday morning they behaved in the classroom very much as they had the week before. The problem of the inquiry-learning Kilpatrick was proposing is that there is no *one* way; indeed, the idea of *the* way is definitionally and philosophically contradictory to the message conveyed.

Joyce and his colleagues remind us that there is no one best model either of the condition they have in mind or for achieving it. The steps they propose are appropriately broad, comprehensively encompassing many elements simultaneously and spreading over several years of concerted effort. Yet, within this broad framework, they cite enough examples of specific steps that can be taken to remove some of the inhibitions to the improvement process. The juxtaposition of the conventional school we recognize instantly with others that we have the power to create is a particularly useful device. Similarly, the authors avoid formulas for school improvement and precisely ordered logistics by consistently invoking the larger context and reminding us that there are myriad ways of travelling if the guiding mission is not lost to view.

Two decades have slipped quickly by since I wrote the foreword to Bruce Joyce's *Alternative Models of Elementary Education*. In that book, I first encountered his concept of Responsible Parties. The idea of establishing a reasonably representative group of persons who would give attention to the long-term mission of a school and continuously review its progress intrigued me then and intrigues me now. Establishment of such a group is the cornerstone of *The Structure of School Improvement*.

The fact that so little progress has been made in constituting groups of Responsible Parties as an integral part of schooling reminds me forcefully of the continued bureacratic resiliency of our formal educational system. Centralized control intensifies while it becomes increasingly clear that parents in particular want important decisions for their schools to be made close at hand—by persons who can be both reached and held responsible. The resulting tension is not in the best interests of school improvement.

Bruce Joyce and his associates say relatively little about the larger structure of schooling, although they say a good deal about the social context of change. The structure they address is primarily that of the single school. What they propose for the school requires a loosening of state and district restraints, accompanied simultaneously by decentralization of much decision-making authority to Responsible Parties at local schools. The assumed shift does not remove the need for policies to guide local action but it does call for considerable rethinking of the decisions most appropriately assumed at each of the several levels of authority and responsibility. This is the kind of thinking and planning we have been ill-disposed to do. However, unless policies and practices are aligned with rhetoric regarding the individual school as the key unit for change, I see little prospect for more than marginal improvement in the schools we have.

The beauty of the structure for school improvement proposed in what follows is that it applies both to a loosened-up, decentralized system of schooling and to schools of choice cut loose from a system. The book provides guidance, then, for those who wish to create responsive, satisfying schools and especially for Responsible Parties seeking to lead the way.

John I. Goodlad

Acknowledgments

Pete Mesa and Roger Pankratz helped greatly, especially as we tried to harden the structure and figure out just what we were trying to say.

Bob Bush was particularly generous and wise as we tried to think out the problem of just what to include about the considerable problem of staff development and how to approach the area.

Literally hundreds of teachers and school administrators (2500 in 1981 alone) have helped us by filling out the questionnaires we and Bob Bush mailed to them and by letting us interview them (300 or so in 1981–82).

René Clift generously helped us with chores and ideas in the final stage of manuscript preparation.

Elinore Brown did all the really hard work. She managed to read our handwriting and turn it into typescript, cheerfully changed it, and changed it, and must be awfully glad that these are the last words—until next time.

Lane Akers of Longman Inc. provided serious reflection and shared the intellectual burden of thinking out the best structure to hold the mass of complex material in a form that readers could absorb with profit.

Bruce Joyce
Richard Hersh
Michael McKibbin

...the training of men by any occupation...requires the understanding of (a) culture as a superstructure which can maintain "remnants" of the past alive in the substructure undergoing revolutionary transformation and (b) the occupation itself as an instrument for the transformation of culture.

Paolo Freire
Pedagogy of the Oppressed

The guiding question is no longer whether the innovation produced effects but why it was not installed.

John I. Goodlad
The Dynamics of Educational Change

Nowadays much of the preoccupation with creativity seems to stem not so much from interest in artistic and scientific originality as from anxiety about preserving any human impulse toward spontaneity and initiative.

Jules Henry
Education and Culture

Part I
SETTING THE STAGE

The improvement of schools takes place in a social context that both impels innovation and complicates the process. We open with the current theoretical and empirical bases for establishing a process of school improvement as a part of the regular business of educational life. Our strategy depends on the development of an organization that we will call the Responsible Parties to scrutinize the health of each school and oversee its improvement. The Responsible Parties examine the program of the school and make decisions about how to refine it to make it more effective, renovate particular curriculum areas, and eventually, redesign the entire educational program.

1

School Improvement
as a Way of Life

Richly connected to its social milieu, tightly clasped by tradition and yet the medium of modern ideas and artifacts, the school floats paradoxically in its ocean of social forces. It is a cradle of social stability and the harbinger of cultural change. Throughout history its critics have found it both too backward and too advanced. It falls behind the times and fails to keep up in simultaneous cadence.

Its missions are elusive. Basic education is prized but so are creativity, problem solving, academic excellence, and vocational skills, sometimes by the same people, sometimes not. Liberals and conservatives alike seek to make the school the instrument of social policy. It is the sword of the militant and the warm bosom of the humanist. Its students are varied. Talents and handicaps mingle, sometimes in the same minds and bodies.

The inner city and rural hinterland make their claims on creaky old schoolhouses while shiny surburban schools grope for a coherent mission. Powerful self-concepts march through the front door of the school while timid souls slip in by the back stairs. Cultural differences are mixed together, with problems of identity and adaptation surfacing chaotically to be dealt with.

Technologies strengthen the school's potential and threaten to replace it. Its personnel receive very little training but are asked to manage one of the most complex professional tasks in our society. They have little status but awesome responsibility both for individual children and for the health of the society as a whole.

Because education exerts great influence on the young, society places great constraints on its schools so that they will reflect the prevailing social attitudes and will fit current views about how its children should be trained. Its very size draws attention. (In the United States there are more than 2,000,000 education professionals and about 8 percent of the gross national product is directly or indirectly consumed by the enterprises of education.) The public watches its investment carefully, scrutinizing educational practices, both traditional and innovative (Joyce & Morine, 1976).

Efficiency is highly prized, but innovations are watched with apprehension. Our societal patterns of schooling, established in the early 1800s, have become familiar and comfortable, and we want our children to have an education that has continuity with our own. Thus most citizens are cautious about educational innovation. People like the familiar old schoolhouse as much as they criticize it. They tend to believe that current problems in education are caused by changes (perceived as a "lowering of standards") rather than because the old comfortable model of the school may be a little rusty and out-of-date. In fact, our society has changed a great deal since the days when the familiar and comfortable patterns of education were established, and many schools have become badly out of phase with the needs of children in today's world.

Social institutions tend to deteriorate unless they are continuously rejuvenated, and when patterns of education become routine, life in schools becomes less vital. Schools need constant attention to revitalize them and the lives of the children and teachers who live in them. The public faces a continuing dilemma: to preserve familiar, traditional practices, making them as effective as possible, and yet keep up with the times in order to meet the challenges presented by social change. The result is that schooling exists in a social tug of war between proponents of tradition and change, and thus much that is known about what makes schools more effective is not being used.

Effectiveness, as such, is not controversial. In our society we may debate about what kind of education is best for our children, but there is total agreement that schooling should be rigorous and effective. Even people who are not particularly dissatisfied with the current state of education usually believe that schooling can be improved. How to increase the effectiveness of schools is a more frustrating topic, and the more critical people are about the present state of schools the more frustrated they become.

This book tackles the question of school improvement directly. Research on curriculum, teaching, and schooling is blended with research on school effectiveness to present a general strategy for improving our schools. The strategy includes ways of enlisting the energy of community members, selecting targets for improvement, and developing procedures that make it likely that appropriate changes will actually take place.

THE STRUCTURE OF SCHOOL IMPROVEMENT

This is a book about the structure of school improvement. By *structure* we mean the pattern of relationships among the many individual components of school change: administrative leadership, teacher effectiveness, curriculum improvement, and community involvement. Just as a computer requires connections among thousands of component parts—circuits are a purposeful structure of connections—so too the process of school improvement requires the careful structuring of curriculum, technology, and the social system in order to be successful.

In the past, school improvement has lacked coherent structure. Change has been attempted in additive ways, rarely with an insight into the synergistic nature of the complex process called schooling. Past educational and/or political attempts at school improvement have treated pieces of the school puzzle as if they were each separate entities. "Teacher proof" material, open classrooms, reducing the curriculum to basic skills, and competency testing are but a few examples of the underlying quick-fix school improvement strategies of the past. Yet, these attempts have served only as Band-Aids and ephemeral inoculations which over time have failed to improve our schools. Such lack of success has resulted in a "blaming the victim" syndrome in which students, parents, teachers, or administrators are alternately held responsible for the failed attempts at improvement. More recently researchers and practitioners have taken a more holistic view of schooling. We have begun to understand the ecology of good schools and to tease out the structure or pattern of relationships among the various components of schooling which together have an effect greater than the sum of its parts.

In this book we take a broad look at the school. We try to weave together the best of what we have learned from the literature of organizational change, and teacher and school effectiveness. We ask fundamental questions regarding the purposes of schooling and suggest that the responsibility for improving the quality of schools resides in a combination of Responsible Parties—teachers, parents, administrators, and community representatives—acting together.

Forging an alliance among Responsible Parties is an important but insufficient condition for making schools more effective. There are certain conditions and structural properties of good schools which, through time, must be created by persevering adults. Like all social organizations schools tend toward stabilization. Structural attributes, such as the school's cellular classroom structure, physically and temporally isolates people and helps keep their behavior within narrow bounds. Such structure creates an insidious form of homeostasis—a resistance to change which functions to separate teachers from the community, administration, and each other, and thus effectively neutralizes almost all attempts at serious innovation.

Schools, like other social organizations, are not disposed toward change and from that emerges an important paradox which provides a clue to the solution to the problem. The paradox is quite simple: schools seek stability as a seemingly necessary condition of survival. Yet this condition of equilibrium is also the root cause of the school's inability to improve, for as society changes and/or pedagogical knowledge increases, schools need to assimilate and accommodate to new realities. How then can a school create a reasonable level of stability and constantly be open and able to change?

The answer lies in the creation of a certain type of school culture, i.e., a set of organizational norms, expectations, beliefs, and behaviors which allow the establishment of activities fundamental to school improvement. This means that what must remain constant, what must remain stable in the life of the school, is the emotional and intellectual dispositions toward improvement on the part of Responsible Parties. We call this condition *homeostasis of improvement*.

All schools can improve. Our task in this book is to explain how such improvement takes place, to specify the particulars of the process. *We identify three stages of school improvement—refinement, renovation, and redesign—the three Rs*. In identifying and describing each of the stages of purposeful and evolutionary school improvement, we focus on the structural relationships among the various organizational elements which, when combined, provide a new sense of organizational efficiency.

Describing a process of school improvement is only part of our task, however. As schools increase their capacity to manage their own growth they must also constantly reconsider the purposes of their existence. In the last section of the book, entitled "Through the Looking Glass," we provide a view of the future which can already be predicted based on events of the recent past. It is through this more fundamental pre/reviewing of their function that school organizations achieve a level of maturity, a capacity to accept the necessity of continual growth as a condition of organizational survival.

THE THREE Rs OF SCHOOL IMPROVEMENT

In order to make school improvement a way of life, we envision three successive stages of growth. In Stage One, school effectiveness criteria are used to refine the current operation of the school. Curriculum and instructional practices are examined and sets of refinements developed to make them more effective. In Stage Two, the organization matures, examines curriculum areas in more depth, and selects specific components of its program to be systematically improved by innovation. New content and teaching strategies are introduced at this point, along with increasing amounts and types of staff development. In Stage Three, the overall mission of the school is examined and the entire range of curricular and instructional options is considered. Hence:

Three Stages of School Improvement

		Scope	Tasks
STAGE ONE	Refine:	Initiate the process	Organize Responsible Parties
			Use effectiveness criteria
			Improve social climate of education
STAGE TWO	Renovate:	Establish the process	Expand scope of improvement
			Embed staff development
			Improve curriculum areas
STAGE THREE	Redesign:	Expand the scope	Examine mission of school
			Study technologies
			Scrutinize organizational structure
			Develop long-term plan

SOURCES INITIATING SCHOOL IMPROVEMENT

Who initiates school improvement? Initiatives can be developed at the local site or at any of the various social system levels that surround schools. School districts (local education agencies) can initiate school improvement efforts as can county authorities or regional centers, such as teacher centers that offer services to schools and teachers. State governments, within which resides the traditional authority for schools, can also make initiatives. The federal government has offered increasing amounts of support for state and local authorities over the last 25 years. These legislative initiatives have had an important role in assessing the state of schooling, as well as offering resources for improvement (House, 1974).

Wherever initiatives arise, the condition of the local school is critical to the impact of the effort. Local communities may wish to upgrade the quality of their schools, but unless the school is disposed toward improvement, even close-at-hand initiatives will have hard sledding. District, county, regional, state, and federal initiatives will also be effective only as local school sites are able to receive and adapt them to their particular conditions (Joyce, 1978; 1982). Hence our belief in the development of an organization of Responsible Parties—local administrators, teachers, and community members who examine the health of their school continuously, select targets for improvement, and draw on knowledge about school improvement to implement desired changes. We envision the Responsible Parties as a permanent organization responsible for establishing a climate conducive to change, for assessing the strengths and weaknesses of the school, and for effectively bringing about improvements. Whether or not the early impetus for leadership comes from the district administration, building administrators, teachers, or community members, eventually they must all work together to establish a process that will endure as long as the school itself exists.

The membership of the Responsible Parties will necessarily change. Children grow up and the composition of interested parents changes. District and building administrators move to other jobs or functions within the organization. Teaching staffs, although relatively stable in recent years, also inevitably change. What must be permanent is the process of school improvement. The first task therefore is to develop an organization of Responsible Parties able to establish the process of school improvement in a way that will consider long-run as well as short-run improvements.

KEEPING SCHOOLS ALIVE AND WELL

Any educational plan, however exciting when first used, can become routine and mechanical in time. With this comes a loss of power and joy. Consequently, this book addresses itself to the revitalization of existing schools as well as the creation of new ones. We attempt to provide a map of educational alternatives as well as the processes that can be used to make them happen. We are not in favor of alternatives because they represent change per se; we are concerned that the persons responsible for schools possess a succinct characterization of the available possibilities and know how to make them effective. Knowledge of the alternatives allows us to select those that are most practical for us and the easiest to integrate with our deepest educational values.

The reader may well ask, ''Why don't you simply describe the best plan for schools and tell us how to make it work?" The answer is, there simply is no best model for a school. Every approach to education has costs as well as benefits. There are many effective models for schooling, but they do not work equally well for all children, nor do they achieve all purposes to the same degree. We must decide on our purposes and look realistically at the children before we can create the best plan. Over time our children and our purposes change, so we have to repeat our planning regularly.

Thus, our purpose is to present a framework for analyzing educational ends and means—a framework that can help us see the variety of purposes the school can serve and the different approaches that are available to achieve them.

We feel strongly that schooling has been far too dependent on a few simple methods, mostly mediated through personal, face-to-face encounters between teachers and students. When most of us think about schools, we think of the standard curriculum areas—reading, arithmetic, and so forth—which make up the normal "curriculum system" of schooling. Actually, there is evidence that the social system of the school is as powerful as the curricular system, because the social system provides us with values, ways of thinking and a view of ourselves. Our hope is for a richer, more diverse educational scene, one that matches the variety of people and communities in this society.

Although teachers manage the environmental variables that enhance each child's learning, they are not the only decision makers. The community has an enormous vested interest in the education of its children. Educational professionals and community members must work together to make conscious, systematic decisions about the learning environment. Hence, our belief that individual schools or clusters of schools should be governed jointly by what we call the Responsible Parties working within the policies set by elected officials, with the help of university personnel.

THE CREATION OF SCHOOLS: REASON AND PERSPECTIVE

The world presses on us; even in the most benign circumstances we are not wholly free. When there is no pressure to move in any given direction, we often constrain ourselves by our lack of vision and resources, our sense of what is possible. In every human activity it takes an enormous effort—and perspective and courage—to back off from familiar patterns in order to achieve a philosophical awareness of where we are going and where we might be going.

In the case of a social institution such as education, we are further constrained because the basic processes of the society continually shape the function and character of schools. We are able—by dint of a mighty force of will, to be sure—to step back and observe ourselves, our society, and our schools. Once we gain perspective we can attempt, if we care enough, to create schools that will have deliberately selected goals—schools that will not only be produced by the society but will necessarily return the favor by benefiting the future course of the community.

It is difficult indeed for a society to create an educational system that deliberately pushes the young to generate unfamiliar ideas and institutions, and even more difficult to give children and adolescents the freedom to do something about those yet unborn notions. To do so requires a trust in the growing youth, a belief that the evolving men and women will choose the best of their new ideas.

In the middle of the last century John Stuart Mill grappled with the problem of freedom and conformity and made a number of statements which appear as relevant today as they were when he penned them: "protection against tyranny of the magistrate is not enough; there needs protection also against the prevailing opinion and feelings; against the tendency of the society to impose, by rules of conduct on those who dissent from them; to fetter the development and, if possible, prevent the formation of any personality not in harmony with its way, and compels all characters to fasten themselves upon the model of its own" (Mill, 1947).

He stated succinctly the problem our society has with its schools: how much to use them to perpetuate the society as it is (or was) and how much to generate new forms of education which impel (and free) the young to rebuild their personal and social reality. Obviously we believe the dilemma should be faced squarely—that the curriculum should be made deliberately, whatever course is chosen.

Our first step is to identify and elucidate the set of decisions that bring a school program into existence. We must learn to seek out alternative courses of action that are possible in each decision area, and understand how various combinations of decisions can produce differing schools. Our approach assumes that it is possible to make realistic analyses of educational processes, that important aspects of the process can be coordinated one with the other, and that schools should be produced by conscious decision, wherever possible, rather than shaped only by the force of events.

In essence, our focus is on creating environments that promote continuous examination of school effectiveness at local sites so that specific, deliberated improvements can be made. Schools are social entities and, like the human spirit, require the challenge of improvement not only to soar but to maintain themselves. Just as the body grows supple through exercise and fades without it, the growing edges of the mind are sustained by challenge. Without stimulus to change, the structure of schools and individuals slide into rigid postures, and values reach toward the status of commandments. School improvement thrives only as life in schools is infected by adventure and tested by challenge.

2

A Realistic Beginning

We begin with a scenario of a school in operation. The scenario is based on a case study of a contemporary school although it has been written so as to disguise the place and the people. The scenario is the first case study in the training of the Responsible Parties. It will provide us with a reference point in later chapters as we examine the literature on school effectiveness and reform, consider the process of change and the role of the Responsible Parties in initiating change, and consider ways that we can build staff development into the ongoing business of the school. Later we will present other cases and study what we can do to improve them. This particular school provides elementary education but has many structural similarities to contemporary secondary schools. Although there are differences between elementary and secondary schools the fundamental processes of school improvement are the same at both levels.

THE CAMEO SCHOOL: THE FORMAL ORGANIZATION

In the Cameo School there is a principal, an assistant principal who also works as a counselor, and 20 teachers who are assigned to classrooms where they are responsible for teaching most school subjects. There are several specialists: a full-time librarian, and art, music, and physical education teachers who are shared with other schools. There is a special day class teacher and one resource specialist in special education. One full-time secretary works there, and two building superintendents are responsible for the physical maintenance of the building. In the Cameo School each of the classroom teachers works relatively independently teaching reading, arithmetic, social studies, science, and literature. The principal organizes the faculty to look over textbooks and other instructional materials each year. He and the secretary are responsible for the actual filling of orders. He schedules the art, music, and physical education teachers into classrooms where they provide about one hour of instruction to each class per week. The principal takes responsibility for the overall relationships with the public. However, about twice a year each teacher consults with every parent about the progress of the children. Also twice a year, usually in the early fall and late spring, the school holds an open house for parents, and periodically during the year the classes present "parent's night" entertainments during which they display their work and sometimes put on a play, a dance recital, or a concert. The upper-grade children belong to a band and a chorus both of which are directed by the music teacher. In addition the music teacher is available to give lessons for a small fee.

We begin our study by examining what happens when a new teacher joins the staff, is assigned to a classroom, and goes to work. Let us place Cameo School in a town of 50,000 people. Our new teacher, Maryann, obtained her job by interviewing with the personnel director of the school district; she was appointed by the board of education. She received a teaching certificate from the state on the recommendation of the university which she attended. In the early summer Maryann is informed that she will be assigned to a second-grade classroom in the Cameo School. She has met the principal only briefly, because in that district teachers are assigned to the school by the central office and are not interviewed by the principal or faculty prior to appointment. (In other districts the principal is responsible for assignments, possibly with a committee of teachers, and in a few districts the faculty and community members are heavily involved.) In July Maryann and the principal, George, get together for a day and he gives her a tour of the school, provides her with the available textbooks, shows her the library, and introduces her to JoEllen, one of the other second-grade teachers. JoEllen explains to Maryann what most of the teachers try to cover in the second-grade curriculum and tells her a bit about the other teachers and the children. (The Cameo School is in a working-class neighborhood, the children are assigned to each classroom on a random basis so that each teacher has a range in ability, etc.) JoEllen is very experienced, has a forceful personality, and usually is assigned the two or three children who are thought to be most difficult to teach. From a management standpoint, she likes that because she sees herself as a strong disciplinarian. Both JoEllen and George explain that Cameo is a "quiet school." That is, each teacher is expected to maintain an orderly and quiet classroom and keep the children working at their tasks. If a child is difficult the teacher is expected to inform George and he will arrange a conference with the parents to try to enlist their aid in controlling the child. If a child is very unruly he may be "sent to the principal's office." George likes to minimize this practice, but when a child is sent to him he chews him out thoroughly and threatens to call the parents and "get him in trouble" with them. According to both George and JoEllen the community likes a powerful, well-organized school and most of the parents will assist with discipline when a problem is brought to their attention.

Maryann and JoEllen see each other several times in the few days before school begins. JoEllen tries to explain to Maryann what the community is like, how George relates to the teachers, how the teachers relate to one another, and to give her advice about organizing her classroom.

"We're very friendly here and we're really open with the community. Most of the people in Cameo's part of town are hard working. A lot of them have jobs in the town's big industry which makes private airplanes. They're skilled workers and most of the folks have lived here for several years. They want their kids to do well in school and they really cooperate with you if one of the kids starts to goof off. They don't come to PTA meetings very often, but they really come down on the kids if we ask them to."

"Do the teachers live in this area?"

"Oh, God, no. I don't really think any of us do. We live all over the city. Most of us women are married to professional men. Two or three of the women are divorced and live by themselves or with their children in the downtown area. The men are married and almost all of their wives work. None of them live in this neighborhood, either."

"Do you see the families at social events or anything like that?"

"No, not usually. We have our open houses and our parent-teacher conferences, but we usually don't see them otherwise unless somebody comes in to visit the classroom or we ask for a special conference because we're having a problem of some sort."

"What is George like?"

"Oh, George works real hard at his job. He gets us the supplies and handles severe discipline problems, and mostly just leaves us alone. The district hires pretty good teachers. Most of us have been here for 10 or 15 years and we pretty well know what we're doing."

"Are people warm and close here, or what?"

"Oh, we all get along very well. We commute here, we get our jobs done, and we go home."

"Do you have a curriculum?" asked Maryann. "That is, how do I figure out what to teach in each subject area?"

"Well, we spend most of our time on the basic skills. Most of us follow the textbooks in reading and arithmetic. We don't teach very much science here and everybody pretty well does what they think they ought to do in the social studies."

"Do you have curriculum committees?"

"Oh dear," said JoEllen, "you've probably been told in your teacher education program that schools have committees that look at their curriculums and make plans about what ought to be taught, and so on. Well, that just doesn't really happen in very many places, and it's certainly not true at Cameo. Each one of us does our own job. We take care of ourselves and George takes care of the office. All you have to worry about is to teach reading and arithmetic really well and nobody will bother you."

"How do most people teach reading and arithmetic?"

"About five years ago the district adopted a comprehensive textbook series. We all use it. The trouble is keeping the kids together. When they fall behind and we can't promote them they get the same books again. Some of these kids are just hopeless."

"How about audiovisual equipment?"

"Well," said JoEllen, "we have a lot of stuff. We have a videotape recorder and projectors and tape records and almost everything you could need. To be truthful, most of us don't use those very much. We pretty well teach by the book here."

"Well, if I think out what I'm going to do the first few days, can you give me some help?"

"Oh sure," said JoEllen, "I'll be glad to talk with you."

The First Day of School

Maryann's second grade has 27 children in it. She'd gotten their records from George and found that JoEllen had both the fastest and the slowest kids. Hers were regarded as "in the middle." All of the families have lived in the area for more than five years. Two of the children lived with single parents. Two were classified as having "special needs." One of them was partially sighted but by no means blind and the other was classified as having a behavioral disorder, specifically being highly nervous and easily upset and in need of much nurturance and calming. The resource teacher would work with them part of the time.

The children were friendly and curious when she met them the first day of school. They wanted to know where she'd lived before, whether she was married and had children (no), how many brothers and sisters she had. She was just as curious about them. She decided to mix the day between activities that would help her to get to know the children and exercises that would give her specific information about their achievement. She gave each of the students a short diagnostic test in reading and a general diagnostic test in arithmetic. She felt nervous and elated in the teachers' room. She went with the children to recess at 10:30 and then met JoEllen in the teachers' room for a moment.

"How's it going, love?"

"Oh fine. I'm just as nervous and excited as I can be."

"You'll get used to it," said JoEllen.

George came by about 11:00. He smiled at her reassuringly. She had taken the children to the library and each had selected several books. The librarian was a little annoyed that she wanted them to be able to take more than one but had given in.

"How's it going, buddy?" asked George.

"Frankly, I'm scared stiff," she said, "but I'm excited too."

"I think you're going to like teaching," said George. "Just hang in for a few weeks and get your sea legs."

She laughed, "God," she said, "I wish I could teach as well as I can sail."

He laughed too. "Listen," he said, "if you have any problems in the next few days just let me know. Especially," he said, "don't let them get out of hand."

"Don't worry about it," she said to herself, "just don't let anybody get out of hand."

Nobody did, in fact.

At lunch the other teachers talked about clothes, shopping, some of the textbooks that hadn't arrived, and exchanged opinions about the "fastest" and "slowest" kids. Maryann was amazed at how calm everybody was and how little they said about their teaching.

"Does anybody know Carlos?" she said, meaning the partially sighted child.

"Oh yes, I had him last year," said Louise. "He's okay. He's lazy as hell though, you have to really kick his butt." Everybody laughed.

"His whole damn family is like that," said one of the other teachers.

JoEllen laughed, "They sure are. Every year I get one. Carlos is the first member of the family I haven't had."

"But he's kind of sweet," said Louise. "You'll see what I mean. But, don't let him con you," she said to Maryann.

Maria Torres came in to teach art at 1:30. Maryann wandered down the hall. She had an overpowering urge to look in someone else's classroom and went in to Terry's. Terry was teaching arithmetic. She was drilling the children on the number facts. "Seven times six is...."

"Forty-two."

"Nine times seven is...."

"Sixty-two."

"What?" said Terry.

"Sixty-two," said the child, firmly. And the other children laughed.

"Sixty-three, dopey," said one of the others.

Terry noticed Maryann, who had walked along the wall and sat down next to the bookcase. She stopped teaching.

"Do you want something, dear?" she asked.

"Ah, why no...." said Maryann.

"If you're looking for George, he's probably in his office," said Terry, and waited without saying anything else. The children all looked at Maryann. The world of the classroom had stopped turning.

"Ah, well—okay," said Maryann and she left.

"I'll see you after school, dear." said Terry.

On the way to George's office Maryann felt firmly rebuffed. She found George changing a lightbulb in a projector. "These damn things are always breaking down," he said.

"I just stopped in one of the teacher's rooms and she didn't seem too pleased," said Maryann. "Did I do something wrong?"

George looked at her and smiled. "Well," he said, "I guess the answer to that is both 'yes' and 'no.' Listen," he said, "I've got a call to make after I finish this. Come on by after school. Two or three of us have a beer before we go home and there are a couple of people I'd like you to meet."

When the children left Maryann felt tremendous relief, pleasure, exhaustion, and frustration. Relief, because she had gotten through the day. Pleasure, because she and the children had enjoyed each other. Exhaustion, because all the tension had suddenly been released. Frustration, because she realized she knew so little about teaching and wasn't even sure what to do tomorrow. She sat on a tiny chair in the middle of the classroom ("Is the *whole* world pint-sized?") and stared at the clutter left by the day's activities. "My God," she said to herself, "children are real and understandable, after all." She realized that she had built herself up to expect a mysterious species of people with whom she had nothing in common. Instead she had a group of perfectly understandable little kids who looked to her for leadership.

Leadership. That was the problem. All she had to do was find some way of providing them with 180 consecutive days of useful activities. In some ways she understood the children very well. After all, she and they had grown up in the same culture. She couldn't figure out why she had expected to find them so unearthly. They were, she reflected again, just little kids, like she had once been. At the same time, for all they had in common, at the moment they seemed to be incredibly different from each other. Some of them appeared to know everything that was commonly taught in an elementary school while others could not really read in any functional sense—they were just about where they were as they entered the first grade. Some seemed to want her to make a lot of very specific rules so they knew exactly what to do and could feel secure. Others were very independent. Some were friendly while others were shy and tentative. Some of them obviously attracted friends while a few seemed to be almost isolated from their peers. She looked at her watch and realized she had only a half an hour before she would have to meet George and whatever group of people he had selected for her to "have a beer with." She scrambled around tidying up the room. She got out the materials for a science demonstration she had decided to use to begin the next day. Unlike most elementary school teachers, Maryann was very comfortable with the physical and biological sciences and had decided to lead from her strength. She still couldn't tell how much arithmetic the children knew and stuffed the test she had given them into her book bag. Looking at the test would help somewhat but she decided that she would begin at the beginning the next day and review counting and addition. Just where their skills reached and where they did not was the mystery. She had already realized with a sinking feeling that they would be different. She laughed out loud for a second.

"Why should I even want them *not* to be different," she thought. "What a terrible world *that* would be. And yet, how in the devil am I ever going to take care of them? I mean, how am I going to deal with all their *real* differences?" Her door opened and she saw two big, friendly men she had not seen before. They entered wielding brushes and mops and she realized that they were the building superintendents.

"You must be Maryann," said one, and stuck out his hand. "We're the janitors. They call us something else, but we kind of like being called janitors." He looked around the room. "Hey, kid," he said to her, "ask the children to put their chairs on their desks tomorrow, would you? It makes it a lot easier to clean the place up. Lots of janitors want the chairs kept in rows, but we don't really care about that. But it saves us about 10 minutes for every classroom if they'll just lift up those chairs."

"Why, sure," she said. His companion was looking at one of the blackboards.

"Hey," he said, "let me show you how to clean this thing right. I think the manufacturers are trying to drive us crazy." He made her wait while he expertly wiped the board clean. He grinned at her. "If you want your class to run smoothly," he said, "it's really a matter of a lot of little tiny things."

She laughed again, "My God," she said, "I don't even know how to keep the chalkboard clean."

George took her to a smoky bar which was part of the local pizza parlor and introduced her to three teachers who were sharing a pitcher of beer. She realized from the conversation that they too were relieved after the day, although most of them were 10 or more years older than she. "Are you always nervous on the first day?" she asked and they all laughed.

Kiki, listening, moved over next to her. Kiki was the resource teacher. She was very friendly and casual, but before the end of the conversation wanted to talk to her about little Carlos. "His sight is actually okay," said Kiki. "Oh, he has those monstrous, thick glasses and everything, but you know he isn't really blind or anything. The problem is that for some reason nobody found out that he couldn't see very well until last year because he's so quiet and withdrawn. Everybody thought he was stupid and he certainly didn't learn anything, or that is, very much, so he's got a lot of catching up to do and the worst part of it is that I think his family treated him in such a way that he actually thinks he doesn't have any brains. I want to tutor him once or twice while you watch so we can share some ideas."

"Sure, I'd love the help."

"George actually found him when he was in the first grade. He was doing really badly and his family said he was really dumb. And his teacher agreed with them. George wanted me to find out whether he should be in the special day class, but the psychologist and I found that he is really very intelligent and quite delightful. He just had to hold his head about an inch away from a book in order to read it. Or that is, try to read it, since he hadn't learned to read yet. So we kind of stumbled on him in a roundabout way. That's not so unusual," she said. "If a kid has any kind of a handicap, most people think they're dumb. That's one of my big problems."

"What do you do most of the time?" asked Maryann.

She laughed, "Mostly I cope with the other teachers' resentment because I'm not in a classroom all day," she said. "Actually I do three things here. One is that I arrange for kids who have speech defects and things like that to get some special help from the teachers who work in the county office. The second thing is that I try to identify the kids who need some special help. I test them or get them tested and we try to find out whether they qualify for special services. Anyway, I try to work out individual programs for those kids. I see my real job as helping teachers work with kids like Carlos, including kids who are very slow and hard to manage and so on. About half my time I tutor small groups and the rest of the time I try to work with the teachers. In a sense," she said, "I'm really on the job right now, trying to give you a fix on Carlos."

They walked out to their cars together and Kiki said, "Frankly my biggest problem is that this is such a well-ordered place that any kid who just doesn't sit in his seat and do what he's asked to do gets into trouble. I keep getting kids referred to me whose main problem is that they're not half dead." Maryann looked at her in surprise. "Oh yes," said Kiki, "you'll find out that this is a hell of a school for any kid who isn't a real conformist."

Although the details of Cameo school are, of course, unique to that setting, Maryann is experiencing a process that is common to all people who enter a new human group. That is, the members of the group are attempting to socialize her to the norms and to give her their own perspectives on the social situation. Already she has been told a great deal about how the school is run, how the principal relates to the teachers, how they relate to each other, how they regard the children. In short, she has had her introductory course to the social system. Kiki obviously does not agree with the attitudes of many of the teachers and is trying to enlist Maryann as a confederate. In the next few weeks Maryann will get more and more information about Cameo. She will get accustomed to the children, teachers, and parents. For a time, she will feel submerged by the tasks of teaching and then, as she gets her head above water, she will have a good many choices to make about what kind of teacher she will be and what kind of satisfaction she can get in the school. How she handles herself in that social system will have much to do with how she will eventually see herself as a teacher and a person.

ANALYSIS: THE CAMEO SCHOOL AS A SOCIAL SYSTEM

The organization of the Cameo School seems simple and familiar enough, but how did it come to be? Only 150 years ago a relatively small proportion of the population were in school and most of those attended one-room schoolhouses (two rooms at most), set in the immediate neighborhood or, in rural areas, located centrally amidst the farms or on the edge of small towns. By the middle of the century some schools had increased in population and it seemed convenient to assign teachers to children of different ages. The school might have developed as a series of one-room schoolhouses, but instead some teachers were assigned to work with the younger children and some with the older ones, and the school began to be organized into something called "grades."

In his excellent book *Schoolteacher*, Lortie (1975) points out that one of the reasons for the graded organization was convenience with respect to the hiring of staff. If a teacher left, another was simply hired to take his or her place. If the number of children increased or decreased a teacher could be added, deleted or reassigned to another school. New staff could take up their duties with minimum interaction with other staff members. They were responsible for all or a large part of the instruction of the children in their classes and did not have the complexity of adjusting to a group of fellow professionals, as would have been the case had a different organizational form been used. Lortie calls the organization that resulted a "cellular" structure. That is, each classroom can be regarded as a cell within which the given teacher is responsible for organizing the children, managing discipline, and teaching the several subjects which came to be common in the curriculum. With this kind of organization teachers became accustomed to working alone. They could make decisions about when and how to teach each subject more or less independently of the other teachers. They did not have to ask the person next door when to do things or how to do them. As the school enlarged the role of "principal teacher" emerged, and when the school became large enough to accumulate administrative responsibilities which could occupy someone full time, the nonteaching "principalship" developed, an official management position with responsibility for the other personnel, public relations, and logistics. Principals developed a variety of management styles. Some principals became very directive, telling teachers what and how much content to teach, what textbooks to use, and even how to teach. Other principals were relatively nondirective and consulted with teachers only when trouble appeared. Some school districts and even states established curriculums and asked the teachers to use them, whereas others provided guidelines only and left the individual teacher to make his own decisions. Either way it became customary for principals to relate to the teachers on a diadic basis, that is, in a one-to-one relationship rather than organizing the faculty to take collective responsibility for the management of the curriculum and program. The principal "supervised" the work of the cells.

Since the teachers were assigned primarily to instruct the students, very little time was provided for them to interact with one another. They could see one another occasionally at lunch time or when recess was scheduled with other classes, and some of them would chat after school. But most of the teachers' day was occupied with instruction leaving relatively little time for cooperative planning with their peers.

The cellular organization, thus, served to isolate teachers from one another and they became independent operators, making the majority of their own decisions and taking responsibility for their children. *They did not become accustomed to taking responsibility for the school as a whole.*

Human groups in workplaces not only develop routine ways of getting their jobs done, but also norms which affect many aspects of behavior. Gradually, normative patterns of behavior developed in schools organized like Cameo (and *most* elementary schools were organized similarly). An important example was the rise of norms governing the "privatism" of teaching. Teachers regarded their classrooms as private domains. Their duties isolated them from each other during working hours—they rarely visited each other to observe one another's techniques. Not only was teaching in isolation normative, but violating privacy when teaching became a prohibition. A teacher entering another person's classroom was expected to be there on business. "Can I borrow some chalk?" "Do you have that story book?" "Have you seen the science kit anywhere?" "Can you ask Gwen to take a message home to her sick brother? I'd like to let him know what his homework is." For a teacher to simply come in and sit down in the back of the classroom and watch a fellow teacher became an unusual behavior, so unusual that the staff became uncomfortable when it happened. (Teachers are *supposed* to tend to their own knitting and not bother one another!) It was all right, of course, for the principal to come by, but gradually the teachers came to wonder what he was doing there, too, and in many schools the principal felt that he had to ask permission to come in and observe. Furthermore, he was kept busy with administrative chores. He oversaw the maintenance personnel, answered queries from parents, related to the district office or board of education, chaired meetings of the faculty, preparing its agenda, and dealt with those administrative matters that are necessary to "keep the ship running." It was not written down that teachers and administrators were not supposed to observe one another, but the prohibition was nonetheless powerful. Other norms developed also.

The Cameo School will be a difficult one to improve unless it changes substantially as a socioprofessional system. Most of the faculty work in isolation from one another. They are not close to the community and are somewhat disdainful of it. The principal is concerned with the maintenance of order. He is friendly to the staff but he permits them to work separately and has not organized them, let alone Responsible Parties into a problem-solving unit. He lets Kiki solve her own problems in giving service to children with special needs.

The Cameo staff will "teach" Maryann that their way of life is the normal and proper professional one. She will fumble her way to a reasonable level of teaching competence but will not be informed by the practice of others or by expert supervision.

In the next chapter we are going to look at the formal literature about what makes schools effective and then apply the criteria from that literature to a study of the Cameo School. In preparation for reading that chapter, make some notes about what *you* think needs to be done.

3

What Makes Some Schools and Teachers More Effective?

For the past two years we have been reviewing research to determine what, if anything, makes some schools and teachers more effective* than others. Happily, there emerges from such research a variety of clues, which when put together into a coherent whole, make a great deal of intuitive sense. What is particularly pleasing is that different researchers in a variety of studies are reaching similar conclusions about effective schooling, and that these conclusions are reinforced by teachers and administrators who bring to research programs the critical eyes of experience. Because of the conjunction of researchers' knowledge and professional educators' wisdom we optimistically believe that we can improve education in America both on its current terms and by using technology and fresh curriculum alternatives more extensively.

Three important generalizations have emerged. First, people run schools. How teachers, administrators, and students behave in a school setting matters and accounts heavily toward determining a school's effectiveness (Edmonds, 1979). The social climate of the school is extremely important. Second, quality and not just quantity of effort, materials, and time is what counts. However big the school library, however much is spent per child, and however experienced the teachers, wihout a high quality of effort those factors alone make little difference. Third, the curriculum of the school, which includes *what* is taught, *how* it is taught, and the social climate within which it is taught, is very important.

*"Effective" here refers to student academic achievement as measured by standardized achievement tests, usually in reading and math. This is not to suggest that such outcomes are the only objectives we should consider but rather that they are, for the moment, the only variable with which we can easily compare schools.

ATTRIBUTES OF EFFECTIVE SCHOOLS

Table 3.1 lists two sets of attributes associated with effective schools. Under the heading *Social Organization* are items that pertain to the social system—the human community of the school. These attributes (clear academic and social behavior goals; order and discipline; high expectations; teacher efficacy; pervasive caring; public rewards and incentives; administrative leadership; community support) help promote conditions for effective teaching and learning across all classrooms and learning centers. These are the social conditions that help individual teachers and students to excel (Hersh, 1982).

The second heading, *Instruction and Curriculum*, includes those items which are found in the most effective classrooms. These attributes (high academic learning time; frequent and monitored homework; frequent monitoring of student progress; coherently organized curriculum; variety of teaching strategies; opportunities for student responsibility), in the context of the social climate of the school, help promote the classroom conditions for maximum student engagement with purposeful learning activities. Please note that the two sets of conditions (social organization and instruction and curriculum) are not unrelated to each other. In fact they are both overlapping and interactive, complementary and reciprocal. Clear school-wide goals, for example, not only help generate community understanding and support but also allow individual teachers to better assess the fit between their expectations for students, students' expectations of themselves, and the curriculum.

Social Organization

Schools are social entities whose function is puposeful learning. As with all social groupings their organizational power is dependent on adherence to *common* sets of values, norms, beliefs, expectations, rules, and sanctions. Rutter (1979) refers to this as a school's *ethos*. Wynn (1980) calls it *coherence*. Glass (1981) uses the word *tone*. We prefer *community*. Whatever term is selected it is important to note that there is a need in a school for such shared agreements on norms and purposes because it is the existence of common understanding and assent which creates the foundation for trust and respect for others—the glue of social and moral intercourse. The more effective schools create a distinctive sense of community, a community derived from conditions which profoundly affect how and why educators and students treat each other, how much the precious commodity of time is valued, and how well academic and social learning skills are integrated.

TABLE 3.1
Attributes of Effective Schools

Social Organization	*Instruction and Curriculum*
Clear academic and social behavior goals	High academic learning time (ALT)
Order and discipline	Frequent and monitored homework
High expectations	Frequent monitoring of student progress
Teacher efficacy	Coherently organized curriculum
Pervasive caring	Variety of teaching strategies
Public rewards and incentives	Opportunities for student responsibility
Administrative leadership	
Community support	

Clear Academic and Social Behavior Goals.   Effective schools articulate a clear schoolwide set of academic and social behavior goals. Achievement in reading, writing, mathematics, and other areas is heavily emphasized across the entire teaching staff as is student behavior which promotes an orderly classroom and school climate. There is a minimum of ambiguity about the importance of achievement. Teachers, parents, and students share the same understanding of the school's goals (Brookover et al., 1977).

Order and Discipline.   Administrators, teachers, and students understand and agree on basic rules of conduct. Each person may expect that such rules will be uniformly enforced, be they about property, courtesy, or cooperation and that all teachers will work together to ensure this observance. The attitude of each teacher is, "I will enforce the norms whether or not the student is in my particular class."

The concern for an orderly and disciplined school climate is not to be equated with oppression. The 1960s critics of oppressive schools made their point so well (Holt, 1964; Kozol, 1967) that some came to believe that a disciplined environment as such is oppressive. Not so. Chaos is oppressive and confusing. Effective schools seem to find that happy medium between strong discipline and respect and support for growing students. The solitude of a tomb is not required but neither is the noise of a circus tolerated. Effective schools recognize order as a social necessity, not a rigid order that snuffs out spontaneity and individualism, but a strong norm to keep on with the business of learning. Fairness and equity are valued also and rules are clear, not capricious (Edmonds, 1979).

High Expectations.   Teachers and administrators in effective schools hold higher academic and social behavior expectations for their students than do teachers and administrators in less effective schools (Good, 1979). High expectations carry several messages. First, they symbolize the demand for excellence and tell the student, "I think you ought to and can achieve." High expectations are stars to reach for. Second, they communicate to the students that the teacher *cares* by saying, in effect, "The reason I have high expectations for you is that I believe in you." Third, high expectations serve as the adult world's professional judgment which is translated by the student as, "I am really more capable than even I at times think I am. If my teacher continues to have high expectations for me, even when I screw up, then maybe I really can do better." In a high-expectation environment, the students achieve in a manner that surprises them.

Teacher Efficacy.   Effective schools have teachers who have a strong sense of efficacy—a belief which says, "I *know* I can teach any and all of these kids." Efficacy is a sense of potency, and it is what provides a teacher with the psychic energy needed for the relentless and persevering effort required to maintain a high task orientation by the students. A sense of efficacy combined with high expectations for one's students communicates powerfully to students that they *can* learn and that they *will* learn.

Pervasive Caring.   Students in effective schools tell you that their teachers and administrators care about them. It is manifested by the response of one child who, asked, "How do you know your teacher cares?" replied, "Because she gets mad at me when I don't do my homework or do poorly on a test" (Hersh, 1982).
    Caring is expressed in a variety of ways. High expectations, strict but fair enforcement or rules, and homework assignments, for example, all tell the student that the teacher is paying attention to them and cares about their achievement. Observers of effective schools see the caring atmosphere in the informal pats, the rigorous demands, and the staff's collective celebration of student achievement. Teachers, administrators, *and* parents know when a school is a caring place for students and say so when asked.

Public Rewards and Incentives.   Effective schools have a system of clear and public rewards and incentives for student achievement. Public display of excellent student work, honor roll, convocations to honor student excellence, notes sent home to parents, and statements and smiles serve to motivate and sustain students' achievement of a school's high expectations for them (Brookover et al., 1977).

Administrative Leadership. Effective schools have administrative leaders, most often principals, who actively advocate and facilitate the above conditions. Such leadership does not mean that the principal does the curriculum revision, or is the master teacher, or conducts the teachers' evaluations. Rather, it means the principal makes sure these tasks are carried out appropriately. Such a person listens to staff requests and seeks to support such requests whenever reasonable. Such a person initiates dialogues about expectations, schoolwide rules, and the establishment of a good testing program. Most essential, with such leadership the administration is seen by both teachers and students as supportive, caring, and trustworthy, all of which helps create conditions for excellence (Edmonds, 1979).

Community Support. Effective schools have been found to have more parent and community contact than less effective schools. Contact with parents is not limited to concerns of truancy or misbehavior. Parents and other community members are engaged in school beautification programs, tutoring, fundraising, and just plain being kept informed of school expectations, successes, failures. Effective schools usually have more positive parent-initiated contacts than do less effective schools (Brookover et al., 1977).

Instruction and Curriculum

Instruction and curriculum, which comprise the second set of attributes in Table 3.1, refer to that part of schooling which is most familiar to the public. Recent international studies of education found that national differences in curriculum affect what is learned by students (Hussen, ed., 1967). Similar findings appear in domestic studies. Greater attention to literature, mathematics, or social science results in greater achievement in those areas. A number of factors interact to make given curriculums more powerful.

High Academic Learning Time (ALT). Not surprisingly researchers have found that up to a point the more time one spends on a learning task the more one learns. Although this sounds perfectly obvious and perhaps hardly worth mentioning, this rediscovery is actually rather complex and very important.

First, researchers have found that in many classrooms teachers may *allocate* a great deal of instructional time (for example, reading instruction) but the students are behaviorally engaged in learning for only a small fraction of the allotted time. Several studies show that in the classrooms of some second- and third-grade teachers who allocate two hours per day for reading instruction students were actually spending an average of only 12 to 15 minutes a day in learning how to read! Thus, allocated time, or teachers' *intended* time for instruction, has been shown *not* to be the best indicator of what covers effective instruction. Teachers vary considerably in efficiency (as do learners) (Rosenshine and Berliner, 1978).

Consequently, a more precise measure of time has been substituted for allocated time. Called *time on task*, this is a measure of how much time students actually are engaged in the study of a particular subject or skill. However, although this measure approximates more closely the actual time a student spends on a learning activity, it does not, by itself, reveal whether or not the student is successfully learning while engaged in that learning task. Imagine a student who has great perseverance and spends many hours trying to read a history book which is four grade levels above his reading level. Clearly this mismatch of instructional material and time on task would not correlate with effective, much less efficient, learning (Fisher et al., 1980).

Finally, therefore, researchers have arrived at the notion of Academic Learning Time (ALT) (Berliner, 1981). This is the amount of time a student actually spends on a learning activity in which he or she is achieving a high rate of success (90 percent or better) at that task. ALT takes into account the amount of time well spent and requires assessment not only of the time dimension but also of the appropriateness of the curriculum and measures of success. The key research finding here is that effective classrooms have higher ALT ratios than do less effective classrooms. This means that not only do teachers in more effective schools waste less class time in starting and ending instructional activities but they select curriculum materials which are more appropriate to the student abilities.* The student is challenged, but not overwhelmed.

Frequent and Monitored Homework. Teachers in effective schools, after fourth grade, require more homework (out-of-class assignments) more often *and* provide students with feedback about how well their homework was completed. Homework tells the student that learning is more than just a schoolroom activity, that expectations go beyond minimum effort, and that independent learning is valued. Perhaps equally important, out-of-class assignments increase ALT. By checking homework and providing students feedback, teachers tell students that

---

*Ten minutes of lost instruction in each high school class per day totals at least one hour of lost instruction every day, 180 hours per year, over 500 hours for three years of high school. Given that an average high school course requires about 180 to 200 hours of in-class instruction per year, 500 lost hours is considerable.

they care about whether or not it is done (part of the incentive and caring dimension of schooling) as well as find out how well the students are learning on their own.

Frequent Monitoring of Student Progress. Administrators and teachers in effective schools monitor students' academic progress more frequently than do staffs in less effective schools. Such monitoring consists of a combination of more frequent classroom tests and quizzes; formal and informal; written and oral; schoolwide, districtwide, and national. Most emphasis is placed on frequent in-class monitoring coupled with direct and immediate feedback to students. Such frequent monitoring serves an important diagnostic function, prevents students from falling behind, and tells students that what is being taught is important. Effective monitoring can range from very informal to quite formal (Brophy, 1979).

Coherently Organized Curriculum. Effective schools have a curriculum closely related to both school-wide and individual objectives. Teachers do not rely solely on commercial products but alter or create materials and activities to meet the agreed upon goals. The need for a tight connection between curriculum and objectives is perhaps best illustrated by a recent study which found that the five most widely used standardized test items in the U.S. in fourth-grade math had no more than 60 percent correspondence with any of the three most popular-selling fourth-grade math textbook series. Effective schools puposely link goals, curriculum, and evaluation devices in a tightly coupled way to avoid the common mismatch in testing and teaching.

Variety of Teaching Strategies. Several studies have found that teachers in effective schools use a greater variety of teaching strategies than do teachers in less effective schools (Rosenshine & Furst, 1971). That is, teachers in effective schools are able to accommodate better to student differences (as measured by frequent evaluation) by employing an alternative teaching strategy when students do not seem to be succeeding. In addition, teachers with expanded repertoires of teaching strategies can meet more objectives with the "educational treatment of choice" (McDonald, 1976).

Opportunities for Student Responsibility. Effective schools provide students with more opportunities for engaging in responsible behaviors. Such opportunities include student government, hallway monitors, discipline panels, peer and cross-age tutoring, and school fund-raising projects. The student is "taken into the game" of constructing and maintaining an active community for learning (Rutter et al., 1979).

CUMULATIVE AND INTERACTIVE EFFECTS

Each of the attributes above has been shown to exist in some of the effective schools studied. However, it is important to note that simply creating one, two, or three of these conditions would not necessarily result in a much more effective school. The cumulative effects of these conditions is what works. Although no one has shown which ones or how many of these conditions are necessary and sufficient to *guarantee* effective schools, it appears that there is an element of synergy involved. That is, it seems that one has to do many things at once to get the job done. It would be folly, for instance, to believe that simply increasing teacher expectations for students would lead to much increase in ALT or teacher efficacy. But, in combination, several of the factors help create a critical mass of conditions which serve to better promote student achievement.

Tomlinson's summary is instructive. He states that school resources are not the first or generic cause of learning.

The ability and effort of the child is the prime cause, and the task of the schools is to enable children to use their abilities and efforts in the most efficient and effective manner. In the last analysis, that translates as undistracted work, and neither schools nor research have discovered methods or resources that obviate this fact.... We should take comfort from the emerging evidence: it signifies a situation we can alter. The common thread of meaning in all that research has disclosed tells us that academically effective schools are "merely" schools organized on behalf of the consistent and undeviating pursuit of learning. The parties to the enterprise—principals, teachers, parents and *fait accompli* students—coalesce on the purpose, justification and methods of schooling. Their common energies are spent on teaching and learning in a systematic fashion. They are serious about, even dedicated to, the proposition that children can and shall learn in schools. No special treatment and no magic, just the provision of the necessary conditions for learning. (Tomlinson, 1980)

Tomlinson reminds us that in the end it is what students do that ultimately causes student achievement. What is taught, how it is taught, and the social climate combine to increase student effort and belief in their own powers.

Further, these conditions probably apply to schools operated under quite a variety of models of education. Students learning via computer need to have clear goals, believe in themselves, receive support and feedback, and work hard at instructional tasks. Children in drama workshops need the same conditions to learn to act and to understand the performing arts.

Our task is to learn to use what is known to create powerful schooling that is appropriate for students in today's world.

The recent interpretations of research into effective schools and teachers underlined some beliefs that were in vogue before the research was done. In the 1960s the programs that became known as Headstart and Follow Through were generated by the United States Office of Education to develop models to help economically poor children to receive a more powerful early education (Rhine, 1981). A deliberate attempt was made to support the development of models based on different beliefs about early education. For example, some of the programs were based on developmental psychology and used activities designed to accelerate intellectual growth (Weikart et al. in Rhine, 1981). Others aimed at the development of a healthy energized self-concept (Gilkeson et al. in Rhine, 1981). Some used systematic, direct instruction in the basic skills areas (Becker et al. in Rhine, 1981). And some emphasized parent education and developed activities designed to draw parents into the educational process. Each of these approaches represents a distinctive position about what would make education more effective and generates a unique school program. The resulting "models of education" are *really* different! Yet, when they are studied closely, it becomes apparent that they share a number of beliefs:

> That education should begin where children are ready to learn. Thus, information about their capacities should be collected and used to adapt programs.
>
> Instruction should be individualized to a large extent.
>
> Instruction, materials, and other conditions of learning can ensure success for all children. The problem is not the child's, but *ours*.
>
> Goals should be clear to all—parent, child, teacher, administrator.
>
> All children need to learn how to learn—to attend, stay on task, cooperate, to push themselves to achieve.
>
> Emotional development must be enhanced. Success in academic learning is an essential condition of healthy attitudes toward self and others and continued motivation to achieve. (Rhine, 1981, p. 37)

These beliefs sound remarkably like the current formulations. What is important is that they are shared by educators who otherwise espouse and have developed very different approaches to the creation of an effective education.

THE CAMEO SCHOOL AND
THE LITERATURE ON EFFECTIVENESS

Let us now examine the Cameo School in terms of the criteria we have explored in this chapter. One of the first tasks of the Responsible Parties will be to carry out this exercise with respect to their own schools. Such analysis will become one of the bases for their school improvement program.

Clear Academic and Social Behavior Goals. The administrators, teachers and probably most of the community members at the Cameo School believe that reading, writing, and arithmetic are important goals and that the children should be orderly and compliant, but the clarity ends there. They are unsure what to do with children who do not keep up or children who do not in any way fit into the standard, textbook-oriented curriculum in reading and arithmetic. They are clear about what they want for "average" children but faster and slower learners cause them equal problems. Their curriculum is incomplete and in-specific in many areas.

Order and Discipline. This is probably the area of their greatest clarity but they have no operating philosophy beyond the use of parental and administrative authority to ensure conformity. That is, there is no discussion about "what makes children tick" or a view of the developmental nature of children. They do maintain reasonable order, and community, teachers, and administration are agreed about what a school should look like and how children should behave in their school environment.

High Expectations. The experience of the resource specialist and the discussions of the teachers about the children indicate serious lacks in this area. They expect that the children will keep up, but they are not optimistic if a child has difficulty or if his home background does not appear to prepare him for the work that is set forth. Children who have learning problems can be ridiculed and there is no apparent provision for children who master the standard curriculum easily. The attitude appears to be more "you *will* do it" than "you *can* do it."

Teacher Efficacy. The teachers clearly feel that they are in charge of their own classrooms and in that sense probably feel relatively efficacious. They know they can get assistance from the principal when they need it. However, as indicated again by the experience of the resource teacher, most of the teachers probably do not feel that they would be capable of bringing about a change that involved the coordination of persons outside of their classroom. They are dependent on the central office for their curriculum in reading and arithmetic and neither they nor the principal have taken charge of developing curriculums in the other areas or providing for individual differences among the children. Nonetheless, because they feel very much in control of their particular domains, most of the teachers probably do not feel a lack of efficacy.

Pervasive Caring. Cameo has serious lacks in this area, although undoubtedly many of the teachers are kind to the children. The teacher's overall attitude and their feelings about the slower and faster youngsters do not show a philosophy of caring and nurturance.

Public Rewards and Incentives. The incentive system is geared to covering the material in the textbook and children are rewarded for keeping up and keeping busy. The case study does not provide much information about other sorts of public rewards.

Administrative Leadership. Within a very limited range there is clear leadership from the principal about discipline, management, and the need for order and quiet. However, the principal takes no responsibility for curriculum development nor does he offer clinical assistance to his staff. Clearly, curricular and school improvement is not high on his agenda.

Community Support. There is community support but within a limited spectrum. The parents respond when the teachers need assistance with discipline. However, the parents are not active in parent-teacher organizations or in school improvement activities. They would clearly need assistance to elect and support committees of Responsible Parties.

High Academic Learning Time. The children are busy but the activities are appropriate only for the student within a narrow range of capability, that is, those for whom the standard textbooks in reading and arithmetic appear to be more or less well tuned. Students who learn more quickly or more slowly are not productively occupied. Therefore, even though the Cameo School is a busy and orderly place, we would be surprised to find it characterized by high academic learning time in the true sense that the activities are tuned appropriately to the abilities of all the children.

Frequent and Monitored Homework.   In the two areas which receive the substantial energy of the school, that is, reading and arithmetic, there are brief and consistent assignments that are graded and passed back to the children. In the sense of out-of-class work designed to exercise writing ability, research, the study of the community and science, the presence of out-of-class work is dependent on the predilections of individual teachers rather than being part of a coherent curriculum.

Frequent Monitoring of Student Progress.   Again, in the two areas which receive the greatest curricular attention, clearly the teachers know who is keeping up and who is falling behind. A monitoring system based on a standard set of materials falls down where it provides no information about students who are moving ahead or who are capable of more advanced work and no diagnostic information about why a student is having difficulty and what might be done to remedy it.

Coherently Organized Curriculum.   In the sense the two organized areas are built around the textbook they are coherent, but for reasons discussed above it is a primitive organization. In addition, of course, there is no curriculum in many areas. Science, social studies, and the arts are matters for individual teachers and lack structure and cumulative organization of content.

Variety of Teaching Strategies.   The case study does not reveal the extent to which a variety of teaching strategies are used but it is probable that if it is a textbook-oriented curriculum the primary instructional method is recitation (Hoetker and Ahlbrand, 1969). It is probable that relatively few teaching strategies are used; otherwise the manifest problems with students who do not "fit" the standard curriculum would not be so apparent.

Opportunities for Student Responsibility.   Except in the sense of following directions, there are vitually no opportunities apparent in the case materials that have been presented.

In other words, the Cameo School falls short on all of the criteria. It will be easy to find dimensions of the school that can be improved and altogether it can be improved substantially. The school is operating almost as if nothing were known about the character of effective education. In one sense this makes the work of the Responsible Parties very easy. There is clearly no process for school improvement and even the simplest criteria for effectiveness are not being met. On the other hand, without a tradition of school improvement, with leadership that is oriented primarily toward the management of materials and the keeping of order, and so many aspects of the school needing attention, the task of bringing that school up to minimal standards of effectiveness will be considerable.

The Cameo School is clearly an appropriate setting for Stage One school improvement efforts, that is, establishing a process for school improvement and taking steps to get the educational program under control.

4

A Short History
of School Improvement

Before we set about the process of bringing Stage One improvement to schools like Cameo, we need to pause and look at the history of attempts to improve schools and analyze the fate of those efforts. We need to do this for two reasons. First, our experience has left us with an understanding about the social dynamics of school improvement, laying a base on which we can build effective procedures. Many school improvement efforts have not succeeded and we have learned as much from our mistakes (Fullan & Pomfret, 1977) as from our successes.

Second, our attempts to make schools better have come from different visions about what constitutes good education. These visions have given us an array of interesting educational models that we can draw on as we reach Stages Two and Three and begin to consider alternative ways of organizing curriculums, teaching, and the uses of educational technology. Especially in Stage Three we will need to draw on our heritage as we consider alternative missions for the school. To understand how modern schools came into being and why we presently have certain educational alternatives within them, we first need to examine the early social visions that guided our schools and then the visions of the various reformers.

THE COMING OF THE COMMON SCHOOL AND THE INDUSTRIAL MODEL OF EDUCATION

One of the most important American inventions was the "common" school, the school designed to educate everyone in common. It required imagination to envision education as the right and responsibility of every person, rather than the privilege of a selected few. Education had been associated with high social status from the beginnings of the Renaissance, though not all rulers were by any means educated in the contemporary sense. However, as they prepared their children to succeed them, the Renaissance kings developed a limited kind of educational institution, one based largely on the use of scholars to tutor their children. These rulers had very practical reasons for educating their young people. Their children needed information both to govern and also to maintain their advantage over their less literate peers. Also during the Renaissance the Christian church in Europe established schools for educating the clergy and some religious orders made it their mission to educate the upper classes.

Both the religious schools and the tutorial system had much influence on later forms of education. For example, many of the most prominent colleges in the United States were founded to prepare the clergy, and their programs have subsequently had great impact on higher education curriculums. The extent of the church's influence is indicated by the statistic that in 1700 about two in one hundred people were literate and one of the two was connected to the church.

Prior to the Industrial Revolution, there was no overpowering vocational need for education on a wide scale. Most work simply did not require much formal education. Also, prior to the establishment of democratic forms of government, most rulers wanted to keep the power of knowledge to themselves and showed little interest in common education (Cremin, 1965).

The Industrial Revolution of the nineteenth century brought with it the need for a more literate society. This coincided with the extension of the right to vote and the spread of newspapers and other periodicals. Citizens felt a greater need for education than ever before, and lawmakers quickly perceived that both the economic system and the democratic process required at least a modicum of literacy from a reasonable proportion of the citizenry. The expanding commercial class both in Europe and America was vociferous in demanding education for their children, adding to the pressure.

In the United States the movement toward common education began awkwardly. The Constitution did not mention education specifically, so it became the responsibility of the states rather than the federal government. Yet, it is generally assumed that the men who drafted the Constitution intended that an educational system would be established, and it is certainly true that once the states began to establish educational systems, the question of universality arose almost immediately. The 1830s saw the gradual establishment of common schools and laws requiring education. It was assumed that the provision of education would benefit both the individual and the society. The states wished to have a plentiful supply of literate citizens and also to create the opportunity for personal development through education. Thus schools, especially primary schools, appeared across the land, and the states began the long process of making schooling available and requiring all citizens to participate in the educational process.

The curriculum of the early school was dominated by reading, writing, and arithmetic—all useful skills for the simpler industrial and commercial functions, and ones that fitted with the needs the citizens perceived for themselves. (This is probably why those curriculum areas have rarely been questioned in this society; all three simultaneously fit the requirements of industry, citizenship, and personal need.) Education provided the miracle of reading, the ability to communicate through writing, and unpeeled the mystery of arithmetic. In the space of less than 50 years the United States progressed from a situation in which fewer than 10 percent of the population could read or write to one where three-quarters of the white population had achieved functional literacy.

The common school was a Christian school, because anything else was unthinkable to the majority of parents and teachers. There was Bible reading and praying and the singing of hymns. There was strictness and obedience, because fracturing a rule was close to sinning and toeing the mark was the way to salvation.

The teachers were not professionally trained and, for what they were asked to do, little special training was necessary. The content was simple and the teaching methods were straightforward. When special places were set aside to prepare young people to teach, they became training grounds in the original sense of training—the teacher was to administer the common education, not create a unique and personal world of discovery for the students.

By about 1870 half of the children in the United States were receiving some formal public secondary education. At that point, it could be said, the common school was "established," although it had made few dents in the existing status structure. The states established the legal structure for education within their own borders. Of the first 11 constitutions drafted and adopted by states, 6 mentioned education, but in each case left the establishment of an educational system to the legislatures, who were often very slow to act.

The efforts of Thomas Jefferson provide an interesting perspective on the society of the time. In 1779 Jefferson drafted a bill which would have established a universal educational system for the state of Virginia. If the bill had become law, it would have required at least three years of education to be made available to all children. The gifted children of the poor, on the basis of superior academic achievement, would have had free secondary education and college made available to them. The children of the well-to-do would have been able to go, on a tuition basis, through secondary school and finally to William and Mary College.

Jefferson felt that this system would gradually redress the balance between social privilege, educational attainment, and the inheritance of political and social opportunity. The Virginia legislature did not even act on this bill until 1799, and then passed only a watered-down version which was virtually ineffective in establishing any sort of public school system. It was to be a hundred years after Jefferson's proposal before an equivalent system was finally put together.

In addition to the common schools nine higher education institutions were established during the colonial period, but they offered educational services to very few people. At the start of the American Revolution, there were about 2.5 million people in the colonies, about 500,000 of whom were slaves. But only about 750 people were enrolled in the nine colleges altogether! In 1775, for example, Harvard graduated around 40 students, Yale around 35, Columbia 13, and Princeton 6. Except for a tiny sliver of the population, secondary and higher education was almost unthinkable.

The Model of Education

Alvin Toffler argues in *Future Shock* that the school became modeled after the needs of an industrial society.

Mass education was the ingenious machine constructed by industrialism to produce the kinds of adults it needed. The problem was inordinately complex. How to preadapt children for the new world—a world of repetitive indoor toil, smoke, noise, machines, crowded living conditions, collective discipline; a world in which time was to be regulated not by the cycle of sun and moon, but the factory whistle and clock. The solution was an educational system that, in its very structure, simulated this new world...yet the whole idea of assembling masses of students (raw material) to be processed by teachers (workers) in a centrally located school (factory) was a stroke of industrial genius. The whole administrative hierarchy of education, as it grew up, followed the model of industrial bureaucracy. The very organization of knowledge into permanent discipline was grounded on industrial assumptions. Children marched from place to place and sat in assigned stations. Bells rang to announce changes in time.

The inner life of the school thus became an anticipatory mirror, a perfect introduction to industrial society. The most civilized features of education today—the regimentation, lack of individualization, the rigid system of seating, grouping, grading, and marking, the authoritarian role of the teacher—are precisely those that made mass public education so effective an instrument of adaptation for its place in time. (Toffler, 1970)

Toffler's stance is that the institution of the school was created to resemble the factory life that would be the lot of most citizens. It taught people to take orders from others, to work together under close coordination in accordance with instructions, and most of all to put up with enormous quantities of monotonous, imposed tasks, regulated and graded. The early industrial society had a great need for disciplined people who were willing to take orders and work long hours at tasks intrinsically meaningless—meaningful only as they were rewarded or as a person achieved status by being promoted away from them.

In content and procedure the American common school was an almost perfect mirror of the industrial society and reflected in many ways the prevalent status system. The children of the more affluent received greater opportunity for education, and this in turn perpetuated that affluence by being a gateway to higher-salaried occupations. However, for many white children education did partially open the gate to greater opportunity. Contemporary social critics argue that what had been established was a system for perpetuating the "corporate state" and the unequal division of wealth and power (Apple, 1979). Unquestionably the school was heavily influenced by the corporate mentality and undeniably much of its structure did preserve and even accentuate differences in class and caste.

THE REFORM MOVEMENTS

The common school was no sooner established than concerned citizens and educators began searching for ways of improving it and reform movements began to be generated around their ideas. Gradually these reformers came to believe that the kind of school that seemed so obviously "right" to most of us was not necessarily the best climate for mental and emotional growth. They challenged our normal, automatic ways of doing things. They came to believe, and taught us to understand, that punishing children did not help them to learn and that competition was often destructive. They helped us to see how different were those children we were trying to educate in the same way. They urged us to improve our schools.

The most challenging reformers had their eye not only on the child but on the society. Schools they suggested, should not simply transmit the existing culture to the young but should also teach the young to apply the methods of science to the improvement of democratic society. Schools should teach a common faith, one built around the mutual attempt to develop a more humane world (Joyce & Morine, 1976).

The resulting movements never fully transformed the schools, although some of their model schools showed what a phenomenally rich and powerful education could be built, if one had the will. However, they have left a world much less dogmatically sure of the functions of education, because they opened up an infinitely rich spectrum of possibilities. Over the years quite a number of these educational models have been developed, and taken together, they represent the alternatives from which we can choose as we create a plan for any given school.

The *expansionist* orientation was an attempt to broaden and equalize opportunity. This movement began with Jefferson and some of his contemporaries, continued with Mann and his fellow administrators, and is very much alive today. Central to the expansionist movement is the belief that social equality should be promoted, and that educational opportunity is crucial to successful involvement in most social processes. The expansionists sought to change society gradually by extending educational opportunity to children of the economically poor, to blacks, Chicanos, Asians, women of all groups, and to the handicapped. The expansionists concerned themselves less with how education is carried on than with making the mainstream available to more people. The Women's Equity Acts, Public Law 94–142 dealing with persons having physical, mental, or social "handicaps," the bilingual education acts, and Title I, which provides additional resources to schools having large concentrations of poor people, all try to equalize educational opportunity. Thus the expansionist movement contains within it the attempt to enlarge schools, enrich the curriculum, and provide more vocational and cultural avenues at the secondary and higher education levels.

In addition, a number of innovative reformers attempted to change the nature of the mainstream, i.e., to change what is taught and how it is taught. First are the progressive *social reformers,* who focused on the need for citizens to grapple with contemporary political and social problems instead of accepting the status quo without question. The social reformers emphasize the creation of an active citizenry that continually tries to perfect the society. Second are the *academic reformers,* who focused on the need to develop citizens who view knowledge as tentative and testable, who think independently instead of blindly accepting the scholarship of others, but who are well-grounded in the best scholarly knowledge of the time. Third are the *personalistic reformers,* who attempted to make education more relevant to the needs of the individual instead of forcing each individual into a predetermined mold. They emphasize the release of creativity and self-actualization by the unique individuals who make up the body politic. Fourth are the *performance-oriented reformers,* who sought to insure that each individual would achieve competency by learning how to master academic, social, and vocational content.

Because the innovative reformers have worked to bring about change in the form and content of education, they have given us a storehouse of educational methods that represent the riches from which we can create and revitalize our schools. Their views, some radical and some mild, are presented in summary form in the following pages.

The Social Reformers

The progressive movement in American politics in the late nineteenth and early twentieth centuries was devoted to increasing the participation of all members of society in political, economic, and cultural development. The progressives wished to turn the social institutions of society into instruments for increasing this participation. They believed that the larger base of ideas that would flow naturally from that increase in participation would in turn transform those institutions. Political leaders, like Robert Lafollette of Wisconsin, had a vision of very broad-based and egalitarian democracy. They were aware that wide-reaching changes would have to be made in order to actualize those values, since not just education but all the social institutions reflected the prevailing inequalities between castes and classes. Unless those inequalities were reduced, social participation would not increase. The progressive movement in education was a natural part of this wider progressive movement. The thrust of their orientation was directed toward the social and intellectual quality of education.

The Role of John Dewey.   Although many others were involved in the creation of the progressive movement in education, the central spokesman and philosopher was John Dewey (1916). Dewey brought to the task convictions about the nature of knowledge, the process of social life in a democracy, and the relationship of educational process to the preparation of socially effective citizens. As he saw it, intellectual activity arises from the attempt to solve problems, both personal and social, and the resulting knowledge and ideas are constructed and reconstructed as problems are redefined and new information is gathered. He believed that the social construction of knowledge should be shared by all and the ever-changing nature of knowledge understood by all citizens (as contrasted with the view that scholars "discover" unchanging truths).

Children would learn best by being actively involved in solving problems relevant to their daily lives. The scope of the problems would grow as their horizons expanded. Dewey suggested that schools should be places of great activity. The children shold be organized into problem-solving groups. They would attack the problems right about them, such as the economic and political processes of their communities, and reach out to problems of broader scope, such as trying to figure out solutions to international concerns. In Dewey's laboratory school at the University of Chicago at the turn of the century, industrial arts was an important part of primary and secondary education, for he felt that children should learn the basic skills that underlie the industrial society.

According to Dewey, the primary task of the teacher was to help students to identify and learn to solve problems. The teachers should help students to pose progressively more sophisticated questions and then help them find progressively more rigorous sources of information and ideas. For example, children's need to make change in the cafeteria at lunch time could, if properly pursued, lead to the comparative study of different types of number systems, the study of commercial and banking systems, and the international monetary system. To facilitate the process of deepening and expanding knowledge, the teacher needed to balance an emphasis of everyday needs with an ability to conceptualize increasingly broader problems.

Dewey also felt that the social order should be continuously improved, and he had a fervent belief in the perfectability of man and his social processes. Perfection, however, was not simply the pursuit of some utopian social order, but rather the achievement of a state in which all people would continuously participate in the recreation of their social institutions and the redefinition of their social goals. Education should function to commit each person to lifelong activity in political and social reform. New social problems would continue to crop up, and the alive and probing citizenry should be defining those problems, attacking them, and generating yet better ways of living together. Consequently, Dewey felt that the school should be very much a part of the community, and that children should be exposed from a relatively early age to problems which were major concerns of the wider community. Students then would learn interpersonal skills, problem-solving skills, thinking skills, and knowledge about the contemporary world. They would probe into history and into the academic disciplines in an attempt to understand the world and generate solutions to its problems.

Dewey believed that education could be built around the series of steps by which people think through problems (Dewey, 1916).

1. The pupil should have a genuine situation of experience. In other words, there should be a continuous activity that he or she is interested in for its own sake.
2. A genuine problem must develop within this situation that will serve as a stimulator of thought.
3. The pupil needs to possess the information, the appropriate data, and to make the necessary observations required in dealing with the problem.

4. Suggested solutions to the problem will occur to the pupil which the pupil is then responsible for developing in an orderly fashion.
5. The pupil needs to have the opportunity to test solutions by applying them, in order to make their meaning clear and to discover their validity.

At first children would apply these five steps in a relatively naive way. As they became more sophisticated, they would apply them to the solution of increasingly complex problems. Their paradigm was to be the intellectual scaffolding of education—the core mental processes which would be introduced early and exercised and deepened throughout school.

The progressive movement attracted many adherents and a host of philosophers and thinkers during the first half of the century, many of whom concerned themselves with the development of more and more sophisticated methodologies for conducting group-centered education. There was much controversy, however, over whether students in progressive schools would learn as much material as those students who were exposed to the standard curriculum of the industrially oriented school.

Resistance and Retreat. Since the 1930s and 1940s, the formal organization of the progressive movement has declined rather rapidly. The Progressive Education Association was disbanded in the mid-1950s, and its journals passed into history. While there are many educators who still espouse the philosophies of John Dewey, they pursue these beliefs today as individuals rather than as an organized group.

The Eight-Year Study demonstrated the value of progressive education to the satisfaction of the social reformers, but other groups were not convinced. In particular, parents questioned whether their children were learning the basic skills as thoroughly as they might. When reading, writing, and arithmetic were integrated into study of social problems, the emphasis of both pupils and teachers tended to be on solving the problems. Sometimes development of the basic skills did not proceed as rapidly as parents wished (Chamberlin & Chamberlin, 1942).

Reading instruction developed into a national problem with a flavor of scandal about it when *Why Johnny Can't Read and What You Can Do About It,* by Rudolph Flesch, was published in 1955. Others looked at the sales figures for Flesch's book, and quickly joined the attack. Several noneducators became overnight experts on the inadequacies of the public school. The argument was two-fold: that "modern" methods of teaching reading were not as effective as the old phonics method, and that schools were frittering away valuable time on such nonessential activities as field trips and pupil planning. Progressive education was blamed for this state of affairs. (Curiously, probably no more than five percent of schools had adopted progressive methods, even partially!)

While the social reformers protested that Dewey's conception of a progressive educational system had almost never really been implemented in the public schools, their voices went unnoticed amid the general hue and cry. Progressive education had become a bad word. Some progressive educators went "underground," continuing to work toward education that involved children in the real world around them, but not publicizing their efforts. Others continued to preach the philosophy to all who would listen, but the tide had passed them by.

Modern Progressivism and Beyond. Although the progressive movement itself is gone today, the philosophy upon which it was based can be seen in a vast number of present curriculums which emphasize the teacher as a leader of group process. New curriculums have been developed to teach human relation skills directly. Programs of instuction help students clarify value positions and analyze alternative values which can be used to solve contemporary conflicts. Approaches to international education have been devised to help young people comprehend the nature of international society and ways that they can participate in it (Becker, 1979). Approaches to moral development have been generated in which students are taught to think about moral issues in increasingly complex ways and to analyze the moral implications in every day events (Kohlberg, 1966). A number of social studies programs attempt to teach young people systematic ways of thinking about society and its problems and to equip them with the skills to engage in collective activity. Many of these programs emphasize the study of the environment, population, poverty, conflict, and the other vast, critical problems of human life on earth. Programs have been developed to help blacks, Chicanos, and native Americans to discover their heritages and to comprehend the nature of their situations in our society. Some curriculums help young people comprehend sexism and study alternative ways that men and women can better divide labor and status and develop greater mutual respect. And efforts have been made to turn some inner-city schools into community action centers where adults and children study the problems within their areas and engage in collective action to attack those problems.

The orientation of this modern progressivism is obviously as pluralistic and chaotic as was the progressivism of earlier years. Contemporary social reformers still emphasize current social problems, collective action, the reconstruction of society, the evolution of knowledge, and a desire to have values and value development at the core of education.

The Academic Reformers

At the same time that the progressives were under severe attack, another innovative group known as the academic reformers was becoming prominent (Goodlad, 1967). With support from the National Science Foundation and private foundations, these scholars organized committees which undertook to revise each of the major areas of the curriculum by producing curriculum materials for the schools and by increasing the academic components of teacher training programs. They were assisted by the furor that arose when Soviet achievements in space met the American competitive spirit (The Russian launching of the satellite called *Sputnik* marked the coalescence of the academic reform movement). Scientists and mathematicians were suddenly thrust forward as the new supermen, and the academic reformers were launched onto the educational scene, trailing rhetoric about the importance of developing young scholars. But who was to train these young scholars?

The education of teachers was conducted for the most part by the faculties of one-, two-, and finally four-year normal schools rather than within the major universities. The effect of this was to isolate the preparation of teachers from the mainstream of American scholarship and, consequently, educators came to be perceived as outsiders by the professors in other disciplines. Among many academics, education was regarded as a natural consequence of academic knowledge rather than a legitimate field of study. Schools of education had great difficulty obtaining status within their universities. Learning materials also became increasingly divorced from contemporary scholarship since publishers and other producers of learning materials related more closely to educationists than to academic scholars.

By the early 1950s the education of teachers and academic scholars was almost totally separate, and there was resentment on both sides. Teachers resented having to take academic courses that they regarded as unrelated to their work. Academic scholars resented education courses which they felt were second-rate and pedestrian in contrast to the study of the basic disciplines. By the mid-1950s the gulf between academic scholarship and what was being taught in schools was so great that a coalition of scholars began redesigning both the curriculum content and instructional methodology of schools to make them more compatible with the practice of the academic disciplines.

Studying the Disciplines.   The academic reform movement viewed man as a scholar, and its approach to teacher education was direct—to train the teacher to think like a scholar and "to practice the disciplines" with children. Basic to each discipline are sets of ideas and methodologies, sometimes called modes of inquiry, which guide the work of scholars. These sets of ideas, the concepts of the discipline, are under continuous revision as new data are unearthed and organized in new ways. In the newer disciplines, such as social psychology, ideas undergo very rapid revision. In the older disciplines, such as physics, certain sets of ideas have been stable for a very long time, while others are in revision (Joyce, 1964; 1972).

Domains of Study. Scholars in each discipline focus on certain domains of inquiry. Scholars in social psychology, example, study the processes by which human beings interact in small groups, the kinds of influences which they exert on one another, and the individual differences in response to various social environments and types of influence. Anthropologists tend to study human societies as a whole, focusing especially upon the processes by which patterns of behavior and physical artifacts are developed, the processes by which these are transmitted to the young, and the ways in which cultures undergo change. Although these domains change from time to time, sometimes radically, at any given point in time it is usually possible to define their boundaries.

The Structure of Organizing Ideas. Bearing in mind the differences between the disciplines with respect to their focus and the extent to which they are in flux, each discipline tends to have a set of ideas which function in several ways. First of all, they define the discipline. In the case of physics, for example, we find that the area of mechanics is built upon a set of ideas which explains the processes by which force is transferred from one object to another. In the area of mathematics we find sets of ideas which describe number systems and operations upon those numbers. Moreover, some ideas are more unifying than others; they have more "explaining power"; they hold together other ideas and the facts which are subsumed by them. Some of the disciplines are so organized that they have a hierarchical character, with a few major ideas at the top and subordinate ideas slung beneath them in a pyramidal form. This is more true of the natural and physical sciences than it is of the social sciences and humanities, where ideas tend to cluster around specific topics that have been explored by scholars (Joyce, 1972).

Methods of Inquiry. Generally speaking, all of the disciplines share the belief that academic inquiry should be both cumulative and replicable. By cumulative we mean that the scholar is suppose to build on the work of others. He does not have to repeat what they have done but he is supposed to acknowledge their work and to present his ideas in such a way that a clear relationship (or lack of relationship) is shown between what he does and what they have done. By replicable we mean care in reporting inquiry so that other scholars investigating the same ground can examine the same facts and follow the same lines of reasoning that have led to the earlier conclusions. A person whose inquiry is neither cumulative nor replicable is not likely to contribute to scholarly knowledge. Once in a great while a brilliant individualist disobeys these canons and nonetheless makes a contribution. What makes this contribution academic is the painstaking work of other scholars who weld the individualist's work to some larger, related body of knowledge (Joyce, 1972).

Teaching the Discipline to Children. The academic reform movement endeavored to reorganize the public school curriculum so that it reflected the scholarly study of the disciplines. Scholar-led projects in the sciences, mathematics, social studies, English, and foreign languages created materials for children built around the ideas and methods of the academic disciplines. Large-scale programs were launched to train teachers to implement those curricula. In these programs great prominence was given to the information-processing power of the academic disciplines. Effort was focused both on the conceptual capacities of students and on the potential contribution of scholarly concepts to the improvement of their lives. The movement clearly intended to make academic thought more intelligible to the citizen and to prepare more students for a life of scholarship. The teacher was to be the surrogate scholar in the classroom.

A conference at Woods Hole, Massachusetts, which marked the beginning of the movement resulted in the popularization of the term, "the structure of the disciplines." Jerome Bruner, reporting on this conference in *The Process of Education* (1961), cited four advantages for organizing instruction around the central concepts of the academic disciplines:

1. Organizing teaching around the structure of the disciplines would increase memory by providing students an ideational scaffolding with which to organize and retain information.
2. Understanding the structure of the disciplines would give students greater intellectual power by providing unifying ideas to help them comprehend the world.
3. The major concepts would increase the transfer of education to problem-solving situations by providing an intellectual structure for thinking about problems.

4. The education of children would be brought closer to the forefront of knowledge. They would be learning the types of concepts which advanced scholars used, rather than distillations and assertions far removed from ideas that drove advanced technique.

This view deemphasizes emotion. Nowhere in *The Process of Education* are the emotions of the student discussed, except for the assertion that knowledge is itself intrinsically motivating. The act of knowing, the act of increasing comprehension, was seen as so satisfying that students, once exposed to ideas of quality, would be motivated to continue their education. The scholars obviously saw children as they saw themselves.

Most often the view of the teacher that derived from the academic stance was that of the logician and academic scholar. This view was perhaps most eloquently expressed in the handbooks which Schwab (1963) and his associates wrote for a well-known biology curriculum. Schwab clearly felt that it would not be possible for teachers to teach biology unless they also practiced it. It would not, of course, be necessary for them to be prize-winning scholars, but they should have the kind of intellectual interests that would lead them to explore the modes of inquiry of the discipline and to apply them to solving problems in which they themselves were interested.

Thus the reformers emphasized a mode for training teachers that would make them practicing members of the discipline. Acting as models they would subsequently induct their students into the processes and concepts of the disciplines.

Reform and Resistance. The academic reform movement viewed man as an information-processing creature (Joyce & Weil, 1982), and saw the disciplines as the source of the most important knowledge. Both its deductive and inductive branches created materials for children which assumed the teacher to be a practitioner of the disciplines. Teacher and child were seen as receivers either of the concepts of the discipline (the deductive approach) or its methodologies (the inductive approach). Socialization into the academic community was central to both variations on the academic theme.

It is debatable, however, to what degree the academic community resides within the mainstream of American society. The existence of a vast number of higher education institutions and the predominance of academic content within the schooling process might be taken as evidence that the scholar enjoys high recognition within our culture. Likewise the role of scholars as advisors to government attests to a certain degree of acceptance. Nevertheless it is possible to have a postsecondary education without a high degree of intellectuality, and the scholar is certainly not embraced by all segments of the culture. Hofstadter (1963) and his students have taken great pains to point out and document the extent to which anti-intellectualism characterizes mainstream America.

It is not so surprising, therefore, that the attempts to socialize teachers and students into the academic community met with some resistance from parents and teachers. Not all teachers welcomed the new curriculum materials that were thrust upon them. Many were unclear about the new concepts they were supposed to be teaching while others were uncomfortable with the new instructional procedures they were told to use. These teachers tended to use the techniques of passive resistance: the new curriculum materials sat on the classroom shelves, but somehow the class was always too busy to use them. A typical comment from a resistant teacher was: "The state law says I have to use this teacher's manual. But it doesn't say how I have to use it. I'm using mine as a paperweight."

For those teachers who did make an effort to use the new materials, it was not all clear sailing. Suddenly, parents found that they couldn't understand the homework their children were doing. The new math was using terms like *sets, elements, union,* and *intersection.* What had happened to addition and subtraction? The new English was teaching about determiners, morpheme strings, and sentence transformation! What happened to good old grammar? Many parents found it difficult to believe that the new concepts and methods were establishing a good foundation in the basic skills of reading, writing, and arithmetic. In some cases, they raised objections to the new textbooks.

As a result, the academic reform movement never took over the school curriculum to the extent that the scholars had hoped. New curriculum materials were produced, but they were not used as extensively or as effectively as originally envisioned. There were important changes in some teachers' instruction, but the traditional forms of instruction remained dominant (Goodlad & Klein, 1970).

The major thrust of the academic reformers occurred between 1955 and 1965 and in the decade that followed efforts were made to consolidate their advances. Further advancement will probably require some new and innovative ideas to reenergize the academic reformers, ideas that do not abound at present. Consequently, it is difficult to predict the future direction of this group.

Personalistic Reformers

As the power and energy of the academic reform movement declined, yet another group of innovators seized the spotlight. Powered by the increasing disaffection of young people with what they considered to be the repressiveness of social institutions, the personalists stepped forth to proclaim the importance of individual freedom and fulfillment and to lead the protest against an educational system that rewarded "normal" or standard behavior above all else.

Of course, the establishment of universal education was originally designed to bring about mass education. Its substance and form had been tailored to the needs of the early industrial society. Although it was expected that the acquisition of education would in itself be beneficial to the individual's life, it was also intended that the educational system would function as a powerful socializer and would make us more alike than different. To the personalists, however, the educational system had become too weighted in the direction of mass socialization.

From the time of Rousseau, long before any mass educational system had developed in Europe or in the United States, there were those who doubted that socialization to the prevailing norms was entirely beneficial. They put their faith instead on the development of individual personalities, trusting that well-developed individuals could negotiate better lives for themselves than could possibly be planned by others. They worked to insure the flowering of individual liberty and the development of idiosyncrasy. However, the major emphasis during the development of the common school was not, and probably could not have been, the individuality of students. It was difficult enough to make any kind of formal education available and to increase, thereby, the possibility of mobility through the social system. Since the late 1800s, however, psychologists, therapists, philosophers, and political liberals have waged a considerable battle to make education more responsive to individual personalities. They desire to free individuals from the excessive social constraints that are often transmitted through formal education (Joyce & Weil, 1980).

One of the major strains in the progressive movement was fueled by those who placed the individual first. Schools such as the Bank Street School in New York City were established around principles of individualized education and whole schools of psychology (e.g., Gestalt psychology) were developed around conceptions of the individual self and techniques for helping each person to flower on his or her own terms. Therapists such as Carl Rogers spoke out against the repressiveness of mass education and developed procedures for building education around counseling theory. More recently, spokesmen such as John Holt, Jonathan Kozol, Herbert Kohl, and Robert Coles have made urgent pleas for the reform of the educational system with emphasis on individualism rather than conformity.

While some theorists and practitioners would develop all of education around the nondirective stance (that is, facilitating the individual's planning of his own education), the personalist orientation has more commonly been implemented through the provision of some form of individual counseling by the teacher within the classroom setting. From clinical psychology (Rogers and Glasser, for instance), individual psychology (Combs and Maslow), Gestalt psychology (Perls and Schutz), and personalistic philosophy (Friere, Buber, and Greene) have come strands of thought that have represented a very strong reform effort in the educational literature. The effort has had only occasional, but nonetheless dramatic, effects on schooling and on teacher education.

The personalist stresses the uniqueness of each student and the importance of their emotional makeup. Individual psychology and Gestalt theory both stress the importance of the personal perceptual field. Peering at the world from their unique perspectives, students create their individual reality and make their world meaningful. Their relations with others are characterized by a process of continuous negotiation as they seek to exchange differing frames of reference. The unique configuration of the self controls the kinds of life activities that are perceived as possible and the kinds of learning that are accessible.

Curriculum Adaptations. The personalist orientation has produced certain approaches to training. In reading, for example, the experience approach, in which reading is taught through stories that the children make up and dictate to the teacher, grows out of the belief that pupils will better comprehend these self-produced reading materials, since they reflect their own unique perspective of the world. Self-selected reading programs, where children select books of personal interest, are another expression of the personalist approach to educational reform.

From the personalist orientation, one does not presume to teach. Rather teachers provide environments with much diversity and flexibility, ones which confront learners with many choices and allow them to shape their own educational configurations. The curriculum is not planned in the sense that objectives are set and learning activities organized in advance. Rather, the teacher gently helps students to reflect on their own experience, and negotiates goals with them.

When this view guides the design of a whole school, the result is markedly different from traditional schools. Summerhill, for example, is delineated not only by what it focuses on, but by what it avoids. Its founder, A.S. Neill (1960), believes that personal development should not be subverted by a highly structured curriculum no matter how well intentioned. His school avoids imposing learning on the student and gives primacy to their emotional life.

If the student is unique, what of the teacher? Teacher educators who emphasize the uniqueness of children and the importance of their emotionality must do the same for teachers. Their education, too, has to be a process of freeing the personality and helping them to develop on their own terms. The act of teaching has to be seen as an interaction between two equal selves, teacher and learner, in which the more experienced serves as the gentlest sort of guide.

The chief spokesman for the personalistic education of teachers has been Arthur W. Combs. Combs assumes that each person strives as best he can for self-fulfillment, that they are filled with energy that expends itself on self-maintenance and self-enhancement.

It is not the physical self that each seeks to maintain, however. It is the self of which we are aware, our self-concepts, we seek fulfillment for. Even behaviors which at first glance seem to be self-destructive turn out to be self maintaining or enhancing when they are seen from the point of the individual. So it is that the hero may give himself up to certain death rather than see himself a coward or a traitor to his fellows. In our own experiences we often place our physical self in jeopardy for the sake of enhancing our concepts of self. For example, we drive too fast, eat too much, work too hard, even when we know better.

The need for adequacy is the fundamental motivation of every human being from conception to death. The drive towards health does not have to be learned; neither does the characteristic of life itself and provides the motor power for every human act.

This drive has a tremendous implication for education. Its existence means it is not necessary to motivate people—a problem we have often struggled with. Everyone is always motivated to be and become as adequate as he can be in the situations as he sees them. Students may not be motivated as their teachers would like, but they are always motivated in terms of their own basic needs.

Knowledge of this unique drive changes the whole structure of the educative process from that which our ancestors felt was essential . . . the task of the teacher is not one of prescribing, making, molding, forcing, (etc.) . . . the role required of the teacher is that of facilitator, encourager, helper, assistor, colleague and friend of the students. (Combs, 1965, p.16)

Thus teachers should develop the capacity to engage in a helping relationship, one which includes the ability to relate to people and help them on their own terms. Teachers need to orient themselves so that their own fulfillment is derived from helping students enhance themselves. Teaching becomes an idosyncratic process that depends on the individual character of the teacher relating with the individual character of the student. Combs says that teaching competencies stem from the unique way in which an individual teacher develops a helping relationship with a unique class and each individual student therein. Since teaching depends on personal exchange between two participants, each on their own terms, the primary teaching competence is the ability to understand one's self and to learn to understand others.

To change behavior a person has to change his perceptions: that is, any significant change in behavior involves a change in one's perceptual field. Thus, the individual self has to be the focus of education. People's adjustment and perception, interpersonal relations, and ability to educate themselves all come from their views of themselves. Combs is concerned much less with the discipline-derived substance of teacher education (particularly the details of the substance) than are advocates of other approaches. Rather, he deals with what is done to help teachers develop their individual views of themselves as persons and as teachers. Combs agrees that the teacher needs to achieve competency and knowledge, but he believes these will develop only in relation to the teacher's personal and professional self-concept rather than as the product of an imposed curriculum.

Problems for Personalists.   Because all reform movements face resistance from some quarter, it was predictable that the personalists would encounter some opposition. Interestingly enough, many parents have protested against the personalistic innovations in schools for the same reasons that they protested against the social and academic innovations. They have complained that children who are designing their own learning patterns are being short-changed on the all-important basic skills of reading, writing, and arithmetic. They suggest that children are basically lazy and, if left to set their own goals, will never push themselves hard enough to develop their real potential. They imply that teachers who permit children to organize their own instruction have abdicated responsibility for the professional decisions they are paid to make.

It remains to be seen how strong the opposition will become and how convincing the personalists will be, for the personalistic reform movement recently hit a new crest, one of several peaks in its historical development, and it will probably continue to influence American education for several years. Although strong, it is not the only important movement presently on the educational scene. Competing for the attention and commitment of educators are the advocates of performance-based education.

The Performance-oriented Reformers

In recent years a new reform movement has developed, one which is probably receiving the widest attention as this is being written. It is focused on systems approaches to instructional management—an attempt to increase the precision and directness of teaching. It is characterized by learning objectives in precise, behavioral terms, diagnosing the learner's readiness to achieve (the development of a diagnostic profile), and prescribing learning activities directly matched to those objectives. In addition, careful monitoring of progress and adjustment of instruction to learner progress is advocated.

The movement is heavily oriented toward instructional materials developed on these principles. Such materials have been developed at all levels and within all subject areas. In some cases large curricular systems provide objectives, modules, and diagnostic and management materials. In other cases the objectives are provided and teachers invent the rest of the system as they go along.

In many ways the competency orientation is a logical extension of the industrial model of the school. It is based in part on the desire to make schooling more efficient and to hold teachers and teacher educators accountable for the results of their efforts. It employs many techniques originally developed in industrial or military applications of systems technology. Emphasizing computer-based management systems, the use of multimedia instructional devices, and the development of data storage and retrieval systems to store program elements, objectives, and evaluation, it represents a look beyond the traditional age to the emerging technitronic age. In this sense the competency orientation is futuristic. Even futuristic movements have historical roots, however, and the antecedents of the performance-oriented movement can be most clearly discerned in the years since 1940.

Systems Planning: An Essential Ingredient. An individualized (let alone personalized) education program cannot be conceived for a large student body without the capacity to obtain and store vast amounts of information about students and to maintain and deliver a wide variety of alternative instructional experiences (Joyce, 1972). Although educators have talked about individualized curriculums for decades, they have not assimilated the technology needed to support them. Quality control has been similarly limited. Although curriculum theory has postulated for many years that there should be direct linkages between behaviorally stated objectives, instructional alternatives, and evaluation processes, the actualization of this paradigm has not been possible. For example, even a committed instructor teaching a course to only 20 students simply cannot manufacture enough tests by himself to track progress and adjust instruction to the varying learning rates of his students.

With the advent of technologies for developing large and complex information storage and retrieval systems came the capacity to develop management systems that could coordinate student characteristics and achievement with instructional alternatives, while still maintaining reasonable levels of quality control (Smith & Smith, 1966). To date, however, very few educators have become familiar with these technologies. This is partly because such technology is still relatively new and not yet disseminated throughout the education community, and partly because many educators have reacted adversely and equate management systems with dehumanization.

It is safe to say that system planners are comfortable with the idea of management systems and believe that when we learn how to use them, we will make education much more flexible and human. They look for ways of developing *support systems, choice points,* and *feedback systems;* they develop training in *simulators* with "recycling to a more appropriate alternative" and "increasing complexity of instructional tasks." In other words, they attempt a massive task analysis of the problem of teaching a child to read or preparing an adult to teach. And system planners are confident that the task analysis can be made and the needed management systems created. They recognize that enormous quantities of jargon will be needed to symbolize the concepts of objectives, modular curricular alternatives, evaluation, and support systems necessary to such an effort. They believe that eventually such technology will not only permit instruction to be tailored to individuals but also will enable many instructional goals and means to be shaped by the student himself.

Hence, the performance-oriented reformers live in an assumptive world comprised of management systems theory and a concern with efficiency and systematic training (cybernetic psychology). And they believe that applying these to education will mean a more personal environment for the student, a more effective teacher, and a school in which desirable innovation can be cycled into the system much more easily than with the present organization.

Systems planners have recently developed a wide range of options utilizing computers, broadcast and taped television programs, and other devices that can be used to create a wide variety of responsive options. Some of these options are used to develop very responsive educational systems while others are utilized to transmit relatively fixed courses. The spectrum of media options is so complex that we have chosen to give it a separate treatment and place it at the point (Chapter 13) where we begin to think about Stage Three school improvement efforts.

Opposition to Performance-Oriented Reforms. The use of systems procedures implies that the analogy of "system" to describe schools, teaching, and training is a valid one. Controversy over the reasonableness of this analogy focuses around the question, "Does systems technology partition man—and education—in an inhuman way?"

Support for the movement comes from those who feel that a precise education is most powerful. Opposition comes from those who fear that schools will become an institutional maze in which students will be directed and managed by computers through an impersonal honeycomb of instructional systems (Oettinger, 1969).

PLURALISM IN EDUCATIONAL INNOVATION

Each of the innovative reform movements attempted to achieve an important goal. The social reformers sought to develop schools in which students engage in concerted action for the purpose of societal re-creation. The academic reformers worked to achieve student self-realization by improving their independent thinking skills and their understanding of important bodies of knowledge. The personalist encouraged students to develop their own unique talents, of whatever variety. The performance-oriented reformers argue that self-realization is a vague, unrealizable dream until every student develops certain basic skills and competencies.

Not one of the innovative reform movements has yet achieved its goal. Each has met resistance in one form or another, and in fact, the movements have served as forces of resistance to each other. Each has tended to present itself as the solution to the complex problems of educational improvement. But no single solution can ever solve a complex problem.

The real contribution of the innovative reform movements is not that each of them has established a beachhead, captured the flag, and guarded its turf for a period of time. The real contribution is that each has furthered the possibility of educational pluralism. Together they provide multiple avenues which expand the diversity of educational experience. Together they enable us to select the options which appear to fit most closely the community and children of every school. For our purposes, they have left us with a marvelous array of views of humankind, society, and the role of education.

Our brief description of the ebb and flow of orientations toward school improvement is offered as an introductory guide to the alternatives. The serious reader will discover that the world is not as discrete as we have depicted it—some progressives were personalists, some personalists are performance oriented, and so on. Also, the various movements overlapped to a good extent. We can find traces of them all in the writings of the ancient Greek philosophers! Taken together they force us to ask the questions: "What are *our* beliefs about the central purpose of education?" "What is our social vision?"

Effective Schools from Different Orientations

The criteria presented in Chapter 3 for judging the effectiveness of a school apply regardless of the orientation that is taken toward education. Personalistic, social, academically oriented, and behavioral systems frameworks all require some of the same conditions. A clear understanding of goals, a positive and pervasive caring attitude toward students, a coherent curriculum, instruction that involves the students vigorously but in ways that are appropriate to their abilities and learning styles, the use of alternative teaching strategies when appropriate, and effective leadership are all necessary regardless of the orientation that is taken. In Stage One school improvement we apply those criteria to make the school better on its own terms and establish the process for improving it. In Stage Two we begin to consider some of the options from our heritage as we focus on particular curriculum areas and try to make them better. In Stage Three we draw more heavily on our heritage in order to think about the various missions our school can seek to attain, and the variety of technical and human resource options that can be brought together to achieve these missions.

Part II
ESTABLISHING THE PROCESS

The history of attempts to improve schools combines with studies of the nature of the school as an organization to give us a base on which we can develop a strategy for school improvement. The organization of the school has developed homeostatic forces; that is, forces that keep behavior within narrow bounds. An effective strategy must deal with those forces and establish a homeostasis of improvement so that the flow of activities necessary to maintain the social organization and educational programs do not submerge improvement efforts.

5

Homeostatic Forces and School Improvement

The motive for school improvement can originate with the Responsible Parties of a local school or with district, county, or state education agencies. Federal government and national interest groups sometimes provide resources designed to motivate local agencies toward national educational needs. School improvement efforts can center on neighborhood schools or on the development of services that cross school boundaries. External agencies can create entire new systems such as open universities, institutes or centers that concentrate on particular substance (as the performing arts), and initiate courses using broadcast television or other media that cross school boundaries. In addition, as we described in Chapter 1, efforts can concentrate on refining the kind of education that is presently carried on, or can introduce new substance, process, organization, or technology. Thus we can think of school improvement as:

	Locally originated (within school)	or	Externally originated
and:			
	Refinement oriented (Stage One)	or	Innovation oriented (Stages Two and Three)

Whether an improvement effort is fueled by energy within or outside of the local school community, and whether the focus is on refinement or innovation, the *problem* is one of innovation—of bringing about changes or creating new forms of education. The Responsible Parties of a local high school attempting to improve its science program need to develop and implement curriculum, introduce new materials, help teachers learn teaching strategies they are not accustomed to using, etc. *All of these require changes that have, in the past, proved difficult to implement and sustain.* Even locally inspired refinement is difficult.

61

Refinement or innovation generated by districts or other external agencies are much harder to implement successfully. For example, state agencies that have created courses mediated by broadcast television or television tape have had great difficulty ensuring implementation by local schools even when the only requirement was providing time for viewing, and for minimum follow-up of broadcast episodes. Implementation of externally generated curriculums and technology by local education personnel has run into even greater difficulty.

The history of educational reform has provided us with a large data base for current school improvement efforts. In this and the next chapter we will discuss the problem of innovation and describe a strategy designed:

1. To make it easier for the Responsible Parties of local schools to generate and sustain continuous efforts to improve their schools.
2. To create a climate in which local decision makers can capitalize on externally generated school improvement efforts. External agencies are more capable of generating the research and development necessary for major innovations in curriculum and technology. Unless the local environment can use external developments effectively, they are doomed to fail.

Thus we will concentrate on the local school, on organizing the Responsible Parties to select targets and implement procedures that will permit them to continuously assess the missions of the school, and the means to achieve them.

The history of change contains some spectacular short-run successes and we are beginning to learn from our failures. From the experience of the last 25 years we have accumulated a base of knowledge from which we can operate with some confidence. We now have defensible hypotheses which form elements of a general strategy we can test and improve as we gain experience.

The strategy is aimed directly at the two primary adversaries of educational reforms—custom and habit. Custom operates through citizen pressure. It seems fair to state that any educational practice that is not customary will generate an adverse reaction. Similarly, the habits formed through present educational practice tend to absorb new procedures. In order to overcome these adversaries we must first recognize that educational changes, no matter how desirable, face formidable obstacles. Next we must consider what changes need to be made so that sensible school improvements can be routinely implemented.

THE HISTORY OF CHANGE

If we lived in a social vacuum, changing schools would be as simple as arranging the players on a chess board in the absence of an opponent. We could simply select the arrangement we prefer and move the pieces around until we liked the result.

The real world of educational change is, however, about as far from an opponentless board game as we can get. The fundamental reason for this is the school's relationship to society. Over the years society has become accustomed to the school model that was developed during the industrial revolution. Alternative models are resisted both because they violate social expectations and because habit is so powerful. The prevailing model of education has become ingrained in the patterns of teachers, administrators, and students. To use an alternative model requires that school personnel learn how to make that model work and also that they change deep-seated norms. Although educators can easily learn to make alternatives work, after a time the old patterns tend to reassert themselves and wipe out the new approach. This combination of social expectation and educational habit has been lethal to many reforms as several recent studies have documented (Fullan and Pomfret, 1977).

A 1970 study by John Goodlad and Frances Klein entitled *Looking Behind the Classroom Door* was especially timely for several reasons. First, it followed closely on the heels of 20 years of active educational reform. This period saw the creation of numerous instructional models and efforts to persuade and train teachers to use them. The efforts began with the generation of models for "nongrading" the school, an effort in which Professor Goodlad is one of the leaders. This was also the period of the technological revolution in which mediated instructional systems were developed and disseminated by foundations, industries, and federal programs. New patterns of school organization such as team teaching, and the development of instructional centers and support services were also created along with newer, more compatible forms of school architecture. Curriculum reform movements produced a variety of new instructional models, some highly structured and teacher centered and other primarily child centered and less structured (see Chapter 4). During the same period the "great debate" over reading practices reached its boiling point and spawned a variety of new and resurrected models of reading instruction. In summary, the schools Goodlad studied had available to them a vast variety of alternative models of teaching. Finally, school architecture was liberated from the "egg-crate model," and most of the emerging architectural concepts have promoted collegial teaching and the use of newer instructional technologies.

In other words, Goodlad and Klein's report came at a time when it permitted us to see the effects of the reform efforts of the last 25 years including the use of available alternatives. Although they found that principals and teachers "alike spoke frequently of individual needs, individual differences, and provisions for both...our data lead to the firm conclusion that the overwhelming majority of our 150 classrooms— in organization, subject matter, materials and mode of instruction— were geared to group norms and expectancies rather than to individual differences in learning rate and need" (Goodlad & Klein, 1970, pp. 82– 83). Their observers saw very little application of learning principles, either in diagnosis or in prescription, and they concluded that although the teachers were generally relating positively toward the children there was very little evidence that most of the innovative teaching models were being used.

Goodlad and Klein concluded that the traditional grade school, a product of our industrial past, with its commitments to grades, lower-order objectives, and convergent activities continues to dominate the American scene. They argue:

The highly recommended and publicized innovations of the past decade were dimly conceived and at best partially implemented in schools claiming them. The novel features seem to be blunted in the effort to twist the innovation into familiar conceptual frames or established patterns of schooling. For example, team teaching more often than not was some pattern of departmentalization and nongrading looked to be a form of homogeneous grouping. Similarly, the new content of curriculum projects tend to be conveyed with the baggage of traditional methodology. (Goodlad and Klein, 1970, p. 72)

This conclusion held even for schools selected because of their innovative reputations. Although many of the principals and teachers in those schools believed that the teaching was innovative, the observational records indicated otherwise.

The instructional environment of the classes we visited, more in grades 1 and 3 than in the kindergarten, were characterized by telling, teachers' questioning individual children in group settings, and an enormous amount of seemingly quite routine seat work. Rather than probing, seeking, inquiring, children were predominantly responding and covering. Even when using the materials of curriculum projects presumably emphasizing "discovery" methods, people appeared bent on covering the content of textbooks, workbooks and supplementary reading material. (Goodlad & Klein, 1970, p. 79)

Goodlad and Klein also comment on the homogeneity which their observers frequently reported:

We were struck. . .by the sameness of activities within any given room, whether or not designed for enrichment or individual supplementation of the regular program. We rarely saw an abrupt turnabout from the kind of instruction we have described to vigorous, constructive, play acting, or dancing. Independent activities when provided meant more of the same reading (but with different books), writing, and coloring. (Goodlad & Klein, 1970, p. 91)

They go on to ask, "Is some stereotype of schooling so built into our culture that it virtually shapes the entire enterprise, discouraging, or even destroying deviations from it?"

Goodlad and Klein conclude that the extensive reform movements of the last 25 years barely touched the classroom. They attribute this to two causes. One is that the entire organizational and social context of the schools has not been conducive to innovation. Schools have not developed a dynamic self-concept nor have they organized themselves to select from the available models of teaching. They have not chosen consciously and forcefully, those models which best suit their mission, their preferences, or the characteristics of their children. Most schools, in other words, adopt the prevailing mode of education without serious reflection about the alternatives. Second, they blame teacher training. Teachers not only work alone for the most part but "it would appear that neither preservice or in-service teacher education programs have provided them with the precise pedagogical understandings and skills required for diagnosing and remedying the learning programs and needs of individual pupils" (Goodlad & Klein, 1970, p. 97). What is so striking about the Goodlad and Klein study is that so few traces were found of the many types of education discussed in Chapter 4. The industrial model of schooling still prevailed, relentlessly absorbing each new effort at innovation.

Recent studies by the Rand Corporation (Berman & McLaughlin, 1975), by the National Institute of Education (Weiss, 1978), by Hall, Loucks and their associates at the University of Texas (1977), and elsewhere have confirmed and extended Goodlad and Klein's results. These studies have documented that when local schools are provided with resources to improve themselves or when external agencies try to improve them there are a variety of results. It is clear that unless a local school environment is congenial to sensible innovation, even minor school improvement objectives, whether locally or externally generated, will have hard sledding.

Should we conclude that the prospects for change are hopeless? Far from it. Studies of curriculum implementation are laying a knowledge base on which we can build strategies that will greatly increase the likelihood of implementing new curriculums and decrease the pain, frustration, and confusion that has so often accompanied change efforts. Simply put, the message from the literature on change and innovation is that schools need to be more congenial to innovation whether generated from within or without.

ORGANIZATIONAL HOMEOSTASIS AND INNOVATION: TIGHTENING THE LOOSE COUPLINGS

The last 20 years has seen the emergence of systematic inquiry into the nature of educational organizations, at least in schools and school districts (it seems that colleges have been less systematically studied). And, despite complaints that much more needs to be done, today's knowledge is much more substantial than it was a couple of decades ago. Drawing on our growing store of knowledge we can now begin to clarify how educational organizations receive innovations and limit or extend their effectiveness through organizational contexts and the use of effective training methods (Lehming & Kane, 1981).

In addition to the recent work on organizations we have drawn heavily on the concepts of George Homans (1950), Talcott Parsons (1951), and aspects of Leslie White (1949). The numerous inquiries into the nature of organizations and the persons who have brought that literature together, particularly Ernest House (1981), Matthew Miles (1981), Michael Fullan (1981), Philip Runkel (1977) and his associates in Oregon, and Herbert Thelen (1954) have influenced the ideas that follow.

Homeostatic Forces and Levels of Organization

We will consider the forces within organizations on three levels. The first of these deals with the behavior of the individuals working to achieve satisfaction within an organizational setting. We refer to this, after Getzels and Thelen (1976), as the *idiographic* level. It focuses on personal concerns and, seen from a distance, it is a sea of emotions, values, individually generated behavior patterns, and informal systems of communications. It is the values and imperatives of the individuals gathered in the workplace. The second level, which is easier to discern in terms of traditional organizational analysis, consists of the structure and planned patterns of the organization. It deals with the way in which authority is distributed and formal communication patterns are maintained. We refer to this as the *formal-structural* level. Third, institutions exist within their *external systems*—the social organization and cultural milieu which impinge on it and, in turn, are influenced by it. Important aspects of institutional life can be found at the point of interchange between internal and external systems. (See Figure 5.1.)

Each of these levels of institutional life generates homeostatic forces, that is, forces that tend to stabilize patterns of behavior and keep them within a normative range. Homeostatic forces are similar to those physiological mechanisms in the human organism which keep life support functions within a normal range. In the social domain homeostatic forces resist attempts at innovation, precisely because it is their function to prevent changes that might endanger some essential aspect of life in the institution. Effective innovation strategies are those that manage to neutralize the homeostatic forces. Let us now consider the kinds of homeostatic forces that operate at each of the institutional levels.

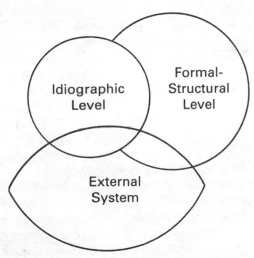

FIGURE 5.1 Levels of the Organization

The Idiographic Level. This is where the people who work in organizations live and function. As Homans (1950) has made clear, people who live in organizational settings learn to carry out their basic functions and satisfy their basic needs within the organizational context. Needs for a sense of belonging, status, predictability, and so forth, are all acted out. In Getzels' terms, these projections of personal need must be reconciled in some fashion with nomothetic, or group, needs including the organization's goals and sructure. To satisfy their personal needs people try to arrange conditions and events within the organizational setting.

Surprises tend to interfere with need satisfaction. As roles become defined and behavior patterns stabilized, changes represent a threat because they create instability. At the ideographic level pressure is created to ensure that roles will be perpetuated so that people will know with whom they are working, what kinds of functions they are to carry out, what kinds of challenges will ensue, etc.

Learning to live within *any* organization generates homeostatic pressure, and schools are no exception. The cellular model of the school (Lortie, 1975), in which individual teachers hold sway over particular domains and functions (the third grade, sophomore English, etc.) has greatly affected the school's receptiveness to initiatives for improvement. Inside these cells there is considerable autonomy (Miles, 1981). Most teachers work in relative isolation, with almost total operational authority over the domains to which they have been assigned. Administrative coordination in most schools emphasizes management matters such as attendance, record keeping, transportation scheduling, the cafeteria, and disciplining specific children, with much less attention to curriculum and instruction. Teachers overtly complain about their isolation but nonetheless often struggle to maintain it because, within their cells, roles are well defined and outside there is a very unpredictable milieu. Many people who enter teaching actually like to work alone and prefer to live in an environment where there is relatively little supervision or collegial activity. They prefer social interchange which does not directly challenge their functioning. In a real sense the classroom is a very safe place for someone who does not wish to have much adult interchange during working hours and prefers a clear separation between their personal and work life.

In most schools there is a tacit understanding between administrators and teachers that their respective domains are not to be encroached on. Informal sanctions are applied to individuals who violate the norms of privacy in the classroom, or attempt to generate systematic change that affects working conditions. Teachers apply social pressure to principals to avoid direct supervision and possible changes. Similarly, principals expect to manage logistics and community relationships with a minimum of collective decision making.

Homeostatic forces are brought into play when "change agents" enter the system. The chief homeostatic mechanism used at the ideographic level is informal social pressure. Teachers in most schools are not well organized in terms of formal collective decision making but they are very well organized in terms of generating negative social pressure. For example, if principals wish to visit their classrooms and offer clinical support, teachers' primary mode of counterattack is to disparage them and suggest that they are not competent to carry out clinical functions. If a curriculum change is initiated by central office personnel resisting teachers dismiss it as "theoretical nonsense." University professors are regarded by many as "uselessly abstract" and innovators as "faddists." Disparagement is the primary mechanism here. As we will see, disparagement is not reserved solely for outsiders who would bring innovation into the scene but is also directed toward other teachers daring enough to innovate. In many schools the innovative teachers have become social isolates. Although the informal social system among teachers needs more study, it is becoming clear that informal social pressure is used to enforce the norms of isolation which characterize the present state of functioning (Joyce and McKibbin, 1980).

The combination of autonomy in the classroom, relative lack of formal structures for decision making, low levels of surveillance and supervision, and the use of the informal social pressure to maintain classroom privacy and resist collective decision making result in paradoxical findings regarding teachers' feelings of efficacy. Surveys report that many teachers believe they have great autonomy *within the classroom* but are powerless with respect to overall *district and schoolwide decision making*. Both findings are correct (Joyce et al., 1982). In most schools and districts teachers are relatively powerful within the classroom but experience low levels of involvement at other levels of the organization. The isolation of the classroom increases teachers' power within it while reducing their power outside it.

For our purposes this duality presents a serious problem because school improvement *requires* collective activity. Any attempt to create a better environment for education will have to decrease isolation, increase cooperative planning, and sharply lengthen the amount of time in meetings. There will be a corresponding lessening of the autonomy of the classroom and an increase in teachers' efficacy in schoolwide and district planning. Unless collective activity becomes the norm and a forum is created through which personal satisfaction can be gained by working for the larger organization, the ideographic forces will operate, on balance, against curricular and instructional innovation.

Such changes will take time. Stage One school improvement should be undertaken deliberately and not rushed. What appear on the surface to be minor changes (such as creating a schoolwide atmosphere of prevasive caring) necessitate below-the-surface changes of great magnitude in the ideographic structure. This is why so many apparently simple changes in curriculum and instruction have foundered—the implementation effort concentrated on the surface change and neglected the social system on which it is founded. (See Table 5.1.)

Thus we want to make clear that in most schools at present Stage

TABLE 5.1
The Idiographic Level:
Characteristics and Problems

Normative Mode	Problems to Solve
Predictable conditions	Loneliness
Autonomy in classroom	Difficulty in collective action
Low surveillance	Alienation from institutional administrators
Cellular structure	Low efficacy outside classroom

One changes are very difficult. Until the Responsible Parties are in place and the *process* of making focused changes is well established, Stage Two (curricular) and Stage Three (structural) changes will be virtually impossible in all but a few schools and even there will be accomplished only with enormous effort.

The Formal-Structural Level. Despite occasional comments on the cellular structure of the workplace, the formal organization of schools receives most of the attention in the literature. One concept which is currently used to explain institutional relationships in education, is that of *loosely coupled* systems (Baldridge & Deal, 1975). Elements within the organization—the superintendent and supporting staff, other departments within the district (fiscal agents, etc.), the schools, principals, and teachers—although associated, have relatively few functions connecting them. School personnel are better organized to maintain logistical smoothness than they are to coordinate instruction. Instructional supplies are generated and dispensed, students are enrolled and records are kept about their attendance. Buses are provided for their transportation, food is assembled and prepared, bond issues are floated, levies are made, curriculum guides are written and distributed, and schools are opened and closed. However, the organizational structure of many districts does not effectively coordinate its major business, which is to educate children.

The loosely coupled organization actually makes it difficult for anyone at any level to generate and maintain an innovation in the curricular and instructional domains. In a number of case studies which we undertook for National Teacher Corps and as part of the California Staff Development Study, we asked school administrators and teachers how one makes a curricular change. Nearly everybody in the schools studied maintained that the lack of a unifying plan among administrators, teachers, and others made it almost impossible to make a coordinated instructional change (Joyce & McKibbin, 1980).

Central office personnel with the school board can open a new school building and select its staff, but the teachers, once assigned to their cells, will create the curriculum. The principals' work is related to the teachers' work mainly with respect to discipline and parent relations. And their work is not necessarily related to that of superintendents or other central office staff who worry continually about gaining the reluctant cooperation of principals and teachers. On the other hand, both principals and teachers tend to feel that the energy of the "real" workplace is drained by the central organization people whose concerns are largely irrelevant to the workplace.

Charismatic superintendents and principals *can* change schools, sometimes quite rapidly, by developing ad hoc executive structures; but the institutionalization of change is very difficult. Recent federal and state initiatives for school improvement have, in most settings, resulted in the development of new "cells"—for special education, vocational education, bilingual education—added on to the old structure but not really integrated with it. The new cells can be added with minimal disturbance to the old ones, and taken away without disruption.

The movement toward mainstreaming has not been greeted kindly by many teachers and administrators precisely because it requires coordination among cells. Special classes and special schools were not disruptive. Cooperative planning and instruction *is* disruptive. Hence most current evaluations of mainstreaming report that PL 94–140 is most often implemented in letter but not in spirit (SRI International, 1982).

Fullan and Pomfret (1977) identified dimensions of implementation—understanding the rationale of a curriculum, using appropriate materials and instructional processes, making appropriate changes in role relationships of teachers and students, and making appropriate evaluation—and suggested that the degree to which these dimensions are used varies considerably. They observed that the use of instructional materials is more likely to occur than is a change in instructional process, pupil/teacher role relationships, or evaluation.

Looking at the studies by Gross et al. (1971), Charters and Pellegrin (1973), Crowther (1972), Downey (1975), Lukas and Wohlleb (1970), and Nauman-Etienne (1974), Fullan and Pomfret suggest that the less explicit the characteristics and rationale of the innovation, the more likely there will be user confusion and frustration and a low degree of implementation. The results seem to boil down to the common sense proposition that the more thoroughly one understands something the more likely one is to master it and be committed to using it.

Although Fullan and Pomfret do not concern themselves with distinctions between various types of training, they have included in-service training as a factor in implementation. Most of the researchers have concluded that intensive in-service training (as distinct from single workshops or preservice training) is an important implementation strategy.

Some of the reports are quite instructive. Downey (1975) reported a low degree of implementation in a well-thought-out and clearly conceptualized social studies curriculum in the Province of Alberta, Canada. The in-service work was essentially a "theory-only" treatment in most cases; that is, in short workshops the rationale was discussed and materials were distributed; practice, feedback, and coaching were virtually absent. From the training literature alone we would have predicted that the implementation effort would have failed in much the way Downey found that it did.

On the other hand, fairly high degrees of implementation were evident in many sites where Follow Through and Head Start developers worked directly explaining the rationale, providing materials, demonstrating, providing coaching and moral support (Stallings et al., 1972). Similarly, evaluation of the Humanities Curriculum Project in England compared a sample of schools in which the teachers received direct training by the sponsors of innovation with schools in which teachers were given materials but no direct training. The training was fairly substantial and included many elements we have identified in the training literature. Not only was implementation much greater for the trained teachers, but pupil achievement scores shifted much more in those schools.

The curriculum literature also supports the notion that consultants provide demonstration lessons, coaching for skill development, psychological support, and materials adequate to support implementation. The recent National Science Foundation studies (Weiss, 1978) show that teachers also need academic knowledge related to new and old curriculums as well as the provision of instructional materials and explicit training about their use. Teachers need much training if new teaching methods are to be acquired and used, and the assistance of consultants who can coach them during the implementation period (see Chapters 9 and 10).

Another characteristic of schools (and other formal organizations) is that energy is increasingly directed toward the maintenance of the organization itself and the comfort of its members. In any relatively mature bureaucracy the structure gradually drifts away from the original goals of the organization in an effort to make life routine and comfortable. The principalship is an example. The role gradually evolved from "teaching principals" who knew their fellow teachers well and regarded themselves the lead teacher, into members of a management team who do much paperwork, attend meetings, and busy themselves with other tasks which prevent them from fulfilling their original function—that of leading the school toward ever improving instruction. Except for a few small, very high quality districts nearly all administrative working involves maintaining logistical functions (McKibbin, 1982). The more the position becomes removed from instruction and the more isolated it becomes from the educational process, the harder the functionary has to work to generate a feeling that the job is worthwhile. Even where there is argument about discernable but nonnormative practice, few principals will violate the norms.

Virtually everyone agrees that instruction can be adapted to individual differences, but almost everyone also agrees that it is easier for teachers to teach children collectively as if individual differences did not exist, and nearly all of them do so. Nearly everyone understands that meetings are necessary in order to bring about coordinated efforts, but teachers' organizations actually bargain for limits on the number and duration of teachers' meetings. This not only places limits on the length of the school day, but also protects individuals working in the school from attempts to organize them to collective action. Thus administrators are both drawn and pushed away from the instructional process. Their energy becomes directed more and more toward noncurricular matters.

The establishment of the Responsible Parties has the express purpose of changing the nature of the formal-structural dimension. At the district level they are to establish standards of improvement and mechanisms to stimulate and support improvement at each school. At the school level they are to establish executive authority (the ability to make decisions *and* to carry them out). (See Table 5.2.) In sum, the organization needs to be tightly coupled so that careful decisions about curriculum can be made and the members of the organization coordinated to implement those decisions.

TABLE 5.2
The Formal-Structural Level:
Characteristics and Problems

Normative Mode	Problems to Solve
Logistical smoothness	Energy drawn away from educational quality
Unilateral decisions	Low vertical solidarity
Ad hoc school improvement loose coupling	Low executive authority

The External System. Schools are both a part of and products of their communities and, consequently, community members have a definite need to understand their schools. Because many community members believe that laymen are as close to if not as expert in education as are the teachers, they don't hesitate to provide their opinions about how the schools should be run. They readily react to nonnormative educational practices and a number of mechanisms now operate to stabilize the school in its present form. One of these is the tendency of many school boards to regularly fire the superintendent on short notice. The average tenure of a superintendent is less than three years and relatively few leave voluntarily. The effect is to keep all superintendents "on notice" that everything they do will be scrutinized and anything they do that displeases a significant proportion of the community will be sanctioned. New superintendents know that they will be judged by conservative criteria and that the price of innovation will almost surely lead to failure.

Compounding the problem is the fact that community members are by no means unified about educational objectives or means. Thus, the community is a fickle master. Almost anything might be attacked by someone. Probably the most publicized and surely one of the most competent superintendents of the last 20 years, Dr. Mark Shedd, was a major issue in the campaign for mayor of a former Philadelphia politician. The mayoral candidate promised that he would fire the extremely competent superintendent as soon as he was elected, which he did. Shedd had initiated scores of activities designed to improve education in the city, and almost every professional educator throughout the country believed he had succeeded in generating excitement in a previously moribund school district. He certainly did not calculate harm to the education of the students. Yet the mayoral candidate maintained that the sorry state of education in the city of Philadelphia was a direct product of Shedd's activities, and Shedd had little support except from those he had brought in and nurtured in their jobs. Among those who were notably absent in his defense were other administrators in the city. Many of the "old line" administrators were uncomfortable when he was appointed and delighted when he left.

Having observed the fate of Shedd and others, many superintendents devote relatively little time to long-term planning and organizational development. The best ones do, stubbornly, but they know how unlikely it is that they will be around to benefit from their efforts.

The press senses this instability and often gives voice to the complaints of self-proclaimed experts and critics. Consider the following passage from one of our more moderate and fair-minded newspapers.

Parents' Groups Purging Schools of "Humanist" Books and Classes

In Onida, S. D., birth control information has been removed from the high school guidance office, and the word "evolution" is no longer uttered in

TABLE 5.3
External System: Characteristics and Problems

Normative Mode	Problems to Solve
Permeability	Guardedness
Watchful disunity	Short-term planning
Administrative turnover	Low efficacy of leadership
Reactive leadership	Atmosphere of turbulence

advanced biology. *Brave New World* and *Catcher in the Rye* have been dropped from classes in literature. The award-winning children's book *Run Shelly, Run* has been banned from the library.

In Plano, Tex., teachers no longer ask students their opinions because to do so, they have been told, is to deny absolute right and wrong. In Des Moines, Iowa, a high school student production of *Grease*, the hit Broadway musical, was banned. In Mount Diablo, Calif., *Ms. Magazine* is off the school library shelves; it is available only with permission from both a parent and a teacher.

Lobbying Methods Sophisticated

Emboldened by what they see as a conservative mood in the country, parents' groups across the nation are demanding that teachers and administrators cleanse their local schools of materials and teaching methods they consider antifamily, anti-American, and anti-God.

Armed with sophisticated lobbying techniques and backed by such national organizations as the Moral Majority, the Eagle Forum and the Christian Broadcasting Network, these parents are banding together to remove books from libraries, replace textbooks, eliminate sex education courses and balance lessons of evolution with those of Biblical creation, at least. They also seek to revise such things as the open classroom, new math and creative writing, asserting that these relatively unstructured academic approaches break down standards of right and wrong and thus promote rebellion, sexual promiscuity and crime. (*New York Times*, 1981)

Unless there is substantial community involvement, even minor and patently sensible improvements usually run a gamut of criticism that can easily erode the spirit of improvement efforts. School personnel begin to think that, whatever they do, criticism will ensue. The Responsible Parties' major task is to create a dialogue that permits opinions to be aired but requires sensible arguments, and brings about a commitment to the improvement process and a faith that reasonable improvements can be agreed on. It is essential to establish the process of examining the school against effectiveness criteria so that focused efforts for improvement are begun and the process "sells itself" by achieving satisfying gains. Otherwise, the critical atmosphere mitigates against solid, long-term planning and produces a reactive, crisis-oriented mode of leadership.

Innovation and Homeostatic Reaction

Thus we have a picture which cannot please the heart of the innovator. Idiographic adaptations are tuned to the cellular organization and not to collective activity. Teachers are comfortable in their isolation and use the sanctions of the informal system to protect their autonomy. The loose couplings of the institutional level mirror the cells but at a macro level. Additive innovations are possible but integrated school improvement efforts are extremely difficult, as indicated by the curriculum improvement literature. The failure to develop an executive role keyed to educational improvement renders impotent all but the most exceptional leaders. The community's watchfulness and disunity creates a hazardous environment for the innovator.

Curricular innovations generated at the idiographic level have to survive the informal system. A group of teachers who get a good idea must persuade their peers that it has validity and justifies violating the norms of privacy and autonomy. Then they have to capture the attention of the organization and co-opt some of its resources. Finally, they have to interest the community and persuade any objectors that it is beneficial.

The same innovation, generated at the formal organizational level, first has to capture the interest of administrators who now occupy themselves with other work. Then, an ad hoc executive function has to be created (in the absence of a permanent one) and resources corralled. Schools and community have to be persuaded to participate. "Ownership" has to be generated so that the idiographic system does not subvert the process. Training has to be provided to personnel not accustomed to or comfortable with receiving it. All this must be accomplished *before* beginning the substantive innovation process with its very real difficulties to be faced and overcome.

The external system faces all the problems of the other levels and, in addition, has to depend on the other levels to create the organizational elements to carry the effort. Probably for this reason and because it is not unified, many external system-generated initiatives are quality-control oriented. The community rarely says "create a better science curriculum" (although it has). More customary is the injunction to "make sure the kids have learned the basic skills" (a common-denominator area of community agreement). The California legislature has recently made a law requiring teaching to the literacy tests, a clear injunction based on the unreasonable suspicion that colleges are capable of graduating illiterate teachers, the state of giving them certificates, and school boards of hiring them. The public has generated PL 94–140 and depends on the other levels to carry it out. The external system has generated a number of such initiatives at state and federal levels. Sputnik had a large enough impact to generate governmental support for reform in curriculum, but the public was always divided about those efforts and now is evidently prepared to believe that the new math probably undermined achievement in arithmetic.

Hence, each level has its problems both within itself and from the other levels. The capability to get things done is not great, generally, and should be increased, because education does need improvement and there *are* practices which could make it better. If all levels continue to be stymied, it will get more and more out of step with the potential state of the art.

HOW UNIQUE IS EDUCATION?

Innovation is not easy in any area of human endeavor since homeostatic forces work against it in almost every kind of organization. Education, however, has some unique characteristics, especially with respect to the degree of influence each level has. First of all very few organizations are as loosely coupled as education is. By way of contrast, hospitals make an interesting example.

Physicians pride themselves on their autonomy and they certainly behave in ways parallel to those of the ideographic level of education. Doctors do things (not unreasonably) that make their lives predictable and relatively comfortable. They maintain role relationships rather strictly. Relationships with other practitioners and nurses are standardized throughout the profession so that everybody knows what to expect from everybody else. Pecking orders are quite clearly established and maintained, and their violation is sanctioned. However, once an innovation is introduced into a hospital and its board or leading doctors decide to act on it, then any illusion that it is a loosely coupled organization disappears immediately. Things get done. We do not mean to imply that in hospitals things always get done smoothly, but once a new practice has been agreed on at the institutional level and the decision made to implement it in a given setting, that implementation will take place. Individual practitioners within the hospital can move to other settings where that innovation does not exist if they wish. However, hospital norms generally encourage adopting technological innovations and place the dissenting professional in serious peril (a decision which is risked by some physicians).

As in the case of education, medicine belongs to the community and the external system is extremely important to it. The community knows that it is in its best interest to sanction the best medical practice possible. Although some religious sects do not believe in medicine at all and certain others have notions about what kind of practice should be permitted, American society generally expects that medical innovations will be continuous and will get better and better. Very few community members will fight innovations involving the choice and implementation of treatment, although innovations are not always embraced.

Private industries also have to please their public and certainly have to deal with idiosyncratic and role-related issues. But they can hardly be referred to as loosely coupled organizations. Industries have much greater integration among all levels. The board of directors are generally stockholders and in a sense represent that community. Stockholders *expect* their companies to keep up to date and expect their executive to implement agreed-on changes. Most industries also lobby in an effort to co-opt government regulation. The institutional level is *organized* to generate changes. Like education there is the phenomenon of energy draining toward the maintenance of the organization rather than the achievement of its function, but there is no question at all about the relationship between the institutional level and the idiographic level. Innovations, having been chose, will be implemented, and there is no question that the organizational structure is capable of bringing about almost any kind of change that is within the law. Workers, if they object, can and do block innovation by exerting massive collective power through unions. To mention just one example, typesetters have slowed the automation of printing. However, workers must exercise overt collective action to block innovation. In education teachers (and administrators) operate through unorganized passive resistance. They just don't participate, and in most school districts there is no clear executive role to force a confrontation. Many principals do not refuse to act as instructional leaders, they just don't fulfill the role, and except in unusual districts no one confronts them with executive authority.

Because the community is often not in agreement about education some aspect of the public nearly always reacts to innovation with suspicion: "The new mathematics is dangerous to the basic skills." "Basic skills are often taught in such a way that is dull and unmotivating," etc. Whenever a visible innovation is generated in the education domain some objection arises.

Norms are important also. In the electronics industry, for example, an engineer who did not keep up with developments based on silicon research would soon be left behind and lose out in the formal and informal systems. In education it is more normal for teachers and administrators *not to keep up* than it is for them to be abreast of developments in their field. On the whole they believe they are competent, but few of them study their profession and many prefer not to believe that educational research and development actually take place. At the institutional level there is little pressure regarding ongoing professional study and insufficient executive authority to generate such norms.

PREPARING FOR INNOVATION: A HOMEOSTASIS OF CHANGE

Because homeostatic forces are more powerful than innovative forces at every level of education, ad hoc structures have to be created to promote innovation and to protect against homeostatic forces. In the absence of an executive role that promotes innovation, the necessary conditions (vertical solidarity, ownership, marshaling of resources, development of training, and community involvement) have to be created *each time* a decision to innovate is made *and these conditions have to be sustained if the innovation is to persist.*

To eliminate the need for ad hoc executive and protective authority calls for a substantial organizational change, one that permits reasonable and continuous innovation to take place. The condition that must be created is a *homeostasis of change*, a condition in which organizational stability actually depends on the continuous process of school improvement. Innovations, occasionally large but mainly small and practitioner induced, need to be normalized. To make this happen is no small order and there are no "five easy steps" to success. What we propose requires hard work, patience, and satisfaction with gradual progress rather than dramatic achievements.

As Miles (1981) has pointed out, the lack of coordination, integration, communication, and surveillance by persons representing the formal-structural level have not resulted in anarchy because teaching is so much controlled by norms which are reinforced by the external system. It is frequently said that young teachers come to "teach as they were taught" and this is true. Having been to school themselves, most people expect schools to perpetuate the patterns they experienced. By exposing the young to certain patterns and enforcing them with great power, society implants in the young a view of how education should be conducted. Socialization to teaching simply thrusts young teachers into a role where they internalize the existing norms of education. They struggle to find personal meaning within the demands of their cells and begin to see the problems of teaching as ones of managing those cells.

At the formal-structural level the loss of executive control results in an inability to intervene in normative patterns. The executives become relatively helpless. Departments of curriculum and instruction become

separated from the line operations of the school, and building administrators and others responsible for maintaining the educational system
become increasingly divorced from the regulation of curriculum and
instruction. Finally, in the absence of a societal consensus that innovation is desirable, education critics rise to meet whatever innovations
threaten normative practice. In order for educational innovation to
become possible on a regular and consistent basis four general conditions must be developed:

- Instruction-related executive functions
- Collegial teaching units
- Continuous staff development
- Continuous community involvement (education about
  education)

These conditions are designed to affect the way educators think
about the education process, and to create relationships at all three
levels that are conducive to education.

Instruction-Related Executive Functions

The loosely coupled organization simply has to be replaced with one in
which district offices take direct responsibility for the health of the
educational program of each of its schools and can exercise curricular
and instructional leadership. While it is obvious that large systems need
decentralized organizations in order to create effective leadership, we
will not discuss that here. What we do emphasize is that district level
units made up of professional curriculum developers, community
members, and teachers need to insure that the Responsible Parties from
each school become aware of the important criteria for effective
schooling. The Responsible Parties must study current options in each
curriculum area, make choices among them, and then make those
choices happen. Curriculum and instruction decision making must be
legitimate at some level in the system along with the authority to
implement those decisions. The same people who make the decisions
(the local Responsible Parties) must have the authority to carry them
out. The combination is the essence of executive authority.

If executive decision making is to happen, perceptions have to
change at almost every level of the system. Teachers must realize that
curriculum and instruction is important and that the coordination of
instruction through shared curriculum decisions increases their power.
Likewise principals and district administrators must see curricular and
instructional coordination as major part of their work. Although many

other administrative concerns must be tended, these must not replace a primary concern regarding the education of children. At this point in time faculties, district administrations, and other organizational levels are all relatively impotent with respect to the major business of education—the development of an educational environment of the highest quality.

Collegial Teaching Units

The team-teaching movement as originally conceived in the late 1950s and early 1960s attempted to bring together groups of teachers who would be responsible for making collective curricular and instructional decisions (Schaefer, 1967). An important side effect would be that teachers would increasingly conceive of their jobs in terms of collective decision making and mutually shared professional development. A change of organization into collegial teaching units of some sort is essential in order to change the thinking of teachers with respect to curriculum and instruction and the improvement of teaching. Having to work together to make decisions, receive instructions, and improve one another's competence will affect their view of their work.

Continuous Staff Development

Teaching is one of the very few functions in today's world which does not require continuous competence improvement. In a rapidly changing world, with research and developments capable of generating new alternatives at great speed, most professions have developed ways of rapidly transmitting new development to their personnel. For many years educational technologies have "bounced off" the facade of the school and its organization so that extremely powerful ways of teaching are only rarely employed. Just as salesmen have meetings in which new products are explained to them, and actors study new dramatic forms in explicit and continuous fashion, teachers need to be exposed to all options and have the opportunity for training to implement them (see Chapters 10 and 11).

Continuous Community Involvement

Creating executive functions, socializing educational personnel to them, and developing collegial teaching units should break down the homeostatic shields that surround the idiographic and formal-structural levels of the organization. The powerful force exercised by the external system to prevent educational change can not be overcome by political manipulation, nor should it be, since schools serve the people and the people need to have a voice in their governance. The only reasonable solution is to involve the community closely in the organization of the curriculum and to develop councils of teachers, administrators, and community members responsible for modulating curricular changes in each local situation.

No single strategy is likely to bring about greater effectiveness in schools. Greater executive authority, stronger staff development, increased community and teacher participation, and collegiality among teachers are all valuable, but none of them, taken alone, will create an atmosphere sufficient to support sensible decision making or resource mastery. We must use all of them.

We must understand that stabilizing forces and obstacles to change will operate even when minor school improvement efforts are considered. They simply cannot be escaped. The school improvement criteria presented in Chapter 3 might at first appear relatively easy to use as guidelines for implementation. In terms of direction that is so, but the process of change requires a very careful effort. For this reason we suggest that most groups of Responsible Parties begin by planning Stage One school improvements, establish the process that makes improvement a normal part of life in schools, and then proceed to Stages Two and Three. Even when organization has been well developed, it will take one or two years for the educational program in a school like Cameo to assimilate all of the criteria; and because a school improvement process is not built into it *two or three more years* will be needed before the necessary changes and processes are embedded firmly enough to make stronger changes feasible.

The context of the district cannot be overemphasized. A district which provides encouragement for school improvement and the conditions that facilitate it will make the work of the Responsible Parties much easier. Furthermore, if any given school is not improving it is the district officers' responsibility to exercise their executive functions to help that school develop an organization of Responsible Parties and put them to work analyzing the educational health of the school and making plans to improve it. We will say over and over again that a school that is not improving is almost surely deteriorating. The establishment of the conditions for school improvement require the direct assistance of the central office administration to provide the resources for staff development and training for Responsible Parties, and to make clear to the building administrator that the facilitation of school improvement is a major part of her or his duties.

The situation in the Cameo School illustrates the need to face and overcome the homeostatic forces on all three levels. The idiographic system is clearly cellular. Teachers work in isolation, protect the privacy of the classroom, and disparage attempts at coordination. They are quite satisfied with a principal who provides little supervision or clinical support and eschews the duties of curricular and instructional leader. The formal structure provides no leadership for school improvement. Peace, order, and a quiescent community are valued. Concern with the effectiveness of the school is missing in any professional sense as the absence of nearly *all* of the criteria for effectiveness demonstrates. The external system is indeed peaceful but inactive. Activating the community and involving it in the study of the school will activate criticism in a community totally unaccustomed to studying its school. When the community begins to realize just how poor Cameo is, the Responsible Parties will have their hands full.

6

Three Stages of
School Improvement

Having discussed the nature of change and the difficulties of initiating changes within schools, our next step is to identify a clear set of guidelines for improving schools. We will develop a strategy that can be used by local school councils—the Responsible Parties—to ensure continued efforts to make education more effective. We will concentrate on the organization of local Responsible Parties rather than initiation of school improvement by external agencies because the success of onsite and external initiatives are equally dependent on the condition of the local environment.*

A COMMITTEE OF RESPONSIBLE PARTIES

Who are these people who are to be responsible for the direction of the school? They are drawn from several sources:

1. *Representatives of the general public.* For public schools in the United States, local boards of education are the most common means of controlling education. However, state legislatures and boards of education, departments of public instruction, and other agencies frequently exercise some direction over schools. Sometimes they issue general regulations or policies within which schools may operate. In other cases (especially local boards of education in small communities) they may become intimately involved with shaping the school. However, local boards often give great latitude to privately financed schools, requiring only compliance with health regulations and building maintenance standards. In any case, representatives of the general public should be involved in determining the direction of a school program if it is to have a good opportunity to succeed.

*An excellent review of the implementation literature with guidelines for action at state or provincial levels is in Michael Fullan and Paul Park, *Curriculum Implementation* (Toronto, Ontario: The Ontario Government Bookstore, 1981).

2. *Site administrators and representatives of the school district administration.* As early as possible in the development of a new school program— or the regeneration of an existing one—designated officials should be given the executive functions necessary to see the planning through and bring the schools into existence. Whenever possible, the officials who are expected to work in the new school program should be included in this group. Throughout the planning process these individuals are expected to procure the expert assistance that the program planners will need. However, the site and district administrators need not conceive of themselves as the "directors" of the school in the surface meaning of that term since the plan for the school could call for an exceedingly nondirective form of leadership or even self-government by the students.

3. *Teachers.* The planning group needs to include teachers who have the capacity to envision new and alternate educational forms. They represent our accumulated knowledge about the educational process. Representatives of the public usually have limited views of educational possibilities (although in some communities they exceed the professional staff) whereas leading teachers are students of the educational process. As planning proceeds toward the development of implementation strategies the instructional specialists will need to increase their ledership role in shaping specific components of the school and bringing it into existence.

4. *Technical consultants.* Because it is unlikely that any local situation will contain all the expert knowledge that is needed, the Responsible Parties need to augment themselves with specialists in curriculum planning, educational technology, architecture, and school administration. The types of competency needed will become apparent as we describe the tasks involved in creating a model for a school.

5. *Patrons of the school.* The Responsible Parties should also include parents and children. Especially in large school districts, where school boards and other public representatives are likely to be quite remote, it becomes necessary to make special efforts to include patrons in the planning process. Children should not be involved in all aspects of planning, but should react to ideas when the child's view seems important.

Now imagine a committee which is charged with the task of creating a school. It includes representatives of the public, school officials, teachers, technological experts, parents and children. The committee might be set up by the legally Responsible Parties. If a private school corporation is initiating the school, the corporation can set up the committee. If a board of education is responsible, it can determine the membership or set in motion the machinery for assembling it. Or, a school committee might be assembled by people who hope to influence educational practice although they have no legal authority themselves. For instance, a firm of architects might decide to develop school models and, in the process, might assemble a representative body, including members of the public, for reality-testing purposes. Similarly, a group of technologists planning a school might include administrators and parents out of no political motive but simply to test the viability of their model for potential customers.

PRINCIPLES UNDERLYING THE STRATEGY

We now offer five principles to follow in creating a homeostasis of change—a condition that provides stability to the school while enabling regular, thoughtful improvements to be made. After examining them we will proceed to outline the tasks involved in studying the school and planning change at the stage one (refinement) level. The five principles are:

1. Building collaborative local governance (the development of the Responsible Parties)
2. Building a climate of support
3. Building effective training
4. Building a sound organization
5. Making change familiar

Each, in its own way, is essential.

Building Collaborative Local Governance

The first principle on which our strategy is based is to build a social context that involves everyone concerned with the school (the responsible parties). The object of organizing the Responsible Parties is to build a community that can continuously rethink the purposes of the school, select its primary mission, choose its most appropriate means, evaluate how they work, make adjustments, and, over time, repeat the cycle.

By providing ways that community members, teachers, and administrative staff can all participate in the creation of the educational program, the Responsible Parties can ensure that:

1. The school program is intelligible to everyone concerned.
2. Conflict over alternatives is resolved or at least dealt with so that a disgruntled faction doesn't subvert the program.

3. There is support for the new program and debate is open and reasonable.
4. There is coordination among administrators, teachers, and community members.

In other words, the Responsible Parties need to build a community that deliberately and openly builds, supports, evaluates, and rethinks the school program. A recent large-scale study (Berman and McLaughlin, 1978) of federal initiatives to provide local communities with resources to improve their schools indicated the importance of including community members, teachers, and administrators in school improvement projects. It found that if administrators initiate change but do not involve teachers, no real change is likely to take place. If teachers generate ideas but the administration is uncommitted, the idea is likely to remain just that—a thought. If the community does not understand or approve of a change in the program, it is likely to be short-lived.

The solution is to build a continuous program-rethinking process which includes representatives of all three groups. This is not to suggest that the entire school program will be changed each year! Making changes is difficult even when there is broad involvement and firm agreement about what is to be done. As the Responsible Parties study the school they will develop priorities for change and the efforts of any given year will be concentrated on the high-priority areas.

Berman and McLaughlin concluded that innovation begins with a mobilization phase, proceeds to a period of trial and implementation, and drives at institutionalization—ensuring continuation of the change. Collaborative decision making increases the probability that mobilization will be thorough.

The practice of rethinking the school missions and means has to become embedded in the life of the school and its community; the search for improvement has to become normal. The atmosphere has to encourage serious reflection and discourage excesses of advocacy. If fresh ideas are put forth dogmatically they will draw defensive reactions ("What's wrong with the way we are doing things now?") and positive governance will break down.

Also, innovations nearly always stumble at first. When a faculty brings new content into the curriculum they have to experiment with it. The first experiments are often awkward. If the climate is harsh and unforgiving of error, it will be nearly impossible for the period of trial and experimentation to function as it should, allowing new methods to be massaged into comfortable processes.

In the early 1960s, as the Academic Reform Movement propelled new mathematics and science content into the elementary and secondary schools, nearly everyone became uncomfortable. Teachers were learning the principles that govern operations with integers and rational numbers. Parents worried about helping their children with Venn diagrams and Cartesian multiplication. Children labored with "structure and function" in biology. The climate became angry and panicky. It was alleged that the new mathematics content would undermine the learning of basic facts. Teachers who were weak in science became insecure and angry. Administrators watched apprehensively as content they did not understand poured into their schools. Although these new curriculums were well thought-out in most cases and were backed up with excellent instructional materials, implementing them became a serious problem because they rarely became part of the ongoing culture of the school community.

It is clear that careful involvement of the interested groups—community, faculty, and administration—in the adoption and adaptation of curriculum plans can avoid many of the problems described above. Although broad governance of the school will not guarantee smooth sailing, it is an essential element in the strategy.

Pro forma involvement, however, is insufficient. The Responsible Parties need to develop what we call *parity*—relative equality among teachers, community, and administration. Parity is illustrated in the experiment in participating governance of local schools (described in Chapter 9). The Responsible Parties can build such parity-oriented governance systems, but it takes time. The school community councils of the Urban/Rural Program were nearly two years in development before they began to function effectively!

Building a Climate of Support

Collaborative governance provides for broad involvement and generates a forum for rational debate over the ends and means of the school. The Responsible Parties select those areas which will be the focus for innovation in the school program. Now we turn to an exceedingly important element—creating a social climate which supports people as they formulate ideas and try them out on the school staff.

As we have stated several times previously, putting educational ideas to work is difficult and frustrating. Consider the example of a school where there are many students who feel poorly about themselves as learners. The Responsible Parties decide to attack the problem. They decide to experiment with teaching strategies designed to boost the students' feelings of adequacy and self-esteem. The teachers organize workshops in which they study those strategies and how to use them.

The time comes to try them out. At first the new strategies feel awkward to the teachers and students have difficulty responding to them. Parents worry that their children aren't learning enough while administrators worry about discipline. All of these reactions are quite normal. The important thing, however, is what happens next, and that depends to a considerable extent on the social climate that is generated among community, teachers, and administrators.

If everyone understands what is going on, lends support, and helps one another over the rough spots, we can predict that the awkward period will give way to the teachers' efforts. They will become comfortable with the new approach, the students will respond, and the parents and administrators will relax. However, if the climate is harsh and unforgiving, if mistakes are not tolerated, if the atmosphere becomes heated with anxiety, they we can predict that discouragement and anxiety will prevail. Within such a negative atmosphere the new approach will soon give way to the old as teachers return to the safe and familiar ways that aroused few complaints, even if the children feel bad about themselves.

During the 1970s The Rand Corporation study team came to similar conclusions. They found that organizations that successfully implemented agreed-upon changes developed vertical as well as horizontal integration. In terms of school organization this means that the school board, the central administration of the district, the building administrators, teachers, and community members must all be working in concert. A local school group working without the support of the central administration or the school board will soon get into difficulty. A school board and central administration which fails to include local community members and teachers in their organization will be equally doomed. Although there is much emphasis these days on the contrast between "top-down" and "bottom-up" initiatives for change it appears that change can be initiated equally well from either level. Regardless of who presents the initiative, vertical integration of the various levels of the system is essential.

Creating a supportive organizational climate was also found to be vital. Innovation involves risk taking and without a climate that supports risk-taking behavior or at least avoids punishing experimentation, we can hardly expect that people will be encouraged to take the first fumbling steps that are essential as innovations are tried out.

The choice is clear. Without a climate of support, new ideas will not have time to develop and new procedures will not have the opportunity to mature. The climate of support is a second essential element of the strategy.

Building Effective Training

Nearly every worthwhile change includes the use of instructional strategies. Teachers and students alike have to take on new patterns of behavior. Consider the example of a science curriculum designed on the premise that students should learn to think inductively—to collect and analyze data, build and test hypotheses, and generate concepts for organizing information. To implement such a design requires inductive learning processes, which in turn require inductive teaching strategies, ones by which teachers demonstrate to students how to think inductively.

The curriculum implementation literature indicates quite clearly that unless very intensive staff training accompanies a curriculum change in either content or teaching process, the level of implementation will be very low (Fulland and Pomfret, 1977). Put positively, training is essential. Teachers can provide much of the training for one another, but time and opportunity must be organized if they are to do so (see Chapters 9 and 10).

Building a Sound Organization

As we have said before collaborative governance takes time to develop. People have to learn to work together, become familiar with the available models of schooling, choose among them, and mobilize to implement the decisions. Judging from the experience of the Urban/ Rural Program, councils of Responsible Parties require a maturation period of about two years during which time procedures for making decisions and a common knowledge base are developed. During this period the Responsible Parties may need assistance from consultants in both *process* (how to work together effectively) and *substance* (what are the options and how can they be implemented).

The maturation period is extremely important. The Responsible Parties must avoid making decisions that would radically change the character of the school before they have acquired an adequate knowledge of alternatives and implementation problems. There are a large number of alternatives and it takes time to become educated consumers of them. Also, it is wise not to attempt radical change at first. Until the decision-making process is well established and resources are adequately mobilized, changes should be minor. The Responsible Parties can select a single curriculum area and work on it, learning how to make decisions cooperatively and how to make small changes happen. This is an ideal activity for the maturation period.

Louis Smith (1971) has provided a wonderful study of a group of talented administrators and teachers who attempted a quick, radical change of an entire school program. They had to retrain themselves, develop community support, assemble instructional materials, and deal with their critics—all within the space of a few months. The new program came awkwardly into existence, was the focus of angry social ferment, and was eroded within a year. By taking our time and learning by degrees we can have a reasonable chance of avoiding the kind of experiences Smith describes.

Making Change Familiar

In most communities educational change has been a nervous, controversial process attempted on an inadequate social and technical base. Innovation in education will remain uncomfortable—and largely unsuccessful—until we build communities of laymen and professionals who will take the time to plan realistically and mobilize powerfully. Until the goal of continual school improvement becomes a familiar and regular feature of the educational scene, innovations will remain only so long as forceful people hold them together. The society needs to understand its schools, and resistance to change is natural. Only when citizens and educators regularly and comfortably institute changes, when the improvement of schools becomes familiar and normal, will innovation become as natural as resistance to it is at present.

STAGE ONE TASK ANALYSIS

Assume that a committee of Responsible Parties has been formed and is just starting to work. What do they do? At the risk of being too specific, we set forth the following 12 tasks for them to engage in at the Stage One improvement level.

1. Organize the Responsible Parties to study the school program and environment
2. Develop relationships among the community, district, administration, sources of technical assistance, and the council
3. Commence studying the school using the effectiveness criteria
4. Select a focus for improvement
5. Assemble the necessary resources
6. Provide time for training
7. Communicate, communicate, and communicate
8. Prepare the pilot study
9. Carry out the pilot study
10. Revise the innovation
11. Commence implementation!
12. Evaluate and fine tune the innovation

Let us now examine each task in turn.

Task 1: Organize the Responsible Parties to Study the School Program and Environment.   At its beginning stages, the organization and functioning of the Responsible Parties will require considerable time and effort. The administrators of the school and the faculty need to meet and determine a method for electing or appointing members to a school-community council which will be the executive committee of the Responsible Parties. This council then needs to call a community meeting to explain its purpose and to discuss methods of securing representation from the community. In some communities the parent-teacher association can take on much of the responsibility for developing community representation but in other communities its activities are probably best confined to teacher-parent relationships.

In complex communities it is probably wise to establish a pro tem council responsible for establishing a method that insures full and adequate representation on the school council. In demographically complex communities, for example, the achievement of adequate representation takes time since all economic and ethnic groups should be represented. (See the description of the National Urban/Rural School Development on pp. 152–60.)

Task 2: Develop Relationships Among the Community, District Administration, Sources of Technical Assistance, and the Council.   It will take some time for the council to establish a process for studying the school, determining needs, establishing priorities, and developing a plan of action. At the outset the community members on the council need to establish a network of relationships throughout the community to ensure efficient two-way communication. As the study proceeds opinions and ideas need to be solicited from and transmitted to the community. It will take a considerable period of time to establish a network that will accomplish this comfortably and easily.

In addition the council needs to contact the school district administration to solicit its advice about the directions of education for the community. Curriculum guides and governance regulations should be assembled and examined, and the relationships among the council, the district administration, and the board of education established. Generally speaking, councils can achieve wide latitude for themselves provided they do not violate board of education regulations. Also central district offices periodically tend to initiate districtwide changes in certain aspects of the school program and these initiatives need to be respected. If the school district is making a considerable effort in the area of science, for example, the council may simply want to facilitate that effort, developing its own initiatives in other areas. The exact relationship between councils and the central governance structure of the district will vary from situation to situation and needs to be negotiated carefully and openly. The board of education and district office should welcome the initiates of the Responsible Parties and in turn the Responsible Parties should welcome initiatives originating at the district level.

County, state, and federal guidelines can also be ascertained through the district offices as well as sources of funding for initiatives originating at those levels. For example, federal and state guidelines now mandate that handicapped students be provided the "least restricted education" available and provide resources to bring about certain changes. As this book is being written, there are considerable resources available in the area of special education, especially for teacher information and training.

Resources need to be marshaled, however, and procedures established for obtaining them. Also, supervisors, higher education personnel, and technical assistants from the county, state, and curriculum and teacher centers need to be identified. The council may want to secure the services of a consultant to help them organize and learn to function efficiently. Evaluations of school-community councils such as the National Urban/Rural School Development Program have generally concluded that most councils can use considerable technical assistance both in studying their school and implementing their plans. The council of the Responsible Parties must quickly learn a great deal about education in order to make informed decisions. Membership essentially constitutes an agreement to embark on a long course of study and at many points in that course expert assistance will be needed and appreciated.

Task 3: Commence Studying the School Using the Effectiveness Criteria. The Responsible Parties now begin to study the school and its community. They acquaint themselves with the school program and how it is conducted. They interview teachers, community members, administrators, and children to ascertain what is going on and gather opinions about areas needing attention. They begin to draw a picture of the present missions which the school is fulfilling and the means being used to achieve them. What is our school like? What are the parts of its program like? What is it accomplishing? What might it accomplish?

Refer back now to Chapter 2 in which the Cameo School is described, and Chapter 3 in which the characteristics of effective schools are listed and used to analyze the Cameo School. The Responsible Parties need to do just what we illustrated at the end of Chapter 3— examine their school environment by applying these criteria.

The guidelines to school and classroom effectiveness provide a good beginning although a general consideration of the missions of the school and appropriate means for achieving them should not be neglected in the long term (Stages Two and Three). The attributes described in the following checklist of questions provide a convenient tool for commencing the study of the school. The Responsible Parties can ask:

Are the academic and social goals of the school clear to community, students, faculty, and administrators?

Is there good order? Is discipline consistent with the methods of the school?

Is the school permeated with high expectations for student growth and achievement?

Do the teachers feel efficacious?

Is the climate caring and supportive? Do the students feel accepted and do they understand that the high expectations are the result of caring about them?

Is accomplishment praised publicly?

Is administrative leadership clear, strong, and responsive?

Does the community support education? Are parents involved?

Are students busy with learning tasks that are appropriate to their learning abilities?

Is progress monitored and are students kept informed about their development and achievement?

Is the curriculum coherently organized?

Is an appropriate variety of teaching strategies in use?

Are there opportunities for students to share responsibility for the health of the school?

It is virtually certain that any organization of Responsible Parties that asks these questions will find ample opportunity to refine current practice and generate innovations.

Task 4: Select a Focus for Improvement. Gradually a list of priorities develops and the task becomes one of deciding on an area of focus. When a council is just beginning it is wise to begin with the effectiveness criteria and get Stage One (refinement) moving. Attention can turn to curriculum areas and staff development in Stage Two (renovation). Finally, fresh missions and means for accomplishing them can be explored in Stage Three (redesign). As a council matures, their continuous study will create a situation where in some areas improvements have been implemented, in others the implementation is just starting, and in others the debate is still raging about what to do and how to do it. A beginning council, however, should always focus quite specifically. Nearly everyone who studies a school using the effectiveness criteria finds numerous ways of improving it. It is easy to set too many goals and achieve none of them. In Chapters 7 and 8 we will simulate the process of determining a focus by making selections for Cameo School. The focus should be one in which there is relatively high agreement and in which procedures can be easily developed.

Task 5: Assemble the Necessary Resources. Once the focus is selected and the missions and means within that area have been identified they should be communicated thoroughly to the community, the central district administration, and the teaching staff. Everyone needs to be alerted that a change is about to take place. The proposed change should be communicated as an experimental attempt to improve education, one that will be modified as experience is accumulated, and which may be discarded if it proves ineffective. It is a serious mistake to present any proposed changes as a panacea to the problems of education. A modest approach which does not exaggerate the possibilities and which emphasizes the experimental nature of any innovation is the wiser course.

In addition, resources need to be assembled and detailed plans made. If the area of improvement is the recruitment of volunteer aides, for example, the teachers need to be surveyed to determine how aides can be used and what training will be necessary for them. The Responsible Parties need to advertise the positions and identify criteria for service. The process must be orderly, and a high level of communication is essential. In a curriculum area the guidelines need to be established and the instructional materials brought together. Curriculum planning fails when the plan is not backed up with the resources to make it work. There are many great ideas for teaching which are supported by a very thin base of materials. The Responsible Parties must ensure that the resources are brought together in the areas of focus.

Task 6: Provide Time for Training. There is probably no area worthy of change which does not require that people learn some new behaviors. Curriculum changes require new teaching strategies and the mastery of new content by teachers and others. Changes in organization and community relations require new kinds of conferences and counseling. Parents who volunteer to be aides find that they need skills in tutoring. The development of appropriate training and time for training is essential to successful innovation. One of the major reasons why change has proved so difficult in many schools is simply because adequate personnel training has not been provided. We are going to discuss this subject extensively in Chapters 9 and 10. At this point it is sufficient to point out that new skills need to be identified and ways of learning them provided. In certain areas teachers can provide training directly to one another. In other areas consultants or university personnel will be needed. To omit training will virtually ensure failure. Also, for many schools this will be the first step in the development of regular substantive in-service training, and it must lay the base for the more complex staff development required in Stages Two and Three.

Task 7: Communicate, Communicate, and Communicate. Formal meetings should now be held with community members, the teaching staff, and the district administration to make clear what is going on and how it will be accomplished. All parties concerned need and have the right to know what is about to happen and why. Questions need to be answered at this time and unanimity developed. Teachers and community members should enter the process with a feeling of friendly, supportive experimentation.

Task 8: Prepare the Pilot Study. At this point a plan should be developed for testing, evaluating, and revising selected elements of the innovation. It is important that representative elements of the innovation be tested since their effectiveness will vary according to the plan and the setting. If the change is within a curriculum area, several teachers may volunteer to try out elements of the new procedures. The pilot can be accomplished by observation or an informal evaluation.

Task 9: Carry Out the Pilot. Maximum support should be given to the individuals involved in testing elements of the innovation. Especially if the new teaching strategies and content are involved both teachers and students will be uncomfortable with the new material and procedures for some time and this discomfort should be expected.

Task 10: Revise the Innovation. The pilot will almost surely indicate the need for adjustments and perhaps for further training. This task can occupy a considerable period of time depending on the complexity of the innovation. The pilot will help determine the steps necessary to implement the change and the final plan for implementation can be generated at this time.

Task 11: Commence Implementation. This is the period during which a supportive social climate is most essential. Any change worth making involves new procedures which will be awkward at first. There will be a sense that things are not going as well as they were before and for a time this will be true. For example, when volunteer aides are first brought into a school there is generally some feeling of chaos. The aides feel insecure and the teachers are uncertain how to employ them productively. There is a period of excitement combined with dismay. However, if the social climate is positive and all hands assist one another the adjustment period is soon gotten through. A lengthy curriculum should be implemented in stages and training should continue throughout the early parts of implementation. It is extremely helpful if teachers can regularly share information about what is and is not working.

Task 12: Evaluate and Fine Tune the Innovation. Over time, appropriate evaluation procedures should be used to find out how things are going. Further revision will usually be necessary and the need for it should be taken in stride. Many innovations fail because the first implementation efforts are awkward and appear ineffective. Frequently they are discarded when revision, adaptation, or further training would have been the better solution.

Evaluation should be planned into each part of the innovation to insure that it is under continuous study. As the process of generating and implementing changes and evaluating their effects become established the Responsible Parties will have a continuous flow of information that can be used for further decision making. On the basis of this information efforts should be made to "fine tune" the school program on a continuous basis.

STAGE TWO TASK ANALYSIS

After several discrete innovations have been successfully made, Stage Two (renovation) is ready to be launched. At this point the focus of the Responsible Parties shifts to such major tasks as:

1. Survey the curriculum areas and the overall social climate
2. Clarify the goals of the area being studied
3. Identify alternative means of accomplishing the goals
4. Repeat Tasks 5 through 12 of Stage One

A brief look at the preceding Stage Two tasks is now in order.

Task 1: Survey the Curriculum Areas and the Overall Social Climate.   Now the major curriculum areas (science, mathematics, reading, etc.) come under scrutiny and the ones needing attention are selected for focus. In addition to the curriculum areas the focus might be on matters such as:

> The school climate (developing a warm cooperative atmosphere)
>
> School organization (developing teaching teams, etc.)
>
> Community action programs (involving students in social service)
>
> Developing additional personnel resources (obtaining and training volunteer teaching aides)
>
> Securing and developing a continuing education program for adults (recently communities into which Vietnamese refugees are moving are finding a considerable need in this area)

Even the basic skill areas (reading, writing, and arithmetic) which receive considerable public attention are not easily brought into focus. Although well established in most schools it takes some time before the council can unravel their complexities and develop a clear idea about direction. When a new school is being established, all areas will need to receive some attention and the problem of study is one of considerable complexity.

Task 2: Clarifying the Goals of the Area Being Studied.   Just what the goals are of the area being studied is the next question. Most aspects of the school program contain possible competing missions and it is important to clarify them before the question of means is approached.

Task 3: Identify Alternative Means of Accomplishing the Goals.   Once the goals have been identified the next question becomes, "What are the alternative ways of accomplishing them?" In every curriculum area there are several alternatives; there are a number of ways of changing the social climate of the school; recruiting and training aides can be accomplished in a variety of ways. For such tasks the council can probably use the services of consultants in the areas under consideration.

Even the most experienced teachers are generally too busy to keep up with all the curriculum alternatives. At this point the study needs to include not only the teachers representing the Responsible Parties but also representatives from or perhaps all of the teachers who would be involved in any change. Goals need to be circulated and understood both by the community and the teaching staff. Furthermore the teachers must help identify the alternative curriculum plans, materials, and teaching procedures needed to accomplish the curriculum goals. In this book we divide the means into the curricular—the organization of substance and teaching process; the technological—the assembly of materials and other instructional devices; and the social—the organization of people and the development of a social climate appropriate to the mission. All of these need to be studied and thought out.

Task 4: Repeat Tasks 5 through 12. From here we proceed as from Task #5 through Task #12 in Stage One, one curriculum area at a time. Several major innovations should not be inaugurated simultaneously or the school will become unstable. Again, however, the process should become regular.

A Continuous Process

While one area of focus is receiving operational attention (Tasks 5 through 12 of Stage One), the examination of alternative missions and means (Tasks 1 through 3 of Stage Two) goes on in other areas. New focuses need to be selected, resources organized, training commenced, pilot implementations undertaken, and full implementation developed. It is important to estimate how much improvement the school can manage at any one time and to search for an optimal level of change. Undertaking too much too quickly overtaxes the system but undertaking too little too slowly, does not provide adequate stimulation.

The Responsible Parties will eventually need standing committees to oversee major dimensions of the school program. These committees should engage in a continuous review of their particular area and recommend changes. In addition, teachers and community members should be queried at regular intervals in order to identify areas needing attention.

The most efficient way to survey needs is probably through interviews with a sample of the community members and teachers. They should be asked to think through the school and its program, contemplate the nature of the community, and identify areas worth studying. As the community changes, new needs will emerge. Other needs can be identified by studying the children's attitudes and achievement. In addition, each standing committee should study the products of research and development in their areas. New developments in mathematics, reading, science, social studies, the arts, and so forth should be scrutinized as well as new plans for organizing schools, training personnel, and so on. District offices, counties, states, and the federal government will also generate initiatives which need to be examined by the Responsible Parties. Federal and state agencies support initiatives according to perceived social needs which tend to vary among local school situations. The most effective councils look on these external initiatives as opportunities and will select from them the ones most appropriate to their school setting.

As part of their regular development program, teachers should attend conferences and search out materials and ideas in their fields. The Responsible Parties will also want to visit nearby schools and a few outside their immediate area looking for ideas that will be adaptable to their situation.

Clearly, embedding the school improvement process is essential. The first tentative moves will be uncomfortable to communities and schools that are not accustomed to the continuous change process. As time goes on, change will become more familiar, a positive social climate will develop and community members and teachers will become comfortable working together. As each targeted improvement becomes embedded in the school a general climate of receptivity to change and improvement will develop. School improvement will become normal rather than exceptional. Each effort lays the ground for the next...the next...and the next.

STAGE THREE TASK ANALYSIS

We now proceed to the stage where we begin to consider the overall purpose of the school (its major missions) and rethink the entire structure of the school. Part V of this book deals with alternative missions, new technologies and different ways of organizing personnel and resources. The improvement process (selecting missions and the means to achieve them, assembling resources, and staff development) is the same at this stage as it was for Stage Two. The success of implementation efforts, however, will depend on past efforts to lay a base from which a thoroughgoing examination can proceed.

BUILDING RESISTANCE TO READY-MADE SOLUTIONS

We are able to distinguish a number of styles by which educational decisions have been made in the past. One is the use of custom or tradition, which is more common than we sometimes realize. Why, for example, do we have 12 grades in school? Is it because we have *always* had 12 grades? Why do so many schools begin in September and end in June? Is it because agrarian America of the nineteenth century needed the labor of the children in the fields during the summer? Why is history so often taught chronologically? Is it because history is best learned that way, or is it because events occurred that way? Why is American literature taught in the eleventh grade and English literature in the twelfth? Obviously, this is simply the way it has always been done.

The reason that tradition is so attractive is that it provides ready-made solutions to questions that could otherwise become problems, and thus it simplifies the decision-making process. In daily living this is useful, even indispensable. The dangers are that a habitual or customary solution may rule our decisions long after such a solution is outmoded and useless, or that we will come to rely on tradition to the point where we stop seeking creative solutions.

Another way to solve problems is to appeal to an expert or some highly respected source. Should five-year-olds be taught to read? We might ask a psychologist to give us an opinion. Should we have subject specialists in the primary school? Again, we might hope that authorities will tell us. We might ask a mathematician what mathematics should be taught in the elementary school, or a business man what high school curriculum is the best preparation for business.

We certainly should seek authoritative knowledge. Much uncertainty can be dissipated by listening to authority, and there are times when we must trust the judgment of the expert. But it is not wise simply to call in an authority and ask that person to be our decision maker. Educational knowledge rarely points to clear solutions that are appropriate for all situations. The authority should be consulted about the *options*, not asked to give us the answer.

Another way to solve problems is to rely on common sense. The truth, in such cases, is "obvious," "self-evident," or "indisputable." Now, we certainly want to rely on our good judgment. But we need to be suspicious of many common sense ideas about education. Some obvious propositions have turned out to be quite wrong. For example: teachers once assumed that punishment extinguished poor responses—that punishing or correcting a child for misspelling a word would impel him to spell the word correctly thereafter. It has been found, however, that punishment can often *reinforce* the original response; that is, fix the incorrect spelling in the learner's mind. Punishment can also create phobias, turning the learner away from the subject matter.

Another common sense solution to the problem of low achievement is failing a child and keeping him at the same grade level. This procedure is also supposed to encourage the child to learn what he has failed to learn in the past. Yet nonpromotion may actually retard achievement; it has been found that the unpromoted student tends to learn less than he would have had he been promoted (Goodlad & Anderson, 1965).

Similarly, common sense tells us that grouping children by ability facilitates learning and many schools and school districts employ homogeneous grouping. However, grouping by ability has not always proven to be an effective stimulant to learning and in some cases has retarded the achievement of the less able and has stigmatized some children. Segregating the handicapped seemed sensible to policy makers 30 years ago but is abhorrent today.

There is no easy antidote to the usual ways school programs come into existence, which is to let common practice dominate, accept the solutions offered by one or two authorities, or follow common sense formulas. Schools in general are not as effective as they should be precisely because easy, comfortable practices have been adopted without adequate thought or energy. Schools are difficult to improve because current practice feels like the right thing to do. It would be much easier to institute better practice if teachers and community felt uneasy about the condition of their school. But, in most cases, people accept the status quo and have trouble believing that the school can actually become much better than it is.

If the Responsible Parties are to generate effective school improvement they have to develop a systematic process for studying the school program. For most Responsible Parties study of the school will generate a list of possible improvements to be made in:

> *Social Climate (Stage One):* For example, ways of communicating goals to students, ways of increasing a "can do" attitude, or procedures for the public acknowledgement of achievement.

> *Technology (Stage Two):* For example, adding microprocessors to the high school mathematics program.

> *Curriculum (Stage Two):* For example, overhauling the elementary school science and literature programs (most are quite poor).

> *Organization (Stage Three):* For example, deploying some personnel to work in a microprocessing center or linking the school to broadcast courses.

It is important to build gradually to ensure that homeostatic reactions do not undermine the entire school improvement effort or prevent the formation of an effective working unit. Beginning at Stage One establishes the process and improves the climate of education.

Stage Two establishes a process for improving the curriculum areas and embeds in the school the staff development necessary for curricular improvement. Finally, a matured school council can draw the entire community into the stimulating, difficult process of considering the overall direction of the school to bring it into line with preferred missions (Stage Three).

Few Responsible Parties will want to overhaul the entire school at once—to proceed to Stage Three without going through Stages One or Two. This would exceed the capability of most communities to design, implement, or absorb change. However, if the school environment is under continuous study and small improvements are made regularly then it is reasonable to hope that an overall design can gradually be built and changes can be shaped so as to bring that design into existence gradually. The reform movements have left us a rich legacy of school models to build upon.

It is important to remember that school improvement is a process *that should never cease*. We can't get away cheap—studying the school every 20 years, making a few changes, and then letting it roll along for two more decades. The process of school improvement must be built carefully and then made permanent—the Responsible Parties are here to stay!

Part III

STAGE ONE:
REFINING THE SCHOOL

In this stage a school improvement committee is established, the health of the school is scrutinized using information about effective teaching in schools, and plans are made and carried out to refine the program.

7

The Social Dimension
of Quality Education

The world that presses on us also presses on our children. Sometimes it arouses them. Occasionally, it maddens them. It always pushes against them so as to shape them. At all points in their lives the enormous weight of the culture lies over and around them—a veritable sea of values, skills, ideas, and "normal" behaviors.

Social influence does not stop at the door of the school. In both obvious and subtle ways, the human interaction within schools constitutes a social system that has much effect on student development. For example, social influence strongly affects their self-concepts and the rigor with which they will inquire. Social models influence the value they will place on various kinds of content. By modeling their social milieu students learn social skills and values, even how they will respect and behave toward their fellow students. From their environment they learn whether creativity is a good thing or whether originality is dangerous. Much of the learning about self, others, and valuing is a product of living in the community of the school and experiencing the transmission of values and attitudes from the other members of the group.

The pragmatists have taught us that the critical process in education is the point of interaction between learner and environment (Dewey, 1916). They have given us the knowledge that a major task in creating quality education is the arrangement of the social environment. Because so few people have learned to construct a social system deliberately the most difficult intellectual task for the Responsible Parties is to design a social milieu that will achieve the working objectives of the school.

SCHOOL ENVIRONMENTS

The social system is one of three dimensions of the overall school environment that operate in different ways but interact to become the

107

cradle of learning. Although rarely planned for in schools today, the social dimension is the medium in which the other dimensions exist. It is sometimes called the "hidden curriculum" (Dreeben, 1973). Students are told that one kind of learning (the explicit curriculum) is valued and then find that quite another type (the hidden curriculum) is in fact encouraged. In this chapter we will deal with the social system as something that should be explicit and congruent with the overall goals of the school.

A second dimension is the learning resource system of the school— the artifacts and communication apparatus that enable the learner to access information and ideas, to conduct experiments, and to receive feedback about behavior. Third is the curricular system of the school, or the system for initiating, maintaining, and monitoring learning. It involves the planned presentation of content to the learners, helping them attack that content, and tracking their progress.

Thinking of the means of education as three interacting dimensions of the environment may seem somewhat strange at first since most of us have been conditioned to the idea that textbooks, lectures, and demonstrations constitute the means of education. However, education is more complex than that and can only be understood by analyzing the subtle interaction of means and ends. It is pointless to study one in the absence of the other.

All three dimensions of the Cameo School are weak. It does not use diverse learning resources (even the standard audiovisual materials seem unavailable and neglected). Its curricular systems seem weak and textbook dependent and the social system is a disaster area.

If you wish a contrast to the social system of the Cameo School you might refer to the descriptions of the Foster and the Agapé schools in Chapters 8 and 13 respectively. These schools have complex, well-developed resource and curricular systems but their most striking feature may be their carefully articulated social system. Without the powerful norms of their social environment these schools would not function effectively. Their norms surround the students as they engage in a rich variety of learning experiences and as their teachers model an inquiring and supportive attitude and assist them to use the learning resources that are available.

SCHOOL SOCIAL SYSTEMS

Within every human group there soon develops a social order. That is, interaction becomes less random and more patterned so that coherent sets of values, norms, and roles develop to make relationships predictable and relatively stable. Also, the group develops mechanisms that link them to surrounding organizations—what Homans (1950) refers to as the *external system* relationships. The people who create the social system are, in turn, affected by it. It prescribes their behaviors and imbues them with its values. It specifies how decisions will be made and status accorded. It delineates the kinds of relationships people will have—whether they will be cooperative or unilateral, austere or loving, honest or dishonest.

The social system within an institution does not absolutely control all social behavior (in fact, it may confer freedom), but it has a powerful affect on it, and, in the case of most people, sets limits on what they must do, may do, and can omit doing. Some groups are characterized by highly specific rules that cover many aspects of behavior, while in others boundaries are looser and less pervasive. In his fascinating essays on mental institutions, Erving Goffman (1961) discusses the kinds of control exerted within social institutions and coins the term *total institution* to describe the very high degrees of control that characterize mental institutions. Some observers have described schools as total institutions, but aside from a few exceptional cases, the comparison is probably more figurative than literal. However, it does underline the real and potential power of the school's social dimension. Although there is a deplorable dearth of research on the social system of our public schools, some of the factors that operate within school societies have been clarified.

The Student Society

Coleman's (1963) research has confirmed what any observer should expect: that students in a school form values and norms that severely affect the behaviors of their fellow students. Where intellectual activity has improved, for example, students tend to achieve more academic learning. This is true for the most able students as well as for others. Although Coleman's research was done in high schools, it no doubt applies to elementary schools as well. Some of the recent studies of schools characterized by exceptionally high levels of achievement have reported that they are characterized by clear goals, high task orientation, and public recognition of achievement. In the Agapé School several kinds of learning are embraced. The teachers in both the direct instruction team and the learning center create an atmosphere that encourages achievement of basic skills, academic substance, tools for learning, and social skills. The goals in each area are made clear to the students and they are given responsibility for taking charge of their achievement.

Impersonal Interactive Styles

A good many years ago, Waller (1932) observed that within schools impersonal rather than personal leadership patterns tended to develop. Put another way, teachers in many schools use impersonal devices rather than depending on their leadership skills and personality. For example, many teachers say, "We must learn this because the principal (or curriculum guide) says so," thus invoking the authority of the institution, rather than saying, "I want you to learn this." Another example is, "You will need this if you are to get admitted to college," rather than, "This excites and stimulates me and I think it will be important for you, too!" This impersonal mode removes the teacher from personal responsibility for curriculum and instruction, assigns the real authority elsewhere, and lowers the impact of the teachers' own valuing of the material to be mastered. Such leadership, Waller observed, was adequate for lecture methods of instruction, but not good for democratic-process methods or for counseling the students.

Today, we argue, faculty detachment probably hinders any form of education by lessening the power of teachers to influence their students through personal example. Without teachers who actively model the value and rewards of learning it is less likely that students will eventually become self-motivated learners. In the Foster and Agapé schools the teachers make it very clear that learning is important to them and that *they* have responsibility for the curriculum.

Mental Health and Imagination

A fascinating book by John and Elaine Cumming (1962) describes the dimensions of the social environment that affect the mental health of people. Some environments encourage extreme dependence, where others encourage autonomy. Some press us to conformity, others free us. Some are punitive and make us feel guilty, while others are supportive and reassure us. Some climates tear at self-confidence and others induce us to explore new things.

The social climate of schools should be viewed as a crucial means of influencing students' feelings, self-image, creativity, and ability to think boldly. If people are to make democratic decisions, it will be because the environment supports debate, open-mindedness, and the struggle for compromise. Where they teach themselves, it will be because they have confidence in their decisions and in the supportiveness of the environment. The therapeutic—and the damaging—aspects of the milieu serve to remind us again that the social system has to be an integral part of the educational program, whatever model of education is used. In other words, the leadership patterns of the school social system are related to its educational possibilities.

Social Contagion and Modeling

The social behaviors of teachers are often imitated by students. This may even occur among classes of young children. Forty years ago, Anderson and Brewer (1939) demonstrated that in kindergarten classrooms where teachers were "dominative" toward the children, the children tended to be dominative toward each other both in the classroom and on the playground. Where teachers were more "integrative" and respecting of the children, the children were more integrative toward each other. What happens, then, is that the children become infected with the social behavior of the teacher, and their behavior toward each other tends to take on the character of the teacher's behavior toward them. Similarly, teachers who model high achievement will influence their students to achieve.

A number of interesting studies (conducted mostly at the college level) have shown that the social climate of schools is contagious. An idea or value that is part of the normative structure of the school is likely to be transmitted to the students (Jacob, 1956). This is important for two reasons. First, the norms of the school will be transmitted to the students whether planned or not and may work for or against the educational program. Second, the educational program can take advantage of the phenomena. A school that wishes to encourage self-instruction, for example, can try to develop values that will support independent, scholarly behavior.

Patterns of Interaction and Teaching Strategies

Bellack and his associates (1965) investigated verbal interaction within the classroom while lessons were being conducted. They discovered rather stable patterns of interaction that resulted in relatively fixed teacher and student roles. For example, the average teacher asks most of the questions. Students are accustomed to this and are prepared to respond. Teachers, in turn, react by approving or disapproving what the students have said. This pattern is well suited to recitation styles of teaching. What would happen, however, if teachers were to put the question-asking burden on the students and induce them to develop and test hypotheses? More than likely the students would resist any change in their roles. The patterns that Bellack discovered are comfortable ones—students know what to do, how to cope with the traditional classroom situation, and they are likely to undermine innovative attempts to teach them inductively.

Any school that wishes to employ self-instruction, cooperative inquiry, or any other innovative instructional strategy can expect these changes to be accompanied by corresponding changes in the social system of the school. If the social system is not made to cooperate—be a part of—the educational strategy, then all other aspects of educational method will probably have little effect on the student. Students become as entrenched in roles as do teachers. If students are given a steady diet of routine learning tasks, they will quickly learn what to do and how to do it. Then if they are abruptly asked to take charge of portions of their learning, they will tend to resist the change. They will have to practice the new roles until they are comfortable in them before they will fully accept the change.

The norms of order and of attention to a restricted curricular and instructional mode are quite apparent in the Cameo School. Both the teachers and the principal present a very limited educational model to the students, one which punishes those who do not keep up with a single, fixed curriculum. It is almost certain that the net result will be severely damaging to the self-concepts of many students. On the other hand there is virtually no planned place for the talented students to exercise intellectually. They are being taught that conformity to a curriculum is what constitutes education. By contrast the Agapé School has a carefully developed system for modulating learning rates and presents a wide variety of instructional options to encourage talent development of all sorts.

The Agapé teachers are well aware of the contagious effects of the personal behavior they present to their students. They are kind and supportive and organize the students in a businesslike manner. They make visible their own activity as learners. The learning centers offer well-engineered learning resources, creating a sense that the students are in the hands of professionals who know their business.

The Agapé School uses a variety of approaches to learning and helps the students learn how to use them. Part of their plan is to help students diversify the ways they can learn. They offer highly sequenced learning, inductive inquiry, sophisticated electronic "teaching machines," and small, independent group activities. As a result their students should become increasingly effective as learners.

Personality and Educational Methods

The psychologist David Hunt (1971) has carefully studied the effects of environmental structure and teaching method on students' long-term personality growth. His work has given us a series of propositions for predicting the effect of environment on personality growth and for adjusting educational environments to the characteristics of students. Hunt focuses on the capacity of students to integrate new information and ideas into their cognitive structures. In unilateral environments where students are basically the passive recipients of instructional tasks they are more likely to develop rigid personalities, reject ideas that conflict with their beliefs, and not develop their learning capabilities. On the other hand, relatively rule-oriented students who need much structure do not thrive in environments that require a high level of independence. The optimal environment presents a wide range of learning opportunities and supports the students as they learn to use them. It provides enough structure and support that they can manage themselves and comfortably learn to assimilate new information, learning strategies, and social settings. In other words, the overall learning environment interacts with students' personalities to produce long-term effects on cognitive development and learning capability. Schools vary considerably in provision for difference in learning styles.

The Cameo School environment is clearly unilateral. Teachers and instructional materials dominate the scene with students taking little responsibility for their own learning. A limited range of learning opportunities are presented and, consequently, students are unable to expand their learning abilities.

By contrast, the Agapé environment follows Hunt's advice. It presents various learning channels that match its various goals. The students are strongly supported as they engage in the various learning activities and the tasks are modified to be within their reach. Two overall messages are projected: (1) that students can increase their learning capabilities, and (2) that they will be strongly supported while struggling to master new ways of learning.

The School and Its Neighborhood

The more effective schools enlist the community in the service of education. They scoop up community resources and they involve community members in educational roles—as aides, tutors, and as providers of educational resources through businesses, museums, and other settings. The Responsible Parties should carefully assess the resources within the community and decide what should be capitalized on and what is missing and should be provided.

Except for matters of discipline the Cameo School is virtually isolated from its community and eschews the involvement of community members and parents in the school program. There is an enormous loss of potential power. In a real sense the community and the parents constitute a potentially vast and extended school staff. The more community members are involved the greater the energy and the educational modalities that are available to the school. Community members represent "person power" available both at home with their own children and as volunteer aides and in other roles within the active school program. The Agapé program follows these principles. A committee of Responsible Parties designs and oversees the program. Roles are provided for many parents and the curriculum builds on and extends the natural experiences of the children.

Salient Features of the Social System

The community within the school is an extension of the larger society whose features are mirrored in the school. Within each school distinctive social environments develop whose characteristics, as we have shown influence learning. Adults provide the leadership for the social system. Their styles of leadership and the behaviors they model influence the students both as a community and as individuals within that system.

The school community develops distinctive normative patterns that draw students toward and away from particular activities and domains of development (social, academic, and physical). These normative patterns will have a profound long-term effect on the self-concepts, values, and skills that will be developed. Personalities will interact with the social system productively or unproductively with long-term effects on motivation and learning styles. The modulating capability of the school environment will have much to do with whether or not that interaction will be productive. Finally, homes and neighborhoods impart their distinctive patterns and these, too, will interact productively or unproductively with the environment of the school. The school's ability to capitalize and compensate will, again, be responsible for whether the interaction is productive.

DEVELOPING THE SOCIAL SYSTEM

Building the school's social system depends on creating an appropriate normative structure: coherent student roles and integrated roles for teachers that are consistent with the overall purposes of the school.

The Normative Structure

The norms of the school are made up of the values that are espoused by the educational community (children and the school staff), the norms (expected behaviors) that are encouraged in that community, and the informal sanctions (rewards and punishment) that are employed. What is most valued is what will be transmitted most powerfully. For example, students may be exposed to a community who prize creative thinking and wish to promote it among the students. Bruner (1961) has argued persuasively that such schools will have to actively demonstrate their high regard for such thinking. The students will need to see creative hypotheses formulated and tested. If the school values the "right answer" too much, then students may be reluctant to venture the intuitive answers that are essential to creative enterprise. Bettelheim (1982) has presented a very strong argument that the encouragement of fantasy and a rich emotional life will influence not only creativity but personal integration and the capacity to grow.

What we are saying, of course, is that in order to bring about a particular kind of behavior, the school has to value it. For any kind of educational purpose to be believed, the school's normative structure has to radiate its valuing of that kind of behavior. If students are to learn to practice disciplines it will be because the value of such behavior is actively modeled. If self-concepts are to be enhanced, it will be because students know they are valued and because they have come to value each other. If fantasy, imagination, and creativity are to be released, it will be because the social milieu provides a safe space for emotional growth.

It is one thing to decide what goals the school's norms should support. It is quite another to create appropriate norms, because the school society is made up of children and adults who traditionally do not share a peer culture. Usually the school depends on the parents and community to transmit to the children the norms that are needed by the school community. When, as in the case of the culturally disadvantaged, the home and community do not inculcate those values and norms, the school is ordinarily powerless to affect the children—or at least it does not engage very many of them. The school culture, where school teachers and parents do not effectively reinforce each other, frequently becomes a tug-of-war between children and teachers. However, as we are about to see, schools can do many things to develop a normative structure that will facilitate the function of the school.

Sanctions

Through grades, reports to parents, prizes, honors, smiles, words of encouragement, toleration, the faculty rewards and punishes the behaviors of students. These sanctions have two effects—they identify behaviors the faculty approves and disapproves of, and they encourage or discourage those student behaviors. If the faculty gives prizes for creative thinking, writing, acting, composing, and pays little attention to conventional achievement, then we can expect that the students will be drawn toward creative and away from academic achievement. If independence, self-teaching, and personal inquiry are consistently rewarded, we can expect much the same kind of effect.

In the average school of today few behaviors other than achievement of the basic skills in reading, writing, and arithmetic are rewarded to any extent and children usually govern themselves accordingly. If, however, the school has an active, caring, highly visible faculty, it is likely that the students will identify with them and imitate their behavior. In such cases the faculty can actively model the behaviors that they want to encourage in their students. A faculty that reads widely and constantly discusses the arts and contemporary political affairs is likely to have a student body that does the same. Faculties that venture hypotheses for their students to check or share their own creative efforts with their students will find that their example produces results. Not with every child or all of the time, of course, but the effect can be substantial.

Symbolism and Ceremony

A school that is carpeted, book lined, has an attractive theater and areas for music and art, and has paintings hanging is a building that "stands" for academic learning. If it includes opportunities for the youngest children to present plays and concerts and for the older ones to publicly debate contemporary issues, then it becomes a visible symbol of creative, academic inquiry. If it is a supportive, helpful place where student helps student and the library is open and inviting, then it develops character as a place of learning. The better the school communicates its values through the use of symbolism and ceremony the better its chances of influencing its students.

Informal Contacts between Teacher and Pupil

If the school can be a place of informal, personal contact between students and faculty, then the values and norms of the adults have a much greater chance of being absorbed by the children. Generally, there are two devices for accomplishing this. First, regular school operations can be run on an informal basis, with easy leisurely contacts characterizing all activities. Second, opportunities can be created for students and faculty to share extracurricular activities. For example, hobby clubs, trips to plays and ball games, and community improvement activities can all become part of the extracurriculum that facilitates the desired personal contact.

A school's norms tend to be highly stable and, barring catastrophe, change slowly. The use of rewards, example, symbolism, and the development of informal contacts with students will only gradually effect the existing social system. However, one of the characteristics of a school is its ever-changing population and, given a concerted, ongoing effort on the faculty's part, an incoming population of students can be affected. Four-year-olds enter school not knowing what it is. It can instantly become a place of supportive inquiry or a punishing, competitive grind. In some schools today the children flee as soon as they are dismissed and the teachers are glad to see them go. In other schools they linger along with the faculty. In some schools asking questions is sticking your neck out, while in others, it is an invitation to an academic journey. The processes that bring about these different climates are subtle and slow working but are as crucial as any part of the educational scene.

In nearly all present-day schools the normative structure stems from the natural, unplanned relationships between teachers and students. Frequently the resulting social climate works against the other more formally planned means of education, rather than reinforcing them. It should be otherwise.

Developing Student Roles

Another aspect of the social system that develops whether it is planned for or not is the role expectations of the students. By way of introduction to this subject think back to some class where the instructor alternatively lectured and led discussions. A half-asleep student, woolgathering behind his attentive expression, senses a change in the instructor's voice. Rousing himself, his attention swings back to the subject and he concentrates very hard on the instructor's last remarks. Why? Because he senses that the instructor is reaching one of those points where the lecture will cease and the students will bear responsibility for a forthcoming discussion. Put another way, we may say that the students' roles are about to change—but only temporarily!

Instructional modes shape the roles that students learn to play. When Bellack (1965) discovered definite language patterns in the classroom, he drew attention to the fact that the interchanges between students and teachers have a certain gamelike quality and all of the "players" soon learn their roles. For example, if teachers are quizzers, that is, if they spend much instructional time asking students to recite memorized information, the students will soon learn to play roles as reciters. They will memorize material and then wait to be questioned about it. Were the same teacher to begin asking them searching questions, the students would be quite awkward playing the role of discussant or inquirer. The teacher would probably find the students resisting the change in role for that would mean learning to cope with new demands. Until they have learned the new roles they must live with the uncertainty of a new environment. Consequently, they resist change—the resistance is normal.

The student's role in most schools today is fairly passive. They are expected to work hard to master information and skills that have been selected for them. They do assignments with mastery of the material in mind and, when asked, they are expected to produce "creative" writing or "original" ideas. They are expected to be cooperative if not enthusiastic in accomplishing the set work. Students are taught these roles directly by the teachers.

It is possible to teach students alternative roles. However, it must be remembered that the roles have to be *taught*. A school that hopes to shape students' roles will find that it must prepare the students for them. For example, if students are to be responsible for shaping their own learning projects, they have to be taught how to do this. If they are to evaluate their own progress or participate in cooperative projects, they must learn this also. If they are to be wide-ranging inquirers, they must learn how to use resources, plan excursions, interview, debate, and state and test hypotheses.

While the ages and abilities of students do influence the roles they can play, it is amazing to see kindergarteners who have learned to share in the planning of their day, who grow snap beans under several conditions to test hypotheses they have developed, who make up creative stories and dances, who take their own attendance, and most miraculous of all, who teach newcomers to their groups how to play these roles.

The beauty of the social system is that it is self-perpetuating. Once started it maintains itself, or tries to, and needs less energy from outside. However, teaching students to fulfill desirable roles is a taxing business. It needs to be carefully planned, and often requires the services of specialists. For example, some faculty members could construct units of study aimed deliberately at role teaching. Or if students are to analyze and improve their group behavior, some teacher might move from group to group, supporting them as they set goals and procedures, and teaching them how to analyze their performance for greater efficiency. Again, an entire faculty might plan units at the beginning of the school year which require student roles that will be needed throughout the rest of the program.

It is important that the entire school staff be aware of the roles that the students have been assigned and are learning to play. If teachers organize students to seek information independently, then the librarians must be prepared to facilitate that kind of inquiry. School personnel may need to be redeployed. An inquiry-centered school, for example, probably requires more staff members in the instructional resource centers and fewer in conventional classroom roles. The school climate does not have to be monolithic, but it should not tear the student apart by continually demanding contradictory roles that cannot be fulfilled.

Developing a social system is not a piecemeal business. For example, developing abrasive, driving teacher roles and conforming, acquiescent student roles would not do at all. The students would not respond well to the ferment generated by such teachers. If, however, students are taught that their role is that of initiator, seeker, explorer and that they are to support and assist others; if the teachers' role is that of helper, advisor, cheerleader; if the norms encourage independence and self-judgment, exploration and vigor, then the climate is likely to facilitate change. If any of these ingredients are missing, then facilitation is greatly reduced. A derisive group of fellow students, a few punitive faculty members, norms that vacillate between independence and conformity, can all cause the climate to become nervous and behavior more guarded. Teacher and student roles both need to be matched with the school's normative structure to create a mix that makes the social system an effective educator.

THE SOCIAL DIMENSION OF QUALITY EDUCATION

There are two messages in this chapter. The first is that the social milieu of the school is an essential dimension of its functioning. What is often called the hidden curriculum—the messages embedded in the culture of the school itself—cannot be left to chance but has to be planned as carefully as the formal curriculums, the technical supports, and the arrangement of human resources.

Recent research on effective schools indicates rather clearly that schools with clear missions that value hard work on the educational tasks at hand promote better achievement in the basic skills than do schools with flaccid social climates. What is true of the basic skills is probably true of all areas—schools that stand for achievement in all spheres of education will be more successful than those that take a laissez faire position. The social system, that hidden curriculum, is the key.

The second message is that the school's social dimension is quite complex and improving it can be particularly difficult because many educators are not accustomed to analyzing the social climate and taking steps to improve it. In Stage One school improvement, the educational environment is analyzed in terms of the simple principles derived from the literature on effective schooling. The Responsible Parties can focus on one element at a time. However, when Stages Two and Three are reached the Responsible Parties and the school faculty must collaborate to consider alternative ways of structuring the overall social environment to fit a coherent philosophy of education. Then they must work systematically to bring that environment into existence. A good many of the improvements that they will want to make in schools like Cameo have to do with the social climate. For example:

Clear academic and social goals

Order and discipline

High expectations

Pervasive caring

Public rewards and incentives

Community support

Opportunity for student responsibility

All are aspects of the social dimension. Furthermore, the very development of a committee of Responsible Parties will bring about a major change in school-community relations and in the overall social environment. In Cameo the teachers work alone and in relative isolation from the community. Establishing a committee of Responsible Parties means establishing the norm of joint school-community responsibility for analysing and improving the educational climate. The level of overall community support should rise in proportion to the activity level of the school committee.

Application to the Cameo School

As we indicated at the end of Chapter 3, the Cameo School needs improvement in nearly all of the aspects of the social dimension. The study by the Responsible Parties should reveal this. As the picture becomes clearer, the important question will be where to begin.

The school has relatively clear goals but in very limited areas. There is an atmosphere of order and discipline although the system includes very limited responsibility for students and limited kinds of learning opportunities. It would make good sense for the Responsible Parties to begin by creating an environment that combines pervasive caring with high expectations for the students. A supportive, "you can do it" environment and an increase in the nurturance of individuals and groups will probably make an immediate difference to the school. To carry this out, the school might need a human relations consultant who can help the faculty analyze student and teacher roles and teach them how high expectations are created. If resources are available a series of faculty workshops might be organized and led by consultants to teach ways of improving student self-concepts and engaging in positive discipline. It may also be wise for the principal to begin studying ways of developing a positive social climate. He and the faculty might study Glasser's techniques for conducting class meetings. It is certain that a staff development program will be needed.

One of the most difficult aspects of making even a minor change in the Cameo social system will be the fact that its faculty is unaccustomed to working together and has drifted into patterns of exchanging negative comments about the students during their informal interchanges. As they study how to provide an environment that is both caring and achievement oriented the principal will undoubtedly have to take a leadership role and begin nurturing those norms just as he previously nurtured the norms of quiet and order.

It will be difficult to develop many opportunities for student responsibility without making some curriculum changes, but a clear and easy beginning can be made by organizing student committees with responsibility for various aspects of the school environment. At first student responsibility can be directed at such mundane areas as playground behavior, lunchroom cleanliness, and the care of athletic equipment. As the environment becomes more caring and higher expectations are communicated to the children, student responsibility can be directed toward increasingly important areas.

Thus, within the limited curriculum and social structure of the Cameo School there is much room to improve. Success wil depend on agreement by the faculty, salient community members, and administrators that these changes will make a difference. Despite supporting evidence, some members of the faculty and community will remain skeptical until positive changes in student behavior actually begin to occur. That they will occur is certain if the climate and social system are improved. Students who receive support and encouragement and have high expectations directed at them will achieve more and feel better about themselves in the process. Relationships between teachers and students will improve and the Cameo School will be on its way in limited and halting steps, to becoming an effective educational environment.

8

First Steps in Instructional Improvement

The careful improvement of selected aspects of the Cameo School social environment will gradually establish the process of examining the health of the school and working together to improve it. The overall climate of the school will slowly become more energizing; students will become more active in pursuit of their education, will feel better about themselves, and increasingly will help one another to learn. Achievement and satisfaction should rise correspondingly.

Only in reading and arithmetic are there coherent curriculums, and these are based on a textbook series which is administered to all the students. The faculty has great difficulty with students who fall behind and, although they are less aware of it, they are denying gifted students the opportunity to expand their skills and apply them productively. In other words, the curriculum has few provisions for individual differences. Consequently, although the students are kept relatively busy, it is inevitable that many of them are not properly occupied, that at least half of them are frustrated or bored.

Hence, the Responsible Parties cannot confine their efforts to the school's social dimension. Something has to be done to provide a differentiated academic program. Initially it is wise for the Responsible Parties to confine their curriculum and instruction improvement efforts to those areas that everyone agrees have a high priority. In Cameo's case the faculty is clearly unprepared to create curriculums in any areas but reading and arithmetic. As the Responsible Parties become aware that provision for individual differences is lacking (with a consequent low level in appropriate learning engagement) they can begin by seeking alternative approaches to the reading and arithmetic areas, ones that will improve performance within the school without creating radical change.

Let us now assume that such a study has been going on. The Responsible Parties have brought in experts in reading and mathematics instruction and have explained that they are seeking ways to increase the provision for individual differences and, hopefully, increase the monitoring of learning. These consultations have brought the Responsible Parties into contact with a wide variety of programs in these two areas.

They become very interested in one that was developed by an educational research and development center in Pittsburgh in collaboration with Research for Better Schools, a regional laboratory in Philadelphia. Known as Individually Prescribed Instruction (IPI) the approach is based on instructional design principles first developed in military and industrial contexts (Scanlon, 1966). It now operates in more than a hundred schools across the country, and includes instructional materials in five curriculum areas: mathematics, reading, science, handwriting, and spelling. Students receiving IPI instruction usually work independently on materials which are prescribed daily (or every few days) for them, depending on their demonstrated level of competence, their learning style, and particular learning needs.

Although there are a number of other programs that are structured similarly, this one is attractive to the Responsible Parties because it fits their social climate objectives. Although instruction is quite precise and directive, the philosophy of the program is one of care for individual differences and nurturance of the student. Expectations that each child can achieve are high if the program is implemented properly. By using volunteer aides the program will involve more community members in the operation of the school. The provision for individual differences should increase academic learning time considerably by ensuring that the students are working on individually diagnosed tasks. In addition, progress is monitored continuously and out-of-school work is closely connected with in-school assignments.

The program is accompanied by staff development packages that assist administrators and teachers in learning how to operate the program and how to provide instructional training for the aides. Consultants who have long-term experience in the use of the program are available as well as schools where the program is fully implemented so that visiting faculty members can see the program in operation before transporting it to Cameo. Finally, because the program is so highly articulated it should help bring the faculty together in a clearly defined effort to meet the individual needs of their students.

As bad as they are, the curriculums in reading and mathematics are not Cameo's weakest. Why should the first effort at improvement not be directed at those areas where instruction is most haphazard and neglected? The answer is that initial efforts should provide a maximum opportunity for the curriculum improvement process to become established and for staff development to begin on a regular basis. This should happen in areas that can serve as the safest possible laboratory for establishing the school improvement process.

By systematically improving one curriculum area at a time, increasing the amounts of staff development, building an environment where there is pervasive caring and nurturance, and individual differences are respected, Cameo School is gradually improved. Slowly, it becomes more like the school just a few blocks away which we will call the Foster School.

THE FOSTER SCHOOL:
ANOTHER LEVEL OF DEVELOPMENT

Let's begin our look at Foster School by following one of its team leaders through a typical day.

Brian is the head of a teaching team primarily responsible for the education of a group of 11-year-olds. Preparation for the school day begins the preceding afternoon in a brief team meeting to polish up the plans for the next day. The focus of the meeting is a science unit in which Brian is taking the part of the lead teacher. He had demonstrated a Cartesian Diver to the students the day before, working with small groups and leading them through inquiry-training lessons designed to help them build and test hypotheses. One of the team members had watched him and has a number of suggestions.

"Brian, I'm not quite sure where you're heading. I'm having trouble planning my follow-up." Brian explains his purpose and makes a few suggestions for activities. One of the other teachers wants to discuss some of the students' inquiry skills and has a suggestion for skill training that Brian can do with the whole group.

The team members touch base briefly about their activities in the other curriculum areas and disband. On the way home, Brian stops by the teacher center to pick up some materials that he will need for the rest of the week's activities. The science consultant is there and they spend a few minutes discussing how his inquiry-training work is going. She is released from her teaching team on a half-time basis this year to help other teachers in the science area and to work with the district curriculum committee. Brian tells her that he is still not totally comfortable with inquiry training and asks if she can drop by to watch him.

"The other guys on the team have been helping me," he says, "but none of them have ever used inquiry training either and I need some expert criticism."

He arrives home before his wife or children do and uses the hour or so of quiet time to write a letter to the State Curriculum Resource Center asking for a bibliography of children's books on the culture of the South Pacific islands. He's had difficulty locating enough books on that topic to support a social studies unit which he and his team have been planning. His wife, Margie, returns and they catch up on one another's day and prepare dinner. While they are doing the dishes he is interrupted by a call from the principal, Charlie.

"Brian, I'm sorry to bother you at home but I just remembered that you and I were going to visit the primary reading team tomorrow about 10:00 and I wondered if we could rearrange the observation to the afternoon?"

"I'm afraid not; I'm going to do another round of my science lessons and I've just arranged for one of the folks from the teacher center to come over and watch me work. It's not going badly but I need some help."

"Okay, Brian, we'll keep our date at 10:00. Something has come up but I'll just put it off, I think. We ought to keep our momentum going in the reading area."

The entire faculty is reworking the reading curriculum. Part of the program emphasizes literature and the other part uses computer-based instruction for training in skills. The primary team was the first to use the computers and the intermediate teams are observing the process and preparing for the arrival of their own equipment. The computer programs are built around a game-type approach which includes embedded tests. Teachers and aides supervise the skill study time and most of the teachers' instructional time is spent helping individuals and small groups of children who have read literary selections. Brian is responsible for helping his team learn to use the computer terminals and, in turn, to train their children to use them. Some of the primary teachers do not like the computerized approach at all while others appear to be very enthusiastic. The entire process is unfamiliar to most of the school faculty and the replacement of the traditional basal reading series by a part-literary/part-computerized approach has shaken up a good many parents as well. On the other hand, many of the students are used to calculators and computers in mathematics instruction and they are, on the whole, delighted with the approach.

The primary team spent much of the previous summer in a workship in which the theory of the approach was explained and demonstrated with children attending a nearby summer school, and each of the teachers practiced working with a small group of students.

Now the problem is one of getting the system in place. The whole faculty knows that unless they help each other over the rough spots, they probably aren't going to get anywhere. They know that every innovation makes people uncomfortable and that they have to keep explaining the rationale to one another, continue to practice, and help the kids adjust to the new approach.

The purpose of the visit to the primary reading team is twofold: Charlie and Brian will be able to help the primary team figure out how to make things go smoother and, in addition, they are getting ready for the job they will have with the other primary and the intermediate teams. Charlie and the team leaders are members of the school implementation team. All of them have been trained in clinical supervision and in techniques of training. Every teaching team works on a particular emphasis each year. This year, Brian's team is working on improving science teaching, and he and his staff are studying several approaches, of which inquiry training is one. Reading is the thrust of the primary teams and will become the thrust of the intermediate teams next year.

Brian's next day begins on the way to school as he spends a few minutes having a second cup of coffee with the special education resource teacher. A student with severe orthopedic handicaps has recently joined his class. Recently she learned that the optimistic talk about her recovery was not well-founded and that she is likely to spend the rest of her life in a wheelchair or walking only with the aid of braces. She is, to put it mildly, extremely upset. The resource specialist is teaching Brian and the other teachers about the nature of the disease, explaining the common emotional reactions a child may have to discovering how long-term a disability is going to be, and the most promising ways of helping her come to grips with her problem. Brian and the resource teacher have been spending a few odd moments together each week, but he decides that more formal instruction will be useful. They set a date when the teaching team ordinarily has their monthly dinner together and the resource specialist agrees to spend the evening with them. She will try to give them an overview of the kind of problem they are dealing with, her perceptions of the child, and the kind of information the other children need as they live and work with her.

At 9:00 he is introducing a group of 30 children to an area of literature which is new to them. Brian has brought along about 50 books and he talks about a number of them briefly. They are historical fiction and he helps the students identify a variety of categories. Some of the books are biographies, some are narrative history, some describe life at various times in Europe, Asia, and America. He organizes the children into groups. Each child will read a number of the books and report to the others on them. After everyone has read a dozen or so books they will begin to form them into categories according to style and content.

A number of the children have never read historical novels while others have read a good many. He takes a bit of time at the end of the session with some of the children who are wary and helps them find books he believes they will enjoy. Brian himself is an omnivorous reader and has trouble understanding why everybody doesn't like to read almost anything. Angie, a team member, has sat in on his session. They spend a few minutes afterward discussing how things went. She suggests that he read a passage from a number of books the next time they meet so that the children can have some idea about the flavor of the authors. She points out that much historical fiction makes grand adventure stories and that some of the students who are not initially turned on by history will find the adventure appealing.

By 10:00 he and Charlie are with the primary team. The children are working with the computers and the aides are assisting them. It is very clear that there is a differential response to the method. Some of the children are racing through the skills sections; even children who have already mastered many of the skills appear to enjoy the process. The same is true for some of the children whose skills are less well developed. Other students are floundering. A couple of the aides are very positive and helpful toward the method but one of them is relatively negative and one of the teachers seems unable to help the students.

Both Charlie and Brian notice that there are three aides and three teachers in the working area with only 30 students. The other students assigned to the team are in another area with two teachers. It occurs to both of them that the team does not need all that teaching personnel in that small space and some of them could be occupying their time better either planning or assembling materials. Both Brian and Charlie have been trained in Hunter's (1980) variation of clinical supervision, as have all the teachers and aides in the school. Thus it is no surprise when Charlie and Brian ask to meet with the team in order to help them analyze their plans and use of personnel.

Midge, the head of the team, is determined that things will go well and uses Brian and Charlie skillfully. She has noticed some of the same problems but understands that it is difficult to be a prophet in your own country, so she uses their feedback to help underline some of the points that she wishes to make. However, it has not occurred to her previously that they have actually overloaded the area with adult personnel, a result of her desire to have a successful implementation.

Charlie has an early lunch at 11:30 and Brian joins him with the resource specialist in special education. All three of them have noticed that teachers and children alike are still displaying some phobic reactions to physically handicapped children and they decide to bring it up with the policy board. The resource specialist says, "But I'd like to see us have a number of meetings in which specialists on various handicaps talk with us about the specific problems that handicapped children have. Physical handicaps, especially, are not nearly so scary once you become familiar with them. Most teachers still don't know that blind and deaf children and the orthopedically handicapped all learn pretty much the same as anybody else, and very few people realize how much they are able to compensate for their handicaps. Special education isn't nearly as special as people think it is." Brian volunteers to bring the question up and says that he would like to do some demonstrations with her so that the faculty can get a clear idea about the real differences and similarities among the children.

He then hurries off to prepare his material for the scientific inquiry lesson. As a result of their conversation in the morning, Charlie comes, as well as the representative from the teacher center. After the lesson is over they have a 15-minute clinical analysis and then Brian is off once again to the materials center for some items which she suggested. He arrives home with some time to read before Margie gets home and they have their exercise.

Brian lives within a network of services, some of which are present on the school site. He belongs to a council which includes the team leaders, the principal, and several community members. Together they are responsible for acting as a school improvement steering committee. They lead the faculty in reviewing the curriculum, make plans to improve the organization of the school and ensure that adequate training is available to each teacher. The council has been trained to analyze their decision-making processes and they have the services of a consultant from the district office. The district arranges for the local teaching resource center to provide an evaluation consultant who helps them study the effects of the curriculum. Workshops offered jointly by the district, the local university, and the teacher center provide Brian and the other team leaders with training in clinical supervision. They in turn pass on this training to their teachers so that the entire school faculty is accustomed to observing one another and providing feedback.

When a curriculum change is made the teaching resource center offers training in the teaching strategies which are essential in the implementation of the curriculum. In addition, the teaching resource center and the local university jointly offer courses in alternative approaches to teaching. These are offered during the day. Teams arrange to free their members so that they can take advantage of this opportunity to increase their teaching repertoire. School faculty attend these workshops in teams of two so that they can coach one another after they return to school and begin experimenting with the new approaches. The new approaches are rationalized and demonstrated, practice is provided with peers and small groups of children, and the members of each school team are trained to coach one another as they experiment with the new procedures.

Also available to Brian and his team is the on-site special education resource teacher and a consulting psychologist who rotates among schools helping with diagnosis and evaluation and offering special training to the teachers. A local university is responsible for offering sets of workshops on alternative approaches to each curriculum area. The principal attends monthly briefings and reports to the council so they are aware of new developments which are taking place. The local teaching center cooperates with the district to offer a continuous program of training for paid and volunteer aides as well as mini-courses for parents on developmental psychology, parent-child relationships and tutoring skills.

The district office, in conjunction with each local school council, is responsible for building an evaluation plan which is implemented on a continuous basis to provide a comparative picture of pupil progress within each school. These data are fed back to the school improvement councils so that they can assess the effectiveness of each of the dimensions of the school environment.

The school is organized into teaching teams for several reasons. First, it makes available to each child the services of several profession-als. Second, it permits differentiation of functions, with team members taking turns being the lead teacher in each of the curriculum areas, so that individual strengths can be capitalized on. Third, it provides flexibility in grouping for instruction. Fourth, it permits members of the teams to be freed each week for three or four hours of direct in-service training (about as much as any one can absorb and adequately follow up).

Thus, Brian lives in a very rich environment. He has training in supervision and teacher training, studies organizational development, participates in the continuous study of the curriculum areas, has help with children having special needs, is near a curriculum resource center, and regularly studies new teaching strategies. The teachers vary in the extent to which they take advantage of the university courses which are offered. Brian is an omnivorous learner and blocks out one afternoon each week for ongoing study, sometimes in his specialties and at other times in areas that simply interest him. The new units in the upper-grade classes dealing with Far Eastern cultures are a direct result of a course that Brian and several of the other teachers took.

The school governance structure provides for collaborative decision making by all faculty members. Community members are involved as paid and volunteer aides and serve as members of curriculum study groups so that they too can participate in and "own" changes that are made. The principal serves in many ways as the executive officer of the school improvement council. He does not attempt to impose changes unilaterally, nor does he shy away from initiative. An important part of his job is to keep up with curricular and instructional trends and to bring these to the attention of the council so that constant scrutiny and improvement of the curriculum is embedded in the work of the school. Most important, he has brought about a cooperative environment which stimulates the staff to improve the school as a whole and their own skills as individuals. They manage the students *through* instruction, helping them learn how to learn.

FROM CAMEO TO FOSTER: CRITERIA OF EFFECTIVENESS

The Foster School is organized under a school committee which serves as our Responsible Parties. Teachers, community members, and administration are all involved in examining the program and working to improve it. Perhaps the most striking feature in Brian's day is the amount of energy he has devoted to the development of better instruction. One of the reasons the Foster School functions so well is because of the constant attention to school improvement. Staff development has been built into the environment so that teachers can observe one another, especially at points where they are trying to make improvements. Furthermore, although teachers carry out much of their instruction individually they also work within coordinated groups or teams. The school has incorporated a number of recent technological advances, but has done so in the context of the ongoing program so that the teachers are in control of the library, media facilities, microprocessors, and instructional systems.

Academic and Social Goals.   Academic and social goals are kept alive by constant tending. It is much less important that they are written down than that they are discussed and kept in mind as decisions are being made. They have their embodiment in the interaction among teachers; teachers and community members; and teachers, community members, and students. They are embodied in the program and in the texture of the interactions.

In the Foster School the students are expected to take considerable responsibility for their learning, which is to be accomplished in a wide variety of areas. Cooperation is the rule among all parties concerned.

Order and Discipline. The norms for order and discipline are communicated through the way people behave toward one another and through what is sanctioned. Discipline is centered around learning activities. The school provides a great many options and the teachers nurture the students continuously. They communicate a norm of "orderly business." A student will rarely be told to "stop that" and more often will be asked, "What should you be doing and how can I help you?"

High Expectations. These are communicated by the nature of the student-teacher interactions which characterize the school. As students move from activity to activity they are treated by the faculty as if each one of them has much to offer and much growing to do. It is assumed that activities can be found that will enable all children to grow productively.

Pervasive Caring. Caring is manifested not only through the official policies of the organization but especially through modeling. The teachers' behavior toward one another manifests the norms of caring at least as powerfully as do their attitudes toward the children.

Public Rewards and Incentives. These are accomplished quietly and persistently by helping students follow their own progress and by making it known that their progress has been noticed. Public rewards are embodied in a large number of small acts. A child finishes a complex task and a teacher notices and makes it clear that it is noticed.

Administrative Leadership. One striking difference between the Cameo School and the Foster School is the sharing of administrative leadership. The principal and team leaders work very closely together and center leadership around the improvement of curriculum and instruction. They work hard and expend much more energy than they would if they concerned themselves primarily with administrative routine. They take seriously the responsibility of helping the teachers stay alive in their work and continuously emphasize the adventuresome side of teaching. The teachers are part of the decision-making process in all areas that concern them. The secret of building leadership is the creation of a community of leaders. The organization of Responsible Parties decides on the overall shape of the education program and then the leadership team functions to create the details that implement those decisions.

Community Support. We touched on community support earlier. It is accomplished not only through involving community members in decision making but through instruction—making the community members a part of the "extended faculty."

High Academic Learning Time.   As we have repeatedly said, achieving high academic learning time involves not only keeping people busy but keeping them busy at tasks that are appropriate to them. The tasks must also be differentiated—constantly confronting the same kind of task leads to boredom and apathy. The Foster School differentiates instruction according to individual differences determined through careful diagnosis of each student's learning style and level.

Frequent Monitoring of Out-of-Class Work.   Even in the case of elementary school children, probably a third of their engaged time should be devoted to outside assignments and self-directed projects that are connected to the work done in school. A great deal of the skill in teaching is the art of using the contact time with the student to stimulate activities that they carry on by themselves.

Frequent Monitoring of Student Progress.   To keep in touch with the students and provide them with appropriate feedback, observation of their performance is critical. The more the students take responsibility for their learning the more possible it is for the teachers to observe their behavior, find out how they are doing, and let them know.

Coherently Organized Curriculum.   Another striking difference between the Cameo and Foster schools is in the breadth and coherence of their respective curriculums. In the Foster School coherence is maintained not only by written plans but by continuously discussing instruction and how to improve it. Plans are kept alive in everyone's minds by continually raising the question, "How can we do this better?" Objectives are reiterated, major themes are discussed, and cooperative planning of curriculum implementation is the order of the day. Such an atmosphere is obviously lacking in the Cameo School.

Variety of Teaching Strategies.   The difference between the two schools is so obvious in this regard that it seems redundant to mention it. The broader curriculum of the Foster School combined with their attention to the individual needs of students generates much greater variety of instructional strategies. The program of continuous staff development that is embodied in the school is the key. Only with continuous staff development are teachers given the opportunity to expand their teaching repertoire so that they can reach more students with a greater variety of methods.

Opportunities for Student Responsibility. Whatever its educational model, schools do not become highly or even moderately effective unless the students bear a great deal of responsibility for their own activities. The effective school teaches students how to engage in a wide variety of learning tasks and how to ask for help when they need it. The dynamics of instruction changes from a situation in which the teachers are "pushing" the students through the material to one in which the teachers are supporting, redirecting, and introducing new material.

It should be clear by now that the attributes described in Chapter 3 all fit together in a coherent whole. Each one, as it is accomplished, makes the others easier to bring about. The better organized the curriculum, and the greater the variety of available teaching strategies, the easier it is to sustain high academic learning time and to generate meaningful out-of-class work. Where students take responsibility for their work, the less need there is for discipline. The more caring the environment, the more students will take responsibility, and the more they take responsibility, the easier it is to escape from a student-teacher tug-of-war to a cooperative system. The clearer the goals and the broader the base of leadership and community support, the easier it is for teachers to be efficacious and to work together rather than individually to build the social system that is an effectively functioning school.

Part IV

STAGE TWO: RENOVATING THE SCHOOL

Central to our second stage of school improvement is the business of staff development. After analyzing the research-based principles of staff training, we present a paradigm for establishing an effective staff development program. Next we provide several examples of curriculum reform and conclude with a look at two schools, one prepared and the other unprepared, to mainstream their programs.

9

Effective Staff Training
for School Improvement

Thus far we have discussed characteristics of the school's social system and the influence it has on receptivity to change and improvement. Now we turn to a more technical aspect—the provision of adequate staff development.

First, we want to make it very clear that all but the most mild changes *require* training in content or process. The messages of research on curriculum implementation are unequivocal: very little implementation will take place even in positive environments by highly motivated people *unless* training is provided (Fullan & Pomfret, 1977; Hall & Loucks, 1982; Joyce et al., 1981). Thus, strong and regular training is an essential aspect of an environment favorable to school improvement. The nature of training needed to ensure implementation is far more extensive and intricate than exists in most professional environments today.

TRAINING TO ENSURE TRANSFER

The question is: What kinds of training do teachers need in order to implement new curriculum plans?

Let us examine another scenario. This time a team of teachers is using research-based techniques for learning a new teaching strategy.

The eight members of the English department of Lazarus High School are studying new teaching strategies that they are considering using in some of their courses. The current model of teaching on their agenda is Synectics (Gordon, 1961), designed to stimulate metaphoric thinking. Several members of the department think Synectics will be useful both to encourage creative writing and in the study of fiction and poetry. They began their exploration by reading W. J. J. Gordon's book *Synectics* and then an expert on the strategy came to the school, demonstrated it

137

several times, and held discussions with them. They also saw a videotaped lecture of Gordon explaining the theory behind Synectics and visited a school in Stockton where two teachers have been using Synectics for the last two or three years. They then planned little lessons based on the Synectics procedure and tried them out on one another. They taught each other lessons in creative writing and in the analysis of poetry. They examined the use of metaphor in Ionesco's plays. Each teacher practiced the teaching strategy several times with the other teachers before trying it out with students. Then working in teams of two, they began to try it out, first with the most able students in their elective writing classes. One team member taught and the other offered constructive criticism, then they switched places. Sometimes they taught together. Each practiced several times with the "coaching partner" present to reflect on progress and to offer suggestions about how to improve the next trial.

Then, still working in teams, they began to work the teaching strategy into a couple of their courses, picking places where it appeared that it would be the most productive and where they were highly likely to have success. Not surprisingly, they found that the hardest part of using a new model of teaching is less in learning what to do as a teacher than in teaching the students to relate to the model. For example, parts of the Synectics strategy asks the students to generate "personal analogies" such as being a snowman, tennis ball, dinosaur, lawnmower, toothbrush, etc. A few of the students were puzzled by the instruction to "be a toothbrush and describe how you feel and what you think about your users." It took time before some of the kids tuned into the procedures and became comfortable with them. Also, some of the variations on the Synectics model asked the students to share their writing publicly—at best an uncomfortable procedure for some of the students.

As time passed the Lazarus team found it useful to reread parts of Gordon's book and to revisit the teachers who were more experienced users of Synectics. They were fortunate to obtain the consultative services of a Synectics expert for a day and she reviewed the theory and gave them some tips for practicing and coaching one another.

The Lazarus team are engaged in the serious study of alternative models of teaching (Joyce & Weil, 1980) and are using training procedures which are virtually guaranteed to bring almost any approach to teaching within their grasp.

Over the years (Joyce & Showers, 1980; 1981) we have accumulated a number of research reports on how teachers learn to integrate a new teaching approach into their active repertoire. Studying theory, observing demonstrations, and practicing with feedback are sufficient to enable most teachers to develop their skills to the point that they can use a model fluidly and appropriately when called on to do so. Skill development by itself, however, does not ensure transfer. Relatively few persons who obtain skill in new approaches to teaching will make that skill a part of their regular practice unless additional instruction is received. Not until the coaching component is added into the equation and used effectively, will most teachers begin to transfer their new model into their active repertoire.*

The first message we are able to summarize from this research is very positive: teachers are wonderful learners. Nearly all teachers can acquire new skills that "fine tune" their competence. They can also learn a considerable repertoire of teaching strategies that are new to them.

The second message is more sobering, but still optimistic. In order to improve their skills and learn new approaches to teaching, teachers need conditions that are not common to most in-service settings, even when teachers participate in the governance of those settings.

The third message is also very encouraging. The research base reveals what conditions help teachers to learn. This information can be used in designing appropriate staff development activities for classroom personnel.

Components of Training

Most of the training literature consists of investigations in which training elements are combined in various ways, whether they are directed toward the fine tuning of styles or the mastery of new approaches. From our analysis, we were able to identify a number of training components that have been studied intensively. Alone and in combination, each of these training components contribute to the impact of a training sequence or activity. (As we shall see, when used together, each has much greater power than when used alone.) The five major components of training in the studies we reviewed are:

1. *Presentation of theory.* Studying theory can provide the rationale, conceptual base, and verbal description of an approach to teaching or instructional technique. Readings, lectures, films, and discussions are among the most common forms of presentation. In many higher education courses and in-service institutes and workshops, it is not uncommon for presentation of theory to be the major, and in some cases, the sole component of the training experience. In research it is frequently combined with one or more of the other components.

---

*Transfer of new items of repertoire is more difficult than the transfer of skills that polish or "fine tune" models of teaching that lie within the existing repertoire.

Level of impact: Either for tuning of style or mastery of new approaches, presentation of theory can raise awareness and increase conceptual control of an area. It is rare, however, for this to result in skill acquisition or the transfer of skills into the classroom situation (although there are some people who build and transfer skills from theory presentations alone). On the other hand, when theory is used in combination with other training components, it appears to boost conceptual control, skill development, and transfer. It is not powerful enough alone to achieve much impact beyond the awareness level, but when combined with others, it is an important component.

2. *Modeling or demonstration.* Modeling involves enactment of a teaching skill or strategy either through a live demonstration with children or adults, or through television, film, or other media. In a given training activity, a strategy or skill can be modeled any number of times. Much of the literature is flawed because only one or two demonstrations of some quite complex models of teaching are available, thus comprising relatively weak treatments.

Level of impact: Modeling appears to have a considerable effect on awareness and some effect on knowledge. Demonstration also increases the mastery of theory. We understand better what is illustrated to us. A good many teachers can initiate demonstrated skills fairly readily and a number will transfer them to classroom practice. However, for most teachers modeling alone is unlikely to result in the acquisition and transfer of skills unless it is accompanied by other components. A fairly good level of impact can be achieved through the use of modeling alone where the tuning of style is involved, but for mastering new approaches it does not have great power for many teachers by itself. All in all, research appears to indicate that modeling is very likely to be an important component of any training program aimed at acquisition of complex skills and their transfer to the classroom situation.

3. *Practice under simulated conditions.* Practice involves trying out a new skill or strategy. Simulated conditions are usually achieved by practicing either with peers or with small groups of children under circumstances which do not require management of an entire class or larger group of children at the same time.

Level of impact: It is difficult to imagine practice without prior awareness and knowledge; that is, we have to know what it is we are to practice. However, when awareness and knowledge have been achieved, practice is a very efficient way of acquiring skills and strategies whether related to the tuning of style or the mastery of new approaches. Once a relatively high level of skill has been achieved, a sizeable percentage of teachers will begin to transfer the skill into their instructional situations, but this will not be true of all persons. It is probable that the more complex and unfamiliar the skill or strategy, the lower will be the level of transfer. Research supports common sense with respect to practice under simulated conditions. That is, it is an extremely effective way to develop competence in a wide variety of classroom techniques.

4. *Structured feedback.* Structured feedback involves learning a system for observing teaching behavior and providing an opportunity to reflect on those observations. Feedback can be self-administered, provided by observers, or given by peers and coaches. It can be regular or occasional. It can be combined with other components which are organized toward the acquisition of specific skills and strategies. That is, it can be directly combined with practice and a practice-feedback-practice sequence can be developed.

Level of impact: Taken alone, feedback can result in considerable awareness of one's teaching behavior and knowledge about alternatives. With respect to the fine tuning of styles, it has reasonable power for acquisition of skills and their transfer to the classroom situation. For example, if feedback is given about patterns of rewarding and punishing, many teachers will begin to modify the ways they reward and punish children. Similarly, if feedback is provided about the kinds of questions asked in the classroom, many teachers will become more aware of their use of questions and set goals for changes. In general these changes persist as long as feedback continues and then styles gradually slide back toward their original point. In other words, feedback alone does not appear to provide permanent changes, but regular and consistent feedback is probably necessary if people are to make and maintain changes in very many areas of behavior.

5. *Coaching for application.* When the other training components are used in combination, the levels of impact are considerable for most teachers up through the skill level, whether the object is the tuning of style or the mastery of new approaches to teaching. For example, demonstration of unfamiliar models of teaching or curriculum approaches combined with discussions of theory and followed by practice with structured feedback reach the skill acquisition level of impact with nearly all (probably nine out of ten) teachers at the in-service or preservice levels. If consistent feedback is provided with classroom practice, a good many, but not all, will transfer their skills into the teaching situation. For many others, however, direct coaching on how to apply the new skills and models appears to be necessary. Coaching can be provided by colleagues, supervisors, professors, curriculum consultants, or others thoroughly familiar with the new approaches. Coaching involves helping teachers analyze the content to be taught and the approach to be taken, and making very specific plans to help the

student adapt to the new teaching approach. For maximum effectiveness in most in-service activities, it appears wisest to include several, and perhaps all, of the five training components.

Where fine tuning of style is the goal, modeling, practice under simulated conditions, and practice in the classroom combined with feedback, will probably result in considerable improvement. Where mastery of a new approach is the desired outcome, presentations and discussions of theory and coaching are probably necessary as well. If the theory of a new approach is well presented, the approach is demonstrated, practice is provided under simulated conditions with careful and consistent feedback, and that practice is followed by application in the classroom with coaching and further feedback, it is likely that the vast majority of teachers will be able to expand their repertoire to utilize a wide variety of approaches to teaching and curriculum. If any of these components are left out, the impact of training will be weakened because fewer people will progress to the transfer level (which is the only level that has significant meaning for school improvement). The most effective training activities, then, will be those that combine theory, modeling, practice, feedback, and coaching for application. The knowledge base seems firm enough that we can predict that if those components are in fact combined in in-service programs, we can expect the outcomes to be considerable at all levels.

WORKING HYPOTHESES FOR PRESENT PRACTICE

Designers of training can be optimistic about achieving their objectives provided they are willing to create programs that bring together sufficient resources and training components. Where knowledge is lacking, guidelines for training should be based on a conservative interpretation of the available evidence. To show how this works, let us imagine that a program designer is attempting to build a sequence of training activities that will ensure that 75 percent or more of the trainees will achieve the vertical transfer level in learning a new model of teaching. Let us assume that the model is theoretically grounded (backed up by research indicating that it can achieve certain effects with students), is appropriate to the teaching of school subjects, and can be comfortably implemented within the confines of the school day and with classroom-size groups of children. We will break the scenario into a step-by-step procedure:

1. Our designer should include a knowledge-oriented component designed to acquaint the trainee with the model of teaching and

its rationale. This component can include well-designed lectures, print material, audiovisual presentations and discussions.

The prognosis for transmitting the targeted knowledge should be very good. However, were the training to end at this point, perhaps as few as 10 percent of the teachers would achieve the vertical transfer required in learning a new approach to teaching.

2. Our designer should include a demonstration component in which the new approach to teaching is modeled. Modeling may be live, through the media, or (although a weaker treatment) in a written description of the model in action.

The information acquired from the knowledge component should enhance the trainees' ability to identify the essential features of the teaching model. In turn, the demonstration should facilitate the acquisition and retention of the information targeted in the knowledge component. However, relatively few teacher candidates or in-service teachers will achieve vertical transfer at this point in their training. It would surprise us if more than 10 percent of teacher candidates achieved that level of mastery.

3. Our designer should then add practice and feedback activities in which the trainees practice the new model and receive feedback from instructors or other peers who are studying the same model. (The evidence indicates that peers can be taught to do this activity successfully.)

The addition of the practice and feedback component should have a beneficial effect on information acquisition and retention, and should increase the ability to identify the model. The outcomes of the knowledge and demonstration components will also have a very strong effect on the quality of the practice and will facilitate the acquisition of the skill. Assuming that these three components are carried out expertly, we would expect that nearly all of the trainees will be able to demonstrate skill using the new teaching strategy. Keeping our fingers crossed and extrapolating from the very meager available evidence we would still not expect that a large proportion of the trainees would achieve vertical transfer. Judging from the results of McKibbin's (1980) investigation and extrapolating somewhat wildly from Gene Hall's (1976) work and from the results of the literature on curriculum implementation we would be surprised if as many as 20 percent of the trainees achieved vertical transfer. In Showers (1982) study *no* teacher transferred skills without coaching!

4. Our designer should introduce coaching at the point where the trainee attempts to implement the new teaching strategy in the classroom. Coaches may be peers, supervisors, principals, college instructors, or others who are themselves competent in the new approach to teaching. That is, they themselves have achieved or are in the process of achieving vertical transfer. In the classroom they coach the teacher as he or she takes the first halting steps toward the utilization of the model; helps him or her teach the students how to respond to it and adapt it to their characteristics; and provides support as he or she struggles to adjust to the new model.

ATTACKING THE TRANSFER PROBLEM

For most of us, skill attainment does not ensure skill transfer to the workplace. The same problem occurs in training in other professions. While the major portion of this section of the chapter will be devoted to the coaching process as a major element in assuring transfer, we want to emphasize that the other components are extremely important if mastery is to be obtained. Unless people develop skill in a new approach, they have no chance whatsoever of adding it to their repertoire. Coaching without the study of theory, the observation of demonstrations, and opportunities for practice with feedback will, in fact, accomplish very little.

Furthermore, it should be not be inferred from our description that the components must occur in a strict sequence or need to be separated from one another. One might begin the route to mastery of a new approach to teaching by observing a few demonstrations, turn to the examination of its theoretical rationale, observe more demonstrations, begin to practice with frequent excursions back to theory and further observation, and then, during the stages of transfer, receive coaching— but all the while continuing to attend training sessions.

Nearly all of the complex skills training in military and industrial applications assumes that skill development alone will not bring about transfer. We believe that the problem of transfer is really a new stage of learning which becomes a problem only if it is not recognized. We understand that after a teaching skill is learned it needs to be adapted because classroom situations are different from training situations. One cannot simply walk from the training session into the classroom with a new skill completely ready for use. Using the skill in its context requires a clear understanding of the students, subject matter, objectives, and classroom management variables in order to use the skill appropriately and forcefully.

In addition, all of us are less skillful with a new model of teaching than we are with existing ones. Successful transfer requires a period wherein the skill is practiced in its context until it is as finely tuned as elements of the existing repertoire. Sometimes, however, sets of teaching behaviors which support the existing repertoire may actually be dysfunctional to new models of teaching. We can see this when a teacher who is accustomed to running brisk and pointed drill and practice sessions begins to learn how to work inductively with students. The swift pace of the drill and practice, the directive feedback to the students, and the ability to control the content and movement of the lesson are at first somewhat dysfunctional as the teacher becomes less directive, relies more on initiative from the students, probes their understanding, and helps them learn to give one another feedback. The new teaching strategy seems awkward. Its pace seems slow. The teaching moves which served so well before now appear to retard the new kind of lesson. After a while, practice in context smooths off rough edges and the new strategy gradually comes to feel as comfortable and under control as the old one.

In summary, the transfer problem (or, really, prevention of a transfer problem) requires three elements in addition to coaching:

- Forecasting the transfer process throughout the training cycle.
- Reaching the highest possible level of skill development during training.
- Developing what we term executive control; that is, an understanding of the appropriate content for the model and how to adapt it to students of varying characteristics—a "meta understanding" about how the model works, can be fitted into the instructional repertoire, and can be adapated to students.

Forecasting the transfer process is extremely important. Teachers need to understand that they cannot simply walk away from a training session and have no difficulty thereafter. It is not uncommon for teachers who have attended relatively weak training sessions and then tried to apply the product in their own teaching to report, "Well, that doesn't work." *Of course it doesn't work!* If the treatment was weak the product will never work. Even with the strongest training there will be a period of discomfort when using any genuinely new skill. Even very experienced and capable teachers should be aware throughout the training process that they must prepare themselves up for a second stage of learning that will come after skill has been developed.

Skill development, of course, is really essential. Most preservice and in-service teacher programs have offered weak training. When we think of a teaching model of average difficulty, we should assume that to study the theory will take as many as 20 or 30 hours (more for complex models). At least 15 or 20 demonstrations of the model being used should be observed with various kinds of learners and in several content areas. Demonstrations also need to be included when teachers are trying the model for the first time, when they are introducing students to the model, and when they are trying to adjust to using it. Attaining competence requires a number of practice sessions. Each teacher needs to try the model with peers and small groups of students from 10 to 15 times before a high level of skill can be attained. If the transfer process has been realistically forecast it makes good sense for teachers to want to build the highest level of skill they can before using the model in the more complex context of the classroom.

Developing executive control has not been a common concept in training. Essentially it involves *understanding* an approach to teaching— why it works, how it works, what it is good for, what its major elements are, how to adapt it to varying kinds of content and students. It involves developing a set of principles that enables one to think about the approach and to modulate and transform it during the course of its use. Executive principles should be included in training content.

Forecasting transfer, attaining the highest level of skill, and developing executive control increase the odds that successful transfer can take place and, together, set the stage for coaching.

The Process of Coaching

Ideally, coaching teams are developed during the training process. If we had our way, *all* school faculties would be divided into coaching teams, that is, teams who regularly observe one another's teaching and provide helpful information, feedback, and so forth. In short, we recommend the development of a coaching environment in which all personnel see themselves as one another's coaches. But, in the present context, the primary function of coaching is to help acquire new teaching skills. Thus most of the illustrations given here will be of teachers organized into coaching teams much like the Lazarus faculty described previously.

What does the process of coaching actually involve? We see its major functions as:

Providing companionship

Giving technical feedback

Analyzing application: extending executive control

Adaptation to the students

Personal facilitation

1. *Providing companionship.* Its first function is to provide interchange with another human being during a difficult process. The coaching relationship involves mutual reflection, checking perceptions, and sharing frustrations and successes. Two people, watching each other try a new model of teaching for the first time, will find much to talk about. Companionship provides reassurance that problems are normal. Both people find that their habitual and automatic teaching patterns create awkwardness when they practice the new procedures. Concentrating on unfamiliar moves and ideas, they forget essential little odds and ends. Companionship not only makes the training process technically easier but it makes the quality of the experience better. It is much more pleasant to share something new than to do it in isolation. The lonely business of teaching has sorely lacked the companionship that we envision for our coaching teams.

2. *Giving technical feedback.* In the course of training, our team members learn to provide feedback to one another as they practice their new model of teaching. They point out omissions, examine how materials are arranged, check to see whether all the parts of the teaching strategy have been brought together, and so on. Technical feedback* helps ensure that growth continues through practice in the classroom. The pressures of the context tend to diffuse the teaching experience and draw attention away from the new teaching strategy. Technical feedback helps keep the teacher's mind on the business of perfecting and polishing skills and working through problem areas. Nearly any teacher who has been through a training process can learn to provide technical feedback to another teacher.

The act of providing feedback is also beneficial to the person doing it. The coaching partner has the privilege of seeing a number of trials of

---

*Technical feedback should not be confused with *general evaluation*. Feedback implies no judgment about the overall quality of teaching but is confined to information about the execution of model-relevant skills.

the new model by another skilled teacher. It is often easier to see problems of confusion and omission when watching someone else teach than when attempting to recapture one's own process. Also, ideas about how to use the model are collected through observation. When a group of four or six teachers observe each other regularly while they are trying out a model, they can not only give technical feedback to each other, but will receive it vicariously while they are observing it being given. Among them, they will produce a number of fine practices which constitute further demonstrations and from which they can obtain ideas for the use of the model.

3. *Analyzing application: extending executive control.* One of the most important objectives of the transfer period is figuring out when to use a new model and what will be achieved as a consequence. Selecting the occasions for using a teaching strategy is not as easy as it sounds. Nearly everyone needs assistance in learning to pick the right spots for exercising it. Also, unfamiliar teaching processes appear to have less certain outcomes that do familiar ones. Early trials often give the impression that one has worked all day and not gotten very far. Most of us need assistance in finding out how much we have, in fact, accomplished and how we might accomplish more by making adjustments in the way we are using the model. During training the coaching teams need to spend a considerable amount of time examining curriculum materials and plans and practicing the application of the model they will be using later. Then, as the process of transfer begins, practice in the classroom intensifies. We need to pay closer and closer attention to appropriate use.

4. *Adaptation to the students.* Successful teaching requires successful student response. A model which is new to a group of students will cause them trouble. They will need to learn new skills and to become acquainted with what is expected of them, how to fulfill the task demands of the new method, and how to gauge their own progress. In addition, the new model should be adapted to fit the characteristics of the students. More training must be provided for some, more structure for others, and so on. One of the major functions of the coach is to help "players" to read the responses of the students and make decisions about the necessary skill training and how to adapt the model. This is especially important in the early stages of practice when teachers are more concerned with their own behavior than about the response of students.

5. *Personal facilitation.* As mentioned earlier, practicing any new approach to teaching causes a higher degree of discomfort than using one's existing repertoire. All of us feel bad about ourselves as we fumble around. Students sense our uncertainty and let us know in subtle and

unsubtle ways that they are aware that we are less certain and surefooted than usual. At such times we tend to become discouraged relatively easily. The expression, "I tried that method and it didn't work," refers as much to the sense of dismay that accompanies the early trials as it does to the actual success or failure of the new method itself. The fact is that successful use of a new method requires practice. Normally early trials aren't even close to our normal standard of performance. Thus one of the major jobs of the coaching team is to help its members feel good about themselves as the early trials take place. A real tragedy in many schools is that there is so little interpersonal support and close contact with other teachers because classrooms are such terribly isolated places. Coaching reduces the isolation and increases support.

BUILDING AN EMBEDDED
SYSTEM OF STAFF DEVELOPMENT

Creating training on an ad hoc basis whenever a curriculum change is made would be horrendously expensive and disruptive. The kind of training described above needs to be embedded in the lives of teachers as described in the account of Brian's team in Chapter 8. If the education profession is to flourish and if schools are to be a vital force in society, it is necessary to rebuild the school into a lifelong learning laboratory not only for children but for teachers as well. The improvement of staff development is not a matter of deciding how to create and implement ad hoc programs. Rather, it is a matter of generating a rich environment in which every educator becomes a student of education and works continuously to improve his or her skills. If schools are not being improved, they atrophy. Teaching is an experiment in life and, like a marriage, it must be worked on or it will become desperately routine. The environment of the school must regenerate the relationships between teachers, learners, and community members or the school will lose its vitality.

Making schools into learning laboratories will be a long, slow process, but it is time for us to make the commitment and to put our energies into that process and not waste them by repeating the mistakes of the past. *The primary task in staff development is to develop a professional, growth-oriented ecology in all schools.* The purposes are three:

1. To enrich the lives of teachers and administrators so that they continuously expand their general education, their emotional range, and their understanding of children.

2. To generate continuous efforts to improve schools. School faculties, administrators, and community members need to work together to acquire the knowledge and skills necessary to bring those improvements into existence.

3. To create conditions which enable professional skill development to be continuous. Every teacher and administrator needs to be a student of learning and teaching and to engage in a continuous process of experimentation with their behavior and that of their students. They need to study alternative approaches to schooling and teaching, to select ones which will expand their capabilities, and to acquire the understanding and skills necessary to make fresh alternatives a part of their ongoing professional repertoire.

It is quite clear that curriculum implementation and instructional improvement are very difficult unless strong staff development is in place. If teachers and community members do not achieve *their* needed learning, it will be impossible for the students to do so. It is equally clear that effective methods for staff development exist and such programs can be implanted in the ongoing operation of the school. To do so is in itself to bring about a major change in the social system of education. Without it new curriculums cannot be implemented and faculty will have extreme difficulty working together to make instructional improvements.

In the next chapter we will consider another dimension of staff development, one designed to help teachers achieve high states of growth and to help the faculty as a whole increase their problem-solving capability.

10

Staff Development as a Regular Event

We have stressed from the beginning that school improvement will not occur with ease unless the educators who must implement change are in environments congenial to change and are given sufficient training. The Responsible Parties must make it a central part of their business to create productive, professional environments and to provide necessary training. The Foster School illustrates an environment where teachers work together to analyze their teaching, experiment with improvements in instruction, and help each other learn new techniques.

Again we emphasize that a school is a social system that exists within a cultural context that powerfully influences it. When we enter a school, whether as a teacher or a student, that social system begins to operate on us and we begin to operate on it as we become members of the groups that compose it. One of our major tasks as teachers is to understand the school's social system and our role within it. Through this understanding, we can work toward a satisfying personal and professional life as members of that social system.

The social systems of the Cameo and Foster schools would have a vastly different impact on any teacher. The Cameo School is comprised of independent teachers who conduct their classrooms in the absence of a system that provides continuous, collective analysis of the school and collective action to improve it. Except for Kiki, the staff (or the principal) will give Maryann relatively little feedback on her teaching or on how to improve it. In the Foster school she would have ongoing examination of her teaching and be a member of a team—and an entire school faculty— that engages continuously in the process of analysis, not only of teaching, but of the entire curriculum.

There is little question that school improvement is more congenial to the Foster school. The sad history of school improvement described earlier is due partly to the existence of too many schools that look and feel like Cameo and partly to the lack of a system of staff development

151

that makes the study of school improvement a regular feature of the environment. As mentioned earlier, the school environment needs to:

Provide trust and support

Encourage risk taking

Ensure the collaborative study of teaching

Embrace cooperative decision making

Provide avenues for instruction and training.

How can this be brought about? How can we change an environment like Cameo's into one like Foster's? Not easily, for sure. And not with leadership like George's. (George will have to be sent off for thorough training in leadership, school improvement, and the creation of productive environments.) The path to a better environment will be uphill and should be carefully cleared. Although the social system of a school will not bend easily to pressure, transformations can be accomplished if the Responsibile Parties jointly develop a map of a productive environment and then directly and systematically set about creating it. The services of an organizational consultant might be procured. George will have to become active or be replaced. He will need training. Decisions will have to be made about where to begin. (The very creation of the Responsible Parties will have some effect.) Let us now look at a program whose modest success illustrates that persistence does pay off.

THE COMMUNITY AS A PARTNER IN SCHOOL IMPROVEMENT: THE URBAN/RURAL EXPERIMENT

The Urban/Rural School Development Program, a federally sponsored effort to involve community members and school staff from 25 extremely poor neighborhoods in joint decision making, focused on the use of staff development to improve the quality of education in those areas. At the core of the Urban/Rural Program were school-community councils in which, from 1970 to 1977, lay persons and education professionals labored to analyze educational needs and find the means to help teachers become more vital forces in the lives of their children.

The Social Intent of the Program

The major purpose of the Urban/Rural Program was to improve the social process of educational decision making in several ways:

1. *By reducing alienation.* As Emile Durkheim pointed out nearly 80 years ago, the concentration of people in large urban areas in Western

societies has resulted for many in feelings of normlessness and rootlessness. The effect has been to alienate people from their important social institutions. Durkheim called this feeling *anomie*. It is associated with meaninglessness and helplessness, feelings which legitimize a withdrawal from normal social processes and reduce affiliation with one's fellow man. It was intended in the Urban/Rural Program that involvement in the social processes of education, especially in teacher education, would reduce the feelings of alienation for people whose communities are poor, and whose schools appear to have lost the ability to help children develop the tools necessary for successful navigation within their complex technology-based society.

2. *By increasing feelings of efficacy within the social system.* Closely related to alienation is a loss of belief in the efficacy of individuals to influence their social context. Especially in economically poor communities people feel they are unable to make a difference; an individual's solitary vote seems miniscule within a social context of millions of people. This feeling helps sustain a cycle of poverty and makes even the most basic social transactions increasingly impersonal. It was the intent of this program to generate, in a small way, involvement in an important area of local decision making in order to increase participants' feelings of efficacy, and to do this in such a way that the processes and products of the program would be carried out within the system.

3. *By increasing integration among teachers and community members in determining staff development activities.* Integration depends on a mutual frame of reference. Through an exchange of ideas, an honest assessment of community and school needs, and debates over alternative courses of action, it was intended that individuals in these local communities would reach toward one another and thereby develop the attitudes and skills necessary to make common cause.

4. *By increasing the flow of community energy toward the improvement of education.* When citizens feel alienated and ineffective and have few avenues through which to generate ideas and a sense of community with others, energy decreases and social processes become stagnant. This stagnation should be replaced by social ferment powered by a positive flow of energy from those who had previously felt separated from one another, powerless to affect social processes, and unable to interact effectively.

5. *By making local needs the focus of action.* In contemporary America many see the education system as impersonal and unresponsive to the needs of their children. Individual learning styles are ignored, as is the need for curricula that is relevant to conditions in the local community. School boards, while possessing political legitimacy, are viewed as too remote to assess the actual needs of children.

The Urban/Rural School Development Program, then, was an experiment in grassroots democracy. Its goal was to establish a condition of parity between educational professionals and community members, with the purpose of generating staff development activities (in-service teacher and administrator education) through collaborative decision making and the assessment of local needs.

What Were the Sites Like?

Thirteen sites were urban and 12 were rural. The urban sites were concentrated primarily in the northeastern United States, while the rural sites were scattered throughout the country.

Seven communities were predominantly black; four had large populations with Spanish surnames; six were generally white and rural; two were largely native American; and six included broad mixtures of ethnic groups. The student body of the smallest school was about 300 children, the largest nearly 6,000. The Urban/Rural Program schools were staffed by some 2,500 teachers, with a range of 20 to 254 teachers per site.

A Model for Community Development

At the core of the Urban/Rural concept is a school-community council (SCC), consisting of an equal number of educators and community members whose responsibility it is to make decisions about staff development for a particular school or cluster of schools. Council members are elected by the professional staff of each project school and by members of the community the school serves. The essential concept is one of parity, that is, equal representation in decision making. Procedurally, it means equal input from professionals and community members in determining staff development activities. Organizationally, it is embedded in the council.

In 1970 and 1972, SCCs were set up in each of the Urban/Rural Program sites. Each one elected a council chairperson and hired a team manager (project director) as administrator of the project. To varying degrees, the council and team manager employed staff members who were to be responsible for managing implementation of the program (such as resident professors, community coordinators, and curriculum and training specialists).

The Needs Survey

Each council was responsible for conducting a needs survey of the school and the community. This was accomplished in diverse ways—

through meetings, questionnaire surveys, studies by outside consultants, and consultations with school administrators. One community employed a network of 300 "outreachers" to ensure broad input through interviews. The needs thus identified were analyzed by the SCC to determine the chief areas in which staff development activities would concentrate.

Translation of Needs into Program

The councils then endeavored to translate the prioritized needs into staff development activities which would further the children's education. Across the country the needs varied widely, as did their interpretation into programs. Some schools were grappling with integration problems and concentrated on helping teachers relate more effectively to children and other community members. In several cases communities focused on programs to help teachers and other community members work with students and parents to interpret and transmit the heritage of the community more effectively. A focus on cultural pluralism was recognized as a general need even in communities not characteristically comprised of racial or ethnic minorities.

Implementation

Each of the projects then had to determine what kinds of workshops, courses, and other experiences would be needed to implement the programs. One Urban/Rural project combined with other community agencies to develop a radio station to help unify the community and make all members more aware of their heritage.* Some projects concentrated heavily on staff development activities, and as many as 300 workshops and other in-service teacher education experiences have been generated by individual projects. Some projects concentrated on the recruitment, training, and use of classroom aides. The projects were responsible not only for implementing the programs but for evaluating them as they progressed. Sometimes the evaluation was accomplished through survey methods (chiefly interviews and questionnaires); at other times it took the form of assessing pupil achievement with respect to the in-service training which was provided teachers.

---

*A brief history of the Wayne County, Va. project may be found in Chapter 3 of Don Davies, ed. *Schools Where Parents Make a Difference*. Boston: Institute for Responsive Education, 1976.

Recycling Needs

As the evaluation process went on, each community was responsible for periodically reassessing its needs, making new determinations about programs, and implementing new suggestions.

The Local Education Agency: Independence of the Council

The projects were funded through the local education agencies by the U.S. Office of Education; however, decisions about the expenditure of funds were to be made by the councils. Thus, the local education agency was able to maintain control over accounting and budgeting procedures, but the SCC was responsible for the program; the team manager reported directly to the council. In most cases, the team manager and council chairperson worked as coequals in the administration of the projects. Since team managers typically were drawn from professional ranks, and council chairpersons from the local community, this arrangement reinforced the parity concept by providing a formalized council leadership structure which reflected and safeguarded the interests and needs of both educator and community members. Based on a conviction that schooling can be improved through cooperatively operated staff development programs, the division of formal leadership affirmed the potential contributions new educational partnerships can make to the in-service teacher education enterprise. While the local education agency was assured of proper expenditure of funds and reporting, neither school board members nor administrators were in a position to control the decision-making process.

The councils were formed with relative speed (Terry & Hess, 1975). It took much longer, however, for SCCs to develop effective processes. Communities needed to learn how to organize and elect members. Although the educators had less difficulty electing their representatives, all council members needed to work together, and it took councils a year or more to achieve process parity. Once parity was achieved, however, councils were able to proceed with an actual equality of decision making, with comfortable input by professionals and community members, a realistic appraisal of the needs of the community and the school, and the design and implementation of programs that could serve them best.

HOW SUCCESSFUL WERE THE PROGRAMS?

We can draw a number of generalizations from the Urban/Rural experience.

Working Together Works

The 25 projects in the Urban/Rural School Development Program were based on school-community councils in which teachers and community members had equal representation on boards whose responsibility it was to assess local needs and translate these into in-service teacher education programs. The evidence appears clear that this process worked in a variety of ways. First, the school and community council members were able to work together in relative harmony to carry out the processes of needs assessment, program reconstruction, and implementation. In fact, in the Urban/Rural Program as a whole, school and community members made about equal input into the council meetings. Most important, those councils which achieved the greatest degree of equality between school and community generated the most active, responsive, and diverse in-service teacher education programs. Imbalance in either direction (school over community or community over school) reduced either program quantity, breadth of clients, or relevance to local problems.

Community members involved in the process became more positive toward teachers and teachers' organizations than is commonly the case. For example, they became more positive toward matters such as time for training and providing released time for teachers. Although these councils worked in communities under considerable stress, they were able to assess needs, select the most important ones, and implement them in ways that solved many difficult in-service education problems. During the 1976–77 academic year, more than 800 teacher training activities were generated; in many of these, community members, aides, school administrators, and teachers worked together to improve their skills and the educational programs of their children.

Although the Urban/Rural School Development Program design did not include higher education institutions as either basic partners or a source of advisors, higher education institutions and people persistently appeared as trainers in the Urban/Rural projects. Faculty members served as resident professors or consultants, offered workshops, and altogether were valued as colleagues. These faculty members also found ways to bring the power of their institutions with them, and many teachers in the Urban/Rural Program earned higher degrees through onsite courses which were translated into college credits meeting degree and certification requirements.

Job-embedded In-service Teacher Education Can Work

It appears that onsite—hands-on—in-service experiences which are made part of the teacher's job can function effectively. Teachers in the

Urban/Rural Program received most of their training during school hours in or near their schools. They reported greater satisfaction with these activities than did comparison populations in California, Michigan, and Georgia. With the assistance of community members, teachers in the Urban/Rural Program persuaded college faculty members to work onsite with them, dealing with the children as well as with the teachers themselves. In this way, project participants bridged the gaps that often separate universities, school districts, teachers, and teachers' organizations. Community members who were a part of this process also became more committed to the options that would permit job-embedded in-service education to take place.

Teachers who are heavily involved in in-service education have a more positive attitude toward it than those who are less involved. The more the community members and teachers participated in the collaborative governance process, the more positive they felt about it and the more optimistic they felt about their schools. Collaborative governance appeared to produce a more vigorous and integrative type of in-service education, one that was hands-on, job embedded, and course related. Altogether it manifested a positive expression of institutional collaboration.

The Urban/Rural Program did not solve all the problems of in-service education, but did provide a dramatic national experience in collaborative governance and the overall results were almost entirely positive.

Alienation Can Be Overcome

Teachers and community members agreed that their involvement in the Urban/Rural Program was well worth the time and effort. Needs assessments were translated into programs which were then carried out. Nearly all the participants believed the projects had a positive impact on their schools and on their children's learning. The vast majority felt they became more effective in expressing local needs and more closely affiliated with other interested parties than before the process began. In other words, the Urban/Rural Program appears to have been successful in reducing alienation, increasing feelings of efficacy, and generating an integrative process whereby persons who had previously been separated were brought closer together.

In those communities where a clear test was possible, it appears that the Urban/Rural Program may have affected pupil achievement in classrooms where teachers were consistently involved in training. In short:

1. Over the program as a whole, a balance of community and professional input was achieved. Councils took from one to two years to get organized, but once organized did an effective job of translating local needs. *The greater the level of equality achieved, the more active were the teacher education programs which were generated.*
2. Participation seems to have reduced alienation and increased feelings of efficacy among community members and professionals alike.
3. The more the participants were involved in the planning process, the greater were their feelings of integrativeness toward other groups and the greater their perception of the project's impact on their local situation.
4. It appears possible for teachers and community members to assess local needs and to translate them into programmatic efforts.
5. Many projects managed to capture and focus the energy of community members in those communities where members had previously sought participation, but had lacked channels for it. Findings in the comparison sites of Georgia, Michigan, and California indicate that many community members throughout the United States would like to increase their participation in educational decision making and are willing to put time into it. The more they desire this, the more favorable they are toward approaching the hard problems of creating vital schools and supportive staff development programs.
6. Urban projects, on the whole, will be more expensive than rural projects and generally will provide less output for the dollar. This differential, we believe, is the price of the complexity of an urban society.

Summary

The Urban/Rural model was essentially a very simple one: it involved community members, teachers, school administrators, and students in decision making. The Urban/Rural projects were deliberately located in poverty stricken communities where education is generally agreed to have been unsuccessful in the past, and specifically in areas where students were achieving even less than average for that kind of community. The simple business of bringing people together and asking them to assess local needs and to translate these needs into school programs to be implemented primarily through staff development appears to have (1) decreased feelings of alienation, (2) increased feelings of efficacy, (3) brought about a more integrative process, (4) generated a flow of energy into those communities, and (5) demonstrated that local needs can be translated by local personnel into meaningful programs.

The full story, of course, is more complex than this brief account.

THE INNER CURRICULUM OF STAFF DEVELOPMENT: SOCIAL INFLUENCE, SELF-CONCEPT, AND LIFE AS A LEARNER

Now, let us turn to (1) the "state of growth" of individual teachers, and, (2) the influence of the school environment and its supporting agencies on individuals' efforts at personal and professional growth. We argue for an environmental approach to the reconstruction of staff development. Let us begin with an impressionistic peek into the lives of a few teachers.

Philby has taught for 30 years. He grew up in the mountain states, the child of migrant fruit pickers, and attended as many as four schools per year in his childhood. He matriculated at a state college and, after graduation, moved to the rural area of California where he presently teaches. His current life revolves around teaching and a second full-time job. He is presently a real estate salesman. (In the past he has been a logger, a truck driver, and has sold brushes.) He collects glass and antiques and travels about the country when he can, searching for them.

He likes to be left alone in his classroom and prefers administrators who "keep out of his hair" and keep other people "off his back." Textbooks structure what he teaches and, "to keep alive", he changes grade levels every few years. (He is an elementary teacher.) He resents in-service workshops that take him or any other teacher out of the classroom. He takes an occasional short course at the local university.

The last time he watched someone else teach was 15 years ago, and he feels no need to repeat the experience.

Philby's second job leaves him with little time to read, or to attend films or plays. His collections are his primary nonwork leisure activity.

Loretta grew up partly in a metropolitan neighborhood and partly in a rural town. She graduated from a leading urban university and for 15 years has taught English in the secondary school in the same district where Philby works. She sponsors the school newspaper and drama groups, both of which require before- and after-school time. She writes on her own and has just finished a collection of short stories. She teaches creative writing at the local university. A writing project sponsored by the county office of education has greatly stimulated her. Through the local community college she is now offering college-level courses to high school students and works closely with professors of writing there and at the university.

She is an officer of the regional professional organization in her specialty and attends whatever workshops it sponsors. As department chairperson she visits other classrooms and enjoys it greatly. She runs the department meetings as idea-sharing seminars. Her classroom is visited by many others but fewer fellow department members than she would like, primarily because of scheduling problems. She sees very little of teachers not in her specialty.

She draws her primary inspiration from her students and believes that successful teaching requires continuous personal and professional growth.

Philby and Loretta live in the same area and have essentially the same environments to draw from. Philby is consumed by his personal economic activity and stands aloof from colleagues, professional staff development activities, literature, and the arts. Loretta has wedded personal and professional life. Writing, teaching, and learning about writing and teaching are closely connected and she explores the environment voraciously in her search for growth.

In the last chapter we described the transition from credential, course-related in-service work to the development of educational environments which can regenerate themselves continuously. We stressed the importance of improving school environments that would nurture the personal, social, and academic potential of students and enable faculty to live a satisfying and stimulating personal and professional life. In this section we will draw on several recent investigations into the professional lives of teachers, especially those dealing with the influence of the school's informal social systems on the growth–producing activities of individual faculty. We will argue the need for staff development activities that improve the informal system in such a way as to free energy for personal and professional growth.

LIVES OF TEACHERS

In the course of a long-term inquiry into the nature of staff development and the professional growth of teachers in the state of California, we have interviewed about 300 teachers, given questionnaires to 3,000 others, and held group discussions with several hundred more. Our purpose was to explore teachers' perceptions of their states of growth with respect to teaching, academic content, curriculum, and general knowledge (Joyce & McKibbin, 1982). The interviews explore their (1) use of the formal system of universities, workshops, and supervisory efforts, (2) interchange with teachers and other persons in their environment, and (3) personally directed activities—reading, consumption of the performing arts, sports activities, travel, and leisure activities. Although the variation is striking, both among teachers and among schools, there are some common elements. Relatively few teachers receive direct supervisory assistance, and most teach in relative isolation from one another (although they report that the informal contact they have with other teachers is their major growth-producing activity with respect to the improvement of their teaching). Relatively few have experienced workshop or course training powerful enough to implant new teaching skills and strategies into their repertoires, although many do get useful ideas.

Despite the common aspects of schools, there is enormous variation in the extent to which individual teachers pull potentially growth-producing experiences from their environment and exploit formal and informal learning opportunities. Some are close to their principals and draw on them for considerable assistance. Some seek out other teachers and belong to a tight-knit professional group from which they obtain ideas. Some exploit universities, and many are conference goers and workshop users. Some read a great deal and others very little. Some are movie-goers and others haven't seen a movie in years. Some not only consume but participate in the performing arts while, for others, the performing arts are only a memory of childhood.

We uncovered some striking examples of persons who have developed intense growth-producing activities. We found a Spanish teacher who, at her own expense, spent two months in Mexico working on her language skills because she felt they were getting rusty. We found an English teacher who has created a beautiful and intense sex education course as a result of her concern about the ignorance of her

FIGURE 10.1 Growth States and Domains: Possible Configurations.

	Formal System	Domains Informal Interchange	Personal Patterns
Omnivores			
Active consumers			
Passive consumers			
Entrenched			
Withdrawn			

students and of many of her community members. We found autoshop teachers who study new developments by the major domestic and foreign automotive manufacturers. We found teachers who are intensely reflective about their teaching and delighted in interchange with others, and teachers who appear to insulate themselves from interchange which might affect the way they view themselves and their children.

CATEGORIES OF GROWTH STATES

Gradually, we developed categories for describing these people. The terms of our classifications are reminiscent of Maslow's descriptions of psychological states and manifest his considerable influence on our thinking. In colloquial terms, they are:

- Omnivores
- Active Consumers
- Passive Consumers
- Entrenched
- Withdrawn

We describe activities in each of the following three domains: the formal system of staff development; the informal system of interchange within the school and school district; and personal activities initiated in their private lives. Few people maintain the same growth state across all three domains, although some do. However, few behave in widely discrepant states across the domains. The matrix of states and domains is depicted in Figure 10.1.

The Total Omnivore

These people actively use every available aspect of the formal and informal systems available to them. Their lives are rich with books, the performing arts, travel, sports, university courses, and the offerings of teacher centers and districts. They have found professional colleagues with whom they are close and can exchange ideas. They are active in the attempt to improve the state of the schools in which they work. They simply will not be denied. They seem able to overcome obstacles and they do not allow dysfunctional emotions to isolate them from a great variety of activities. They do not spend much energy complaining about colleagues, administration, poor presenters at workshops, etc.; they simply take what they can where they can get it. This does not mean that they are undiscriminating—their energy is simply oriented toward growth rather than possible impediments to it. They tend to be happy and self-actualizing people. Teaching has not jaded them, nor has the rest of life. Some teachers behave omnivorously but over only one or two domains of activity.

Beulah has been teaching at her Parker School for 10 years. She has taught third, fourth, and fifth grades and is now teaching sixth. She works in a school that has weekly staff development activities. She has three grown children one going to a state university and two at the local community college.

She has lots of interests; she skiis, backpacks with her husband, plays the piano, sews, and reads. She just finished reading the Castañeda series. "My kids usually give me books as presents."

When she was asked about her connection with colleges she said, "I'm always going to school to take classes." Recently she took courses in Shakespeare and astronomy. When she was asked about astronomy she told me that her son had become interested in it and she "wanted to be able to talk to him." She is going to take a psychology course this summer for the same reason. She also has designed an astronomy unit for her sixth graders.

When she was asked what the purpose of staff development was, she said that she used it as a refresher: "It lets me know what new programs are around and gives me an opportunity to think." She said a recent muticultural workshop was useful because "it is a tap on the shoulder to remind you."

Beulah is working with a nearby university and also the high school that Parker School feeds into. They are working on composition skills with the goal of reducing the number of students who have to take "bonehead" English at the university. Of visitations in other classrooms: "It helps a teacher keep up. It helps you keep from being overwhelmed and gives a sense of community with other teachers."

Beulah ended our conversation by saying the children will learn what you teach them. "It's up to you. If you have lots to teach, they will learn lots."

The Formal Omnivore

The formal omnivore tends to be somewhat less gregarious with fewer close professional friends, but is a serious student of education. Courses, degrees, workshops, and programs of travel and personal reading are a steady diet. The formal omnivore is sometimes less than pleased with their less assiduous colleagues. Much of the formal omnivore's professional growth is relatively isolated from the informal social system of his or her school. Formal omnivores are in a high state of growth in content areas, tend to be relatively autonomous, and are not as closely connected to colleagues as the total omnivore.

The Informal Omnivore

These people are gregarious and draw strength and ideas from their colleagues. They are not terribly concerned with formal credentials and tend to build a busy and active life around the social situation in which they find themselves. They are well connected to the informal social system of teachers and draw from their professional colleagues ideas and materials that they can use in their teaching.

The Personal Omnivore

These people read a great deal and draw sustenance from activities and the performing arts. This is of no small importance for they lead a rich cultural life and are better connected with the world beyond the work situation in which they live.

Thus there are three kinds of partial omnivores, those who emphasize formal learning opportunities, those who emphasize their own self-study and independent activity, and those who are closely connected to the social system in which they live and work. Some partial omnivores are active consumers in the other domains but others are passive except in their most active domain.

The Active Consumers

Many teachers keep relatively busy in one or more domains. The active consumer state contains less initiative than the omnivore state, but is full of activity. Some teachers are active participants in one or another domains and a few are active across the board.

Fran has been teaching for 13 years, 3 at her current school. She became acquainted with the principal in a course they were taking. When her husband was transferred from the western to the southern part of the large metropolitan area she called up the principal and found there was an opening.

Fran sees the in-service offerings much like a "smorgasbord—you have to pick and choose what you might be able to use." However, she believes that a certain number of workshops should be mandatory "because those that you want to be there might well not come. It doesn't hurt to have some things selected for you."

Fran occasionally takes courses, but receives most of her growth from the staff development workshops and from talking to other teachers. Although she seldom watches another teacher she said, "Very few teachers sit alone in their rooms during breaks. They are usually talking to each other about what they do."

Fran enjoys films and some reading but generally spends her nonschool time doing household things.

The Passive Consumers

Another state is exemplified by persons who are there when opportunity presents itself but who rarely seek or initiate new activities. Thus if the formal system becomes active it will tend to draw them to greater activity. If they are a member of a family which engages in much reading and theater going they will tend to go along, and they may be pulled into workshops or other activities by peers or supervisors. However, they are dependent on the activity levels around them to draw them into the activity. If they are in a low-energy informal system they will tend to interact relatively little. If their district maintains a strong formal system they will engage in its offerings. Some persons are passive consumers in one or two domains and active in another. We have met a few partial omnivores who are passive in the domains where they are not omnivorous. Jane is a good example.

Jane is a third-grade teacher at South Bay School. She has taught for 11 years, all at South Bay. Her classroom always is filled with materials and she provides opportunities for her students not available in many other classrooms in the school. She carries on a rather extensive program in physical education, including a tumbling unit. She does a series of art projects throughout the year which has given her quite a positive reputation among parents. She has students from the local state college science department bring reptile and insect collections to her class to the delight of most of her students.

Jane occasionally takes a course from a college or university. She attends workshops given by a professor who flies into the Bay Area. (One of the recent titles was "10 Bulletin Board Ideas.") She attends the regional inservice activities but generally does not seek out new procedures or materials "because my program is filled. I don't know how I would use them even when they seem to be neat things."

Jane is generally seen as a showoff by her colleagues. She talks to two other teachers to some extent. These teachers send children to her for the tumbling unit. Most of their conversations are short interchanges over logistics or upcoming events in the school.

With respect to the outdoors, Jane is an active consumer or omnivore. She likes camping and backpacking and goes as often as she can. She has held "campouts" on school grounds on a Friday night each of the last two years. She attends an occasional play.

Perhaps in a different environment she would be a more active consumer of the formal or informal system, but at South Bay she has settled in and does her own thing. Even though she is in a somewhat hostile setting she has no intention of transferring because she is let do "what I want to and I like the kids, particularly when I have more than one child from the same family."

The Entrenched

Some teachers manifest a state we term *entrenchment* in one or more domains. When in that state they are not likely to seek out training. Where they do take training it is likely to be in areas where they already are feeling successful. For example, they have a management system that they are satisfied with but will take "Taming the Tornado in the Classroom." They will seldom take courses unless there is a material benefit, i.e., salary increment. Innovations that change the way the school's curriculum operates are usually viewed with suspicion, particularly if they might result in a change that would suggest the current classroom practices are inadequate. Change to them means they are not doing a good job and therefore are threatened. They may see themselves as one of the best teachers in the school. Any question of current practice will generally be rebuffed. In the informal domain entrenched teaching is manifested by the use of the informal system of the school to control and stifle. They are likely to do this in one of three ways:

- actively oppose
- surreptitiously oppose (using their position in the informal systems to intimidate and indirectly veto)
- withdraw—building a fortress around their classroom usually saying something like, "I already do that in my classroom."

Totally entrenched people sometimes, in conversations, appear to be operating at the middle of Maslow's hierarchy of needs. In fact, they may talk the self-actualizing game but when something alters the way the school functions, they revert to a survival orientation bent on sublimating anything that threatens their position.

The Withdrawn

People in a withdrawn state require a great deal of energy from outside if they are to become involved. They may push away activity in one or more domains avoiding the formal system where they can, engaging in few activities that they generate themselves, and participating rarely in informal interaction at work. A few are withdrawn in all three domains.

At this point we would hesitate to speculate about the number of people who fall into each of these categories, especially because the more withdrawn tend to be difficult to interview. Also, we have frequently been deceived in the early stages of interviews, especially with respect to the personal domain. Some people who are withdrawn or passive in the formal and informal domains have turned out to be relatively active in the personal domain.

There are obvious implications to this system of classifications. The omnivores generate considerable energy for themselves and exploit opportunities which are created for them. The active consumers become involved easily. The passive consumers and withdrawn not only initiate little, but are difficult to involve—they consume energy.

Although we are by no means certain, we believe that there is a relationship between these levels and the psychological states as described by Maslow. We can obviously compare the omnivores to the self-actualizing state and the withdrawn to the patterns of survival-level persons. Whether or not there is a direct connection, the effect of being in a state of psychological survival and being withdrawn from major growth-producing dimensions of one's environment are virtually the same. An individual who is withdrawn is exposed to much less stimulation than people who are not and lives much more alone. Such a lifestyle has a tendency to reduce the disposition toward risk taking, probably resulting in a relatively low level of growth, as Grace's story indicates.

Grace has been teaching for 22 years, the last 13 in the second grade at the same school. She supervises the school choir. With the exception of another second grade teacher who is her closest friend both in and outside school, Grace has, for all practical purposes, no contact with other faculty members except for the principal who, like her, came to the school when it opened. She takes breaks and eats lunch with her friend. She is cordial to the other teachers but seldom speaks at faculty meetings; little is known about what she does, with the exception that some students in each class are in her choir.

Grace attends required in-service workshops but seeks out none. When a major federal staff development project was proposed for South Bay School, a meeting was convened at her house. Grace and a few others opposed the project. They went individually to the principal to object to its coming. His way of dealing with them was to assure them that although the project would come to the school they could pick and choose what they wanted. Grace was satisfied. In the four years of the project she attended all of the schoolwide activities held during faculty meeting time or with time arranged by sending the children home early. Generally, she sat through the workshops without trying out any of the ideas or materials presented to her. She tried out a concept-development activity and enjoyed its gamelike nature as a change of pace, but did not see it as relevant to her basic instructional program.

Her family is fully grown. She and her husband live quietly and pleasantly. She is active in her church, playing the organ on Sunday. They read magazines, an occasional book, and take in a film once in a while. They have no regular leisure or athletic program. They travel occasionally.

Obviously people oriented differently toward exploitation of the environment will react very differently to the growth opportunities in a school situation.

SOCIAL INFLUENCE, SELF-CONCEPT, AND STATE AS A LEARNER

Not only do individuals in the same environments respond differently to the same opportunities but there are considerable differences in the energy levels of the social environments of schools. The school environments interact with the individual's predispositions to influence the amount of growth-producing activity which will go on. We conducted a long-term formal investigation of one school's social ecology and a number of briefer more informal investigations which have provided us with the basis on which the following concepts are built.

The South Bay School was the site of a four-year investigation which focused on the effectiveness of various types of in-service education and on the receptivity of the school to initiatives for innovation which originated both from within and without it. Portions of a series of interviews conducted with the staff members, both administrators and teachers, explored the extent to which individuals felt efficacious in the environment and understood and felt that it was possible for them to generate initiatives themselves. There was a curious unanimity in the staff on a number of important issues. First of all, each of the staff members and the principal felt that it was relatively easy for any individual teacher to bring about a change within their assigned classroom. The principal was supportive of most attempts, would make resources available if that were possible, and there was a feeling of trust that would sustain the period during which any new practice was being implemented. *However, each staff member felt that it would be virtually impossible to bring about any kind of change on a scale larger than the individual classroom.* It appeared to be very difficult for teachers to get together and engage in concerted action, even in groups of twos and threes, and they all agreed that it would be *impossible* to bring about a change on a schoolwide basis, whether it was initiated by a teacher, an administrator, or anyone else.

The interaction between teachers and principals was interesting to observe. The principal appeared to have excellent dyadic relations. On a

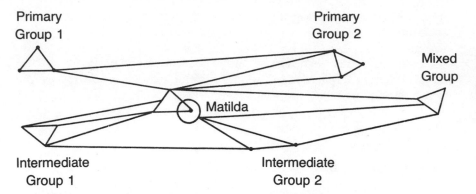

FIGURE 10.2   Friendship Groups in South Bay School.

one-to-one basis he and each individual teacher appeared to be cordial, friendly, and respectful, and to have a relatively easy level of interchange. However, faculty meetings were painful to observe or participate in. Members of the faculty could be seen talking and laughing on their way to the meeting and interacting easily with the principal, but once inside the meeting room the atmosphere became formal and stilted, proposals were greeted with stony silence, guest speakers were treated with bare civility and responded to only minimally, and proposal discussions were filled with obstacles and problems. Usually no action was taken except perhaps to refer the matter to a committee.

Observation of the interaction between the faculty members resulted in a sociogrammatic figure which is depicted roughly in Figure 10.2. Most of the members of the faculty had relatively close interchange with two or three other individuals. There was a tendency for primary teachers and intermediate teachers to consort with others at the same level, although there were some exceptions, and the communications networks converged on one triad of teachers, the most influential member of which we will call *Matilda*. *Matilda* had achieved the position of "gatekeeper" of the social system. She used that position to discredit initiatives for innovation which came from any and all sources. Ridicule was her primary device. If a teacher described something she was doing, Matilda would suggest that the person was showing off and "isn't it too bad that she has that need when she's such a basically nice person." If a staff member came back from a workshop with an idea, she would generally ridicule the idea, suggest that "we all know how Tommy is. Once in a while he gets a bee in his bonnet, but it will pass." Curriculum initiatives from the principal were greeted similarly. Matilda was a master at intimating that whatever was being suggested was simply a new version of something that had been tried before and been found wanting. The result of Matilda's activity was that all of the teachers and the principal knew that each one had heard other's suggestions being held up to ridicule and, worse, they had stood for the ridicule of their friends' ideas. The alienating effect on the informal system of the group was profound. When any individual or group came up with an idea they could be sure that Matilda would cut it down and that their friends would permit that to happen. Thus, by the time an idea got to a meeting the issue had already been decided, not through the formal decision-making process that was part of the meeting, but through an informal system governed by a negative gatekeeper. Matilda, herself, could not initiate anything but was extremely effective at diminishing the effects of any initiative made by another person. The principal was not very skilled in handling the faculty as a group and his pleasant dyadic interactions with the staff had little effect on the overall normative structure that had been developed.

As time passed, it was possible to make a clearer and clearer assessment of Matilda's personality. Matilda is classically entrenched. Although she advertised herself as the best teacher in the school, her teaching was in fact dull and monotonous and as more and more attempts were made to liven the environment of the school the nature of her increasing overt resistance made it clear that Matilda was frightened of innovation. We concluded that an entrenched person had become the most powerful person in the informal system and was using her power to protect herself and, hence, insulate the entire school from attempts to improve it. Not until Matilda's position in the social system was changed could there be sustained attempts at staff development or curricular and instructional innovation in that school environment. Collective action was impossible.

INTERACTION BETWEEN INDIVIDUALS IN THE SOCIAL SYSTEM

Obviously individuals are affected by the social systems of which they are a part. Matches and mismatches can be dramatic. Omnivores are stimulated by energizing schools and will add to the stimulation that is already present. A withdrawn person can be terribly threatened by an energizing environment. If the disparity between their growth state and the social system to which they are exposed is too great they are likely to become overwhelmed. They will have to either become more active or find some way of leaving that faculty situation. At the other extreme, a self-actualizing person who runs into a relatively dormant environment is likely to be appalled. It is also likely that this individual will be made an isolate within the social system where his or her normal mode of behavior will be perceived as abnormal to the depressant environment. All the other interacting possibilities exist as well, of course. A withdrawal-level individual who joins a depressant environment is likely to feel that a home has been found and is also likely not to be stimulated to higher levels of activity. A self-actualizing teacher who joins an energized environment is likely to be delighted especially if the previous environment was relatively dormant.

IMPLICATIONS: A PROGRAM FOR PSYCHOLOGICAL AND ECOLOGICAL STATES

The implications in our long struggle to improve the environments in which teachers work probably are obvious. Initiatives by teacher centers, county offices, districts, states, and the federal government are going to be met by environments and individuals as different as the ones we have been describing. In some environments and with some individuals they will find fertile ground; with others they will have an uphill fight even to a minimal level of implementation. We urge that direct attention be paid to improving the school's social system. Part of this improvement can be accomplished through the help generated by organizational development specialists and part by consultation with social therapists skilled in creating and shaping a new social system, one that is oriented toward self-actualization of the individuals within it.

CREATING ENERGIZING ENVIRONMENTS

There is no simple formula for creating environments that energize groups of people and provide individuals with optimal opportunities for growth. Embedding powerful training opportunities in the school environment helps greatly as does the formation of teams whose members study one another's teaching. Practicing cooperative decision making is also effective. The very establishment of the Responsible Parties, as the Urban/Rural School Development experience indicates, helps people feel more powerful and less alienated and provides greater companionship in the process of making a school effective. The development of a process for self-study is probably the most important. The Responsible Parties need to look carefully at the environments of their schools, determine how energizing they are, and begin to offer opportunities for individuals to grow and for the faculty to gain practice in collective decision making. Unless the principal is an expert in organizational development it will probably be necessary to bring in consultants who can help the teachers and the members of the Responsible Parties examaine the social system and learn how to create a problem-solving environment that encourages growth from everyone.

As the faculty becomes a more efficient problem-solving unit it is important to turn to the improvement of the curriculum areas and push the school toward a level of operation where every curriculum area is under continuous examination.

In a very real sense we become the things that we do. We take on the attributes of the activities that we engage in. It is legitimate to speak of the habit of growing as well as the state of being an omnivore, or the habit of being withdrawn as well as a state of withdrawnness. States of growth are self-perpetuating. The more active consumers of the environment receive great satisfaction from their behavior which tends to draw them into more and more active roles in the re-creation of their own lives. Hence, the adventuresome intellectual and spiritual qualities they bring to their teaching and, ultimately, to their students.

11

Rebuilding the Curriculum

What shall we teach, how shall we teach it, and how shall we organize ourselves for concerted action? These are the questions that beset the curriculum maker. The intellectual life of schools is organized into substantive areas which we speak of as curriculum areas. Once the social system of a school is functioning smoothly, the study of teaching is commonplace, and the Responsible Parties have become established, attention needs to be turned to each of the curriculum areas. In the elementary school these are reading, arithmetic, science, social studies, literature, physical education and the arts. These same areas continue in the secondary school with a widening range of additions. Advanced mathematics, theater, vocational training, and a host of other areas can be added.

In our look at the Cameo School we saw that it had developed a semblance of curriculum only in reading and arithmetic. The Foster School, on the other hand, engages students in the study of society, science, and literature. We now consider the topic of curricular organization, examining some examples of Responsible Parties who take seriously the continuous reconstruction of the curriculum. Like schools themselves, curriculums tend to atrophy if they are not renewed and reconstructed continually. When problem solving is just beginning to be a regular practice, it is wise to take on no more than one area at a time, but when problem solving is normative, committees can work on several curriculum areas simultaneously. The hardest work must be done by the school's faculty, but they can be helped by working with consultants from districts, counties, teacher centers, and other agencies concerned with the reorganization of instruction.

A SUPPLEMENTARY PROGRAM
FOR ECONOMICALLY POOR CHILDREN

To illustrate the decision making processes, let us take an actual case of the Responsible Parties of a junior high school who planned an after-school program for economically poor children. Not all of the many objectives formulated by this faculty can be explored here, but we can attend to some of the more important ones. Nor should the objectives listed here be regarded as universally applicable. The best we can say is that the faculty made reasonably wise decisions, given the specific conditions they were faced with and the currently inadequate knowledge about the teaching of disadvantaged children.

The decisions made by the Responsible Parties were governed by the following conditions: the program was to be conducted after school; the students were to be those who had some difficulty in the regular program; public funds for materials and teachers' compensation had been allocated; commercial teaching materials available to the teachers generally were not suitable in interest level or verbal level; and many materials used in the program inevitably would have to be developed and organized by the teachers on their own or in cooperation with the children.

As a first step toward formulating objectives, the Responsible Parties studied its children. They decided that the children's language problems had the following characteristics:

A small vocabulary (both in recognition and use)

A relatively small number of syntactic patterns (both in recognition and in use)

Poor reading and writing ability

Limited language experiences in the home

The Responsible Parties found that these problems existed in general but with significant exceptions. Some children could use oral language very expressively; some loved to read and could read well; and some were uncommunicative merely because of fear, or rebelliousness or for some other social reason. In other words, although the often-quoted generalities about disadvantaged children held true to some extent, the Responsible Parties learned that they could not ignore individual differences. Thus, some individualized or specialized instruction seemed necessary even though for most students the highest priority was given to overall language development, both oral and written— emphasizing language as a social tool, a means of reading for pleasure, and a tool for acquiring information and communicating ideas.

As a second step toward formulating objectives, the Responsible Parties studied the social milieu of the children and discovered the following conditions of disadvantage:

The children's home life was frequently unstable. The family's transience—moving from apartment to apartment—contributed to this instability, but lack of family cohesiveness often proved a grimmer problem (only 60 percent of the children had known their fathers).

In the neighborhood the dropout rate of teenagers was very high, reflecting the general lack of interest in schools or education.

Employment for graduates and dropouts was hard to come by. Service occupations in particular were often closed to the students because of their unkempt appearance or their unsocial ways.

The problem was intensified for those who were members of minority groups; some two-thirds were blacks or Puerto Ricans.

In view of these environmental problems, the Responsible Parties decided that the children should study how their society really works, how more cooperative personal relations could improve their ability to handle themselves in that society, and how coping with their own feelings of frustration and aggression could obviate some of their difficulties in spite of adverse treatment by society.

As a third step in their decision making, the Responsible Parties decided to concentrate on sociology and economics as major disciplines for study. The central organizing concepts of these disciplines could be identified by the children and applied to their study of their neighborhood and city. In other words, social and economic processes could be studied in such a way that the children could come to understand such things as how social norms prevail in their neighborhood and how these norms effect them. The study of economic processes—such as accumulation and distribution of capital, measures of productivity, divisions of labor, and supply and demand of labor—could be analyzed in relation to the children's own conditions.

As the next step, the faculty studied the particular learning problems of economically poor children. They read the works of major theorists and researchers and concluded that many previous programs for disadvantaged children had suffered because the students had divorced school life from the real world. They had not found their school materials comprehensible in terms of their own experiences. From their study they also concluded that the students would feel fatalistic about failure in school and would expect regimented control from the teachers. They also found that the most successful experimental programs had involved the school in the real dynamics of the city and had emphasized simultaneous development of language and human relations. At length, by studying scholarly views of deprivation and by studying the children they were to teach, the Responsible Parties began to develop a sense of the childrens' needs and the possible remedies.

What might be called "philosophical issues" were also debated in the course of the investigations. For example, some members recommended developing middle-class values in the children, whereas others countered that such an approach was tantamount to telling these children that their upbringing was deficient. Some recommended vocational training as a more immediate, practical need on the part of the children, whereas others felt that a broader linguistic and social development would offer more flexible future choices, including prospects of higher education. Some members emphasized the problems of discipline and control, whereas others believed that cooperation was achievable without imposing traditional notions of discipline.

Finally, after all this investigation and discussion, the Responsible Parties were ready to formulate the following series of general objectives.

Reading Skills
Attacking unfamiliar words, using principles of phonetic, structural, and contextual analysis
Using dictionaries, encyclopedias, and standard reference works to establish word meanings and to find information

Reading Habits
Reading widely for one's own pleasure (at least one hour each day)
Browsing in the library and discussing books with others (at least 15 minutes each day)

Language
Writing a standard manuscript legibly and quickly (at least 15 words a minute)
Applying phonetic and conventional rules to the spelling of unfamiliar words
Dramatizing stories and incidents from life, switching roles and characterizations at will
Saying things in alternative ways, using conditionals and expanded syntactic patterns

Social Study
Understanding the concept of norms and the development of norms
Illustrating a concept in terms of neighborhood, family, and city life

Understanding how societal norms affect other factors in society and the life of the individual

Understanding the division of labor in the city and the neighborhood

Understanding how supply and demand affect the labor market

Understanding the concept of capital, its uses and acquisition

Social Development

Organizing groups democratically to get simple tasks done

Analyzing the adequacy of a group process in terms of group objectives, roles, and plans of actions

Analyzing one's own reaction to failure, interpersonal conflict, and social pressure

The Responsible Parties felt that each of the children had needs of some kind in all of these areas and that whatever differences one might find among the children were mainly differences of degree. Teachers could outline special objectives for individual learners or groups of learners after diagnosing their personal needs more thoroughly. The objectives above were to guide the overall program and to help the faculty find useful ways of grouping the children. The teachers would have to select more specific objectives to guide the instruction.

Selecting Means

Once the purposes have been clarified, the faculty is set to choose the means for achieving those objectives. Again, at the curricular level, the aim is to provide teacher guidelines that will be used later in planning for individual learners and groups of learners. The faculty needs to create an organized environment in which teachers and students can work together for student growth.

The means of education are simply the environmental conditions that have an impact on learners—conditions that cause students to progress toward desired objectives. Several kinds of experiences affect the learner. All are important, and each objective requires teaching skills. Some aspects of the educational environment come in tangible form and are easy to identify and control—books, for instance, and similar media. Other aspects remain more elusive and harder to specify precisely or to produce in given measure—a social climate, for example, offering emotional support for the students.

The means of education can be analyzed into several parts, all converging to produce simultaneous influences on the student. At the same time, for instance, that children are experiencing the study of a particular topic, they are being influenced by the social climate, by the instruction of their teacher (instructional strategies), and by the particular viewpoints of their books and other instructional materials. Thus a faculty must be capable of selecting appropriate means in all these areas and organizing them into a unified curriculum plan.

Flexible and Multidimensional Methods

The task of the faculty is to develop a *system of educational means*—a framework that will guide each faculty member as he or she works with specific learners. To establish this framework, the faculty must shape enough aspects of the school's environment to have a potent effect on the students. Dealing with too few of the environmental variables would be a waste of energy. For example, if the faculty decides to use a cooperative-inquiry teaching strategy, so that groups of students can organize themselves to attack problems, and then fails to provide instruction on how to play the roles demanded by cooperative inquiry, the school is not likely to achieve many of its objectives.

The means that are chosen must also be relatively harmonious. To continue the example given above, if the curriculum in history is organized around the cooperative-inquiry method and students are to carry on research with original documents, then the school library must be stocked with source materials. Otherwise, the students' inquiry will be limited and the experience will be frustrating.

A reasonably adequate range of means can be developed if the faculty makes decisions about the following four variables:

Content. About how specific content will be sequenced over the years and how it will be organized. It also involves decisions about the learning resources that must be made available when students encounter that content.

Social Climate. About the social system that will be developed and the interpersonal climate that will be nurtured in the school.

Teaching Strategies. About how teaching will be carried on. Specifically, the faculty must consider what kinds of approaches are most likely to achieve the objectives of the school given the children who are to be taught and the conditions existing in the community. Also, what technologies will be used and how?

Learner Roles. About what students need to do if they are to learn in this environment. The faculty needs to consider how it will teach students the skills, attitudes, and knowledge that will make them effective, functioning members of their school community.

Numerous other questions will be encountered in formulating educational means. What system will be developed for feedback and evaluation? How will students and teachers keep track of their progress, and by what means will they use this knowledge to readjust the curriculum and alter instructional decisions? Decisions must also be made about how students will be organized for instruction. Will they be grouped by age, or achievement, or interests? Will grouping vary by curriculum area? For example, the grouping system used in social studies might be quite different from the one used in mathematics or science.

Let us return to our junior high school faculty and see how they selected means for their learners. If we were to describe the processes by which means were selected for all 17 of the objectives, our descriptions would be too extensive. Therefore, we will confine our illustration to two objectives with an interesting relationship—the habit of reading widely for pleasure and the skill in organizing groups democratically to get simple tasks done. The following sequence shows the step-by-step development of these two objectives.

1. The Responsible Parties were faced with the selection not only of content but also of context for students who had difficulty reading and who ordinarily did little spontaneous reading. There were many alternative approaches from which to choose. One possibility was to choose books of stories carefully designed to introduce the student to the *structure* of the English language and hence improve basic reading skills. In such books sentence structure and vocabulary are tightly controlled so that structural elements are introduced one at a time. Another possible approach was to choose books about things the student was familiar with—for example, stories about the student's city world. A third possibility was to gather many books and permit the individual student's interest to govern content selection.

The plan that emerged was guided by a combination of principles. The Responsible Parties believed that the content of pleasure reading should be determined largely by the learner. They also believed that the readers needed to be introduced to many kinds of literature they would perhaps not choose for themselves. So they selected a wide range of plays, adventure stories, and other types of literature that would appeal to different interests and reading levels. They then organized this and other content by three devices. First, each student had a daily conference with one teacher who helped with book selection and discussed for a few minutes the preceding day's reading. Thus the children were allowed to select content of interest to them with some guidance from the teacher. Second, certain authors and types of stories were chosen to be introduced to all the children in the hope of expanding their reading interests. Third, the teachers organized the students to write stories about their neighborhood and the city. Their stories were edited by the teacher for reading by other students. Hence some of the children's reading was about the city as they saw it.

In the process of writing stories as a group the children were also developing their skills in democratic group behavior. This process, in turn, provided content for the children's study of the group process itself. For example, tape recordings of group meetings were made and later analyzed by the children.

2. The Responsible Parties also wanted to develop a child society characterized by cooperative inquiry, mutual support, and self-education. The students were organized with this objective in mind. Small inquiry groups were formed with children of different ages and achievement levels. Each group worked together, helping one another in some mutual task. The most troublesome students were assigned to otherwise mature groups and received special attention from certain teachers. At first the problems presented to the groups in reading and other activities were quite structured. ("One member will read the following book aloud. Then the group will select another member to describe the book to the class.") Gradually, more complex problem-solving activities were introduced. ("Select a book and prepare to dramatize it.") Finally, the group was left to conduct its own activities. ("Plan a field trip and report the plans to your faculty adviser. Be sure to identify who will take notes and what questions you will ask. Select someone to identify the group and introduce members to the resource person.")

To further its aims of creating a favorable social climate, the Responsible Parties also agreed to let students try to read difficult books, to reward their attempts, and to be very supportive and sympathetic. Students were introduced firmly and clearly to each activity, but once involved in the activity, they were allowed to speak freely and discuss what they thought of the activities.

3. The Responsible Parties needed to develop an overall plan for carrying out the lessons and conferences. Would they use direct or indirect teaching strategies? Would they structure the activities for the students, or would they help the students create their own study approaches? For reading objectives each child was counseled in the selection of books. Initially little attempt was made to help the children analyze their reading; the first objective was to get them to read. All achievements were rewarded conspicuously. Each child was urged to find out things for him or herself. If a child was not reading during reading time, the student was asked to look up something for the teacher! The tactic depended on counseling the children in book

selection and pressuring them constantly to have a book in their hands. When the child began reading, the teacher helped find goals within the selection ("What do you think will happen next?") to keep the child involved.

To help the students improve their interpersonal skills, an unusual strategy was developed. Tape recordings were made of group planning meetings. These tapes were played back to the children so that they could discuss the effectiveness of the meetings. Gradually the teachers showed the students how to assign roles, select goals, and carry on conversations more effectively. As good leaders developed they were distributed among the groups, and their groups were analyzed on a higher level. Role playing was used to induce each group to demonstrate good organizational procedures.

4. As learners the students had to be taught to select books, to report on them, and to participate in group planning sessions. In the early part of the program demonstrations by the teachers were planned to show the children how to select, report, and plan. Later, children were given more responsibility for reading and reports; tapes of the children's meetings were analyzed, and learner responsibilities and roles were discussed. The groups also made plans for improving meetings. Further demonstrations were given as needed.

To reduce the students' apprehension about assessment (nearly all of them had received poor grades over the years) it was decided that all feedback would be given orally and in terms of observed performance in class activities. Hence in the individual reading conferences each student was informed of his or her progress. The student also kept a log of books read and discussed this log with the teacher. In terms of group activities each class discussed its performance at the end of each day's session and made plans and resolutions for future behavior. The analysis of tape-recorded meetings built into the teaching strategy a good device for evaluation.

Overall, a coherent set of objectives was developed and means selected as general guides, with many decisions to be made by teachers and students during the course of instruction. Content was not highly structured, for example, although faculty had agreed on the means for developing it. Provisions were made for teaching the students the roles they would need to fill, but these were adjusted as the teachers came to know the students better as individuals. With the overall strategy developed, the teachers were ready to develop instructional strategies for their particular groups of learners.

The final plan provided an umbrella of objectives and ways of achieving them, but left reasonable latitude for the teachers to adapt instruction as they interacted with the students.

REDESIGNING A CURRICULUM AREA: AN EXAMPLE FROM SOCIAL STUDIES

Let us now consider the organization of a particular curriculum area. Social studies will be our example. Our Responsible Parties have been trying to increase the effectiveness of social education in their school and a committee has prepared a report that tries to make clear the options. The emphasis can be placed on a particular approach (social science, citizen, or person centered), on a particular discipline (history, geography, etc.), or on a particular social problem. Let us look first at the mechanics of curriculum development and then at a sample curriculum plan that emphasizes one of the three approaches: the social science-centered curriculum.

Curriculum Essentials

A curriculum plan needs to contain the following elements:

1. *Objectives.* These should identify the primary behaviors and the areas of life or content with which students should have experience. Here are some possible objectives for social studies curricula: describe the chief institutions of Western culture and how they developed; explain major issues in national and local elections; recognize the value of equalizing opportunity for all people; show confidence in one's worth as a person. A curriculum can be thought of as aiming at the improvement of thinking, feeling, and doing. Hence, objectives can be divided into three general categories: cognitive, or intellectual; affective, or emotional; and skills.

2. *Broad teaching strategies.* There are many teaching strategies that are useful for different purposes, and the different components of the curriculum will probably require different approaches. For example, one educator recommends that the social sciences be taught by applying social science methods to social problems. Group dynamics skills on the other hand can be improved by teaching students to analyze their group behavior and by devising systems for improving it. Many other skills can be taught through highly sequenced direct instruction.

3. *Sequence.* What will come before what? There are probably some ideas, skills, and ways of thinking that could be introduced early so that they can be built on later. Perhaps some learnings need to be repeated periodically. In the primary grades, one basis for sequence has been the "expanding horizons" approach, by which the child first studies those things that are physically (and presumably psychologically) close to him. Chronology is another possible basis for sequence, but certainly an event need not be studied first just because it happened first.

Curriculum plans can suggest possibilities but leave the choice to each group. For example, a guide might suggest that during one of the junior high years a class study one or two rapidly developing nations and not specify which ones.

4. *Continuity.* This element can be supplied by the essential values, skills, and ideas that are studied and expanded year by year in different ways. For example, group dynamics skills might be begun in the first year of school and developed at first informally, and finally by formal study of methods for improving group processes. Certain methods from the social sciences might be introduced early and developed year by year. Or the study of democratic values might give continuity to the curriculum. One kindergarten through grade seven project (the University of Georgia Anthropology Project) introduces "cultural universals" at the beginning and expands on them yearly so that the child's conception becomes more and more sophisticated in applying the universals to the analysis of more and more situations.

5. *Evaluation and feedback.* The last element in a curriculum plan is a provision for determining what is being learned and communicating progress to the teacher and student. This is an exceedingly specialized problem. Ordinarily a school system requires the services of evaluation experts to help design and implement a system tailored to the local situation. A common and serious error is to impose an assessment system that was not designed for a particular school system. The indiscriminate buying of standardized tests is an example of this error. It is almost certain that an adequate system for assessment and feedback cannot be developed without the help of a measurement expert or testing service.

We will now use these curriculum essentials to examine a curriculum plan which emphasizes social science—one of the three dimensions of social studies. This plan includes only a few objectives, teaching strategies, and plans for continuity and sequence, but it is complete enough to enable us to see how the curriculum essentials are used to make a curriculum plan.

A Social Science-centered Curriculum

To achieve full scholarly control over a discipline, one needs to master its methodology, its frame of reference, and its organizing concepts. For the purposes of general education we have several choices. We can teach those parts of the social sciences that apply naturally as the students study social problems and prepare to be citizens and understand themselves. Or we can emphasize one discipline, teaching it well and letting it be an illustration. Or we can develop an integrated social science approach, teaching the general elements of methodology, the frames of reference of several disciplines, and some of the more important organizing ideas of each. Or we can teach the more general methods and concepts in the early years, and provide opportunity for depth exploration of some of the specific disciplines during the high school years. The following illustrates an integrated social science approach.

Objectives. The student should be able to:

1. name the general elements of social science methodology.
2. collect data, make inferences, and organize hypothecated experiments.
3. recognize the general frame of reference of each social science.
4. analyze small-group interaction using social science techniques and concepts.
5. use social science knowledge to analyze social problems.
6. describe the social movements that are changing the world.
7. form personal values and develop a philosophy of personal and social life.

These objectives emphasize the social sciences, but they also consider social life, citizenship, and the quest for personal meaning.

Teaching Strategy. Several strategies are used according to their appropriateness to the different objectives. Depth studies emphasize the methods of the social sciences. For each depth study, materials are put together to facilitate cooperative inquiries using the social science methods. To introduce the frames of reference of the different social sciences, certain depth studies emphasize specific disciplines. Some of the depth studies each year focus on contemporary social problems, so that the methodologies and ideas learned are applied to contemporary problems. A group-dynamics laboratory method is used to teach students to analyze and improve their group-process skills. Self-instructional units are developed to teach map skills and acquaint students with basic information from several of the social sciences. Independent study units facilitate depth inquiry by individuals into social problems.

Some of these strategies, such as group inquiry, are extremely inductive. Others, like the self-instructional units, are prepackaged for students and use sets of readings or programmed instructional techniques. In addition, *concept units* will be available. These are self-instructional units that can be used to review or catch up on work missed or as preparation for group units. Each concept unit is built around an important concept (*latitude, power, culture*) and provides materials for self-teaching.

Sequence. The pattern of units gradually develops the methodology and philosophy of social science and systematically introduces the frame of reference of each social science. This frame of reference is repeated several times in the 12 years. Two or three social science concepts are introduced early, repeated, and deepened. Group-dynamic skills are also systematically developed.

Continuity. The methodology of the social sciences and the improvement of interpersonal understanding and skills are repeated throughout. At every opportunity, students are asked to examine assumptions, to build and test hypotheses and to weigh values. Frames of reference are stressed throughout. Alternatives are developed—alternative views of human interaction, alternative solutions to problems, alternative ways of seeing things. The spread of topics results from the plans for sequence and continuity as they work together. See Table 11.1.

Evaluation and Feedback. This curriculum plan leans so far toward the intellectual that extensive modification would be necessary to adapt it for use with many children. However, most of these units can be adapted to a wide variety of individual differences because they deal with real events that are easy to see and feel. Also, the use of depth studies permits long periods of data collection so that the students will be less dependent on verbal learnings.

In Stage Three we will consider how deliberate selection of means and overall philosophies can lead us to make systematic decisions about the nature of education and lay a base for the selection of the curriculum type on philosophical grounds. For now, it is important to note that distinctly different approaches result in real differences in the educational options offered to the students. Whether we take the personal, social science, or academic approach to social studies will affect not only the content students will be exposed to, but also the ways they will be exposed to it. It is extremely important that the deliberations over curricular options not simply rely on one or two consultants who put forth their preferences. The decisions should be made consciously from among the best options that can be identified today.

USING TECHNOLOGY: SOME SCENARIOS

There are endless uses for media and communication technology in education. In fact, such innovations constitute a continued challenge to a school's ability to embrace change. Since it is beyond the scope of this book to provide a complete guide to instructional technology,* we will

*We also include a general treatment in Part V.

TABLE 11.1
A Social-Science-Centered Curriculum

Level	Topic	Approach
Primary	What Is a Family? An Anthropological Approach	At length and at leisure, a superficial study of a primitive family (Trobriand Islanders), a Western family (French), and an African family (Bantu)
	What Is a Community? An Anthropological Approach	At length and at leisure, a superficial study of cultural universals in several communities (Trobriand, French, Bantu, Swedish, Thai)
	What Are Tools?	A beginning of the study of civilization; tools, technologies, ideas used by several peoples throughout the development of civilization
	Our Group	A study of ways of having amicable and businesslike groups—study modulated to the character of the group
	Things to Believe In	A study of human interdependence; can relate to culture groups previously studied—family, community, and face-to-face group
	Basic Map and Chart Skills	An elementary self-instructional unit; teaches map and chart making and decoding
Inter-mediate	Our Political World	A study of decision making in families, and communities; follows "What Are Tools?"
	The Beliefs of Man	Follows "Things to Believe In"; studies values in primitive and modern communities
	The Political and Economic History of the United States	A self-instructional survey course: readings, films, programs
	Groups at Work	A depth study of group dynamics, including one's own groups

TABLE 11.1 (Cont.)
A Social-Science-Centered Curriculum

Level	Topic	Approach
	The Social Sciences at Work	Observing methods of validating inferences; the concept of causation; fallacies in reasoning
	Frames of Reference	A study of perception experiments, showing how preconception affects perception
Junior High	What Is a Society?	A study of two small, well-defined societies; Israel and Sri Lanka
	A Study of Law	Freedom and authority in Greece (Athens and Sparta), Rome, and twelfth century England
	Urbanization in America	Economic and political factors
	The Political and Economic History of Brazil	A self-instructional unit
	The Political and Economic History of Japan	A self-instructional unit
	My Community	Political, social, and economic aspects; an inductive study
	Group Dynamics	Laboratory techniques; advanced course
Senior High	International Relations	Using internation simulation—several units
	World Law	A study of international organizations—including NATO, SEATO, the UN—using original sources
	Demography	A study of population distribution and dynamics
	Political Belief Systems	Communism, democracy, etc.
	Macroeconomics	An emerging nation (as Nigeria); a small, well-developed one (as Sweden); a huge one (as India)

TABLE 11.1 (Cont.)
A Social-Science-Centered Curriculum

Level	Topic	Approach
	Group Dynamics, Caste, and Class	A study of the relation between the internation system of a group and its external system or social matrix
	Collecting and Organizing data	Self-instructional units

focus the remainder of this chapter on presenting a few examples of how a school can use technology to (1) increase teaching effectiveness; (2) introduce new content and methods; and (3) generate new ways of delivering educational services.

Practice in Mathematics: Use of a Microprocessor

Many manufacturers of microprocessors have developed systems that students can employ to test their mastery of mathematical facts and processes. The microprocessors can be arranged in skills centers or placed in classrooms or libraries.

In one such program, the student, seated at the keyboard, presses a key to activate a program and is given three options: take a quiz, receive drill, or create and store problems for extended practice. The student selects the operation (addition, subtraction, multiplication, or division) and then decides whether to be quizzed, be given drill, or store problems. Having selected the operation and option (say, drill in addition facts) the student is then asked by the computer to choose the level of difficulty of the problems to be presented: easiest, simple, harder, hardest; the speed with which they will be presented; whether to be given a second chance in case of an incorrect answer; and whether to be given visual prompts in the form of numbers of animals ("three plus five" would be prompted by a picture of three rabbits standing next to five rabbits). Another option is whether to have the problems presented aurally (through a voice synthesizer) or just visually.

The drill begins. On the screen appears a problem: 4 + 7. The student presses 10. A flashing light in the space for the sum indicates an error. The student presses 12. Four rabbits appear, standing next to seven rabbits. The student presses 11. The words "Got it!" appear. A few seconds later another problem appears and the process begins again. The computer will remember which ones were most troublesome and present them again.

The purpose of this type of program is to increase the amount of direct instruction students can receive, especially to increase practice with immediate knowledge of results. Also, as the student advances beyond the beginning stages, the computer can introduce new material (inducing the student who can manage 9×11 to figure out the answer to 9×12) and introduce new operations as well. Extensive libraries of programs are beginning to appear, especially in arithmetic and mathematics. Some companies are building software like this to accompany specific series of textbooks in arithmetic and mathematics, thus creating a role for computer-based instruction in the textbook-based program and facilitating the use of the technology in the regular classroom.

Similar applications are available for high school instruction. Programs can teach students how to create programs and how to use the computer for homework. Software is available in algebra, trigonometry, calculus, statistics, and graphing. A tenth-grade son of one of the authors uses the computer to: do his homework in algebra, receive instruction in programming and statistics, practice topics covered in his class, and for a term project in applying what he has learned to analyze data on baseball players. Such use can strengthen standard courses considerably. Because the computer can administer and score tests, it also permits much closer monitoring of progress and brings the student into the process of assessment.

Practice in Reading

The addition of a voice synthesizer to a computer terminal or microprocessor permits visual material to be accompanied by the sound of a voice (albeit somewhat mechanical), permitting a considerable advance in the development of reading programs.

For example, one program builds sight vocabulary by presenting pictures accompanied by the words that denote them, such as a picture of a tiger and the word *tiger*. The voice says, "This is a tiger." Then it presents several words and asks the children to identify *tiger* by pressing a particular key that moves a marker on the screen to the correct word. When the word is identified the voice praises the child and moves to the identification of another word. In this fashion the child is led to read sentences (*Where is the tiger? The tiger is hiding behind a tree.*) and so on until 75 words can be identified correctly and read in sentences. As in the case of arithmetic and mathematics some of the software programs are keyed to basal readers to facilitate coordinated instruction.

Augmenting the Study of Foreign Languages

Let us turn to an example where the Responsible Parties are concerned about improving foreign language instruction. The French and Spanish teachers are concerned that they are unable to properly manage individual differences in language learning. They are convinced that they are doing a satisfactory job for the average students but not for the more advanced or the slower students. The teachers believe that a language laboratory can improve instruction for all students and the Responsible Parties have agreed to see a demonstration of one and hear presentations about its operation and potential.

The development of the language laboratory represents vivid application of the combined properties of systems analysis, task analysis, and cybernetic principles in the educational setting. Before the language laboratory became commonplace, the classroom teacher served as the model for foreign speech along with the classroom of 25 to 35 students who were more or less accurately reproducing sounds of speech. The individual in such a situation might have a maximum of one minute of speech practice per classroom session, hardly enough to produce fluency or accuracy.

Today the typical laboratory is a classroom where learners use electrical equipment to hear, record, and play back spoken materials. The physical equipment usually includes student stations and an instructor's control panel. Through the instructor's control panel, the teacher has the ability to broadcast a variety of content materials, new and remedial programs, and instruction to individuals, selected groups, or the entire class. The teacher can also monitor the student's performance. The students' stations are often a series of accoustically treated carrells. They are usually equipped with headphones, a microphone, and a tape recorder. The student listens through the headphones to live or recorded directions from the instructor to repeat, answer questions, or make other appropriate responses to the lesson. The instructor may also choose to use the chalk board, textbook, or other visual stimuli to supplement audio inputs. Modern technology has made it possible for near instantaneous situations where the student might:

1. Hear his or her own voice more clearly through earphones than would otherwise be possible.
2. Compare personal speech with a model.
3. Receive immediate feedback.
4. Isolate items for study.
5. Permit pacing for specific drill.
6. Permit more finely sequenced instructional content.

Prior to the language laboratory, it was possible to provide reasonably sequenced visual materials. But the critical elements of language training—the individualized audial practice and dynamic feedback—far outran the human management capacities and support facilities of the self-contained classroom teacher with 25 students. With electronic hardware and software support systems, instructors can now divide their time more effectively between monitoring (management), diagnosis, and instruction. Students are provided immediate, direct sensory feedback so that they can compare their performances with the desired performance and make the necessary adjustments.

Broadcast Television to Enrich Standard Courses

Especially in areas where public and educational television stations are active, students can be exposed to drama, archeological and anthropological studies, and series in many other content areas. There have been a number of very interesting applications of broadcast television over the last 15 years.

The developments by the Childrens' Television Workshop, especially "Sesame Street" and "The Electric Company," bring basic instruction in reading and mathematics to young children (Palmer, 1974) as well as a multicultural perspective on social life. Originally designed to provide instruction to the children of the economically poor, these courses have been highly successful with all children.

The *Twenty-One Inch Classroom* in Boston (Ide, 1974) developed a series of programs in the late 1960s called "Cabinets in Crisis" designed to enrich secondary social studies instruction. The series focused on debates within the United States Cabinet at particularly important times of decision making. Secondary school classrooms were connected to the studio by telephone lines. Actors simulated the deliberations, interrupting them at times while the classrooms continued the debate and used the telephone to communicate recommendations to cabinet members. As the debates progressed the students could see the consequences of their recommendations by listening to rebuttals and counterarguments. The simulated cabinet debates enabled the students to peek into high-level government deliberations and also be, at least to some extent, active participants.

The Ontario Television Communications Authority has been active for many years producing programs to enrich standard courses (and, as we shall see, initiate new ones). TEVEC in Quebec has also been active. One of its outstanding achievements has been to incorporate broadcast television in courses which also include print material and audio-cassettes to help adults complete high school requirements and to help French-speaking Canadians learn Canadian English. The broadcast component of the English course is particularly interesting. It uses a soap-opera format in which the episodes are designed around a variety of real-life situations where English usage can be practiced. These

TEVEC courses introduce no new substance to the schooling process, consisting as they do of standard content, but they do permit instruction to be placed in different settings (particularly the home) because of the application of the broadcast medium and packages of other materials delivered by mail. Essentially, these courses do not deviate from the content that is usually covered, but create alternative ways of taking and completing the courses that are offered.

Cybernetic Principles and Instructional Design: The Simulator

From one perspective, cybernetic psychology represents the machine's contribution to the humanization of man, for in making an analogy between humans and machines, the cybernetic psychologist conceptualizes the learner as a self-regulating feedback system.

Cybernetics as a discipline "has been described as the comparative study of the human (or biological) control mechanism, and electromechanical systems such as computers" (Smith & Smith, 1966, p. 202). The central focus of the analysis is the apparent similarity between the feedback control mechanisms of electromechanical systems and human systems. "A feedback control system incorporates three primary functions: it generates movement of the system toward a target of defined path; it compares the effects of this action with the true path and detects error; and it utilizes this error signal to redirect the system" (Smith & Smith, 1966, p. 203). For example, the automatic pilot for a boat continually corrects the helm of the ship, depending on the readings of the compass. When the ship begins to swing in a certain direction and the compass moves off the desired heading more than a certain amount, a motor is switched on and the helm is moved over until the ship returns to course. As we have seen, steering a boat operates on essentially the same principle as does a human being. In both cases, they watch the compass, and in both cases, they move the wheel to the left or right depending on what is going on. In both cases, action is initiated in terms of a specified criterion ("Let's go north."). And, depending on the feedback or error signal, the initial action is redirected. Very complex, self-regulating mechanical systems have been developed to control devices such as guided missiles, ocean liners, and satellites.

The cybernetic psychologist interprets the human being as a control system, which generates a course of action and then redirects or corrects the action by means of the feedback which is received. This can be a very complicated process, as when the secretary of state reevaluates the foreign policy base, or a very simple one, as when we notice that our sailboat is coming into the wind too much and we ease off just a little bit.

In applying the analysis of mechanical systems as a frame of reference for looking at human beings, psychologists came up with the central idea "that performance and learning must be analyzed in terms of the control relationships between a human operator and an instrumental situation. That is, learning was understood to be determined by the nature of the individual, as well as by the design of the learning situation. Further, human engineering analysis called attention to the concept of the behaving individual as a closed-loop or cybernetic system, utilizing the processes of sensory feedback in continuous control of behavior" (Smith and Smith, 1966).

In any learning situation, we must be able to identify and characterize the pertinent human factors and the instrumental and symbolic features which make up the learning environment. More important, we have to specify the relationships between the capacities of the learner and the instrumentalities of the learning situation. The basis for this analysis is the sensory-motor capabilities of the learner. From this information the learning situation can be designed to fit the feedback capabilities of the learner.

All human behavior, according to cybernetic psychology, involves a perceptible pattern of motion. This includes both overt and covert behavior, such as thinking and symbolic behavior. In any given situation, individuals modify their behavior depending on the feedback they are getting from the environment. They organize their movements and response patterns in relation to the feedback they receive. Thus, individuals own sensory-motor capabilities form the basis of their feedback systems and their ability to receive feedback constitutes the human system's mechanism for receiving and sending information. As human beings develop greater symbolic capability, they are able to utilize indirect as well as direct feedback, therefore expanding their control over their physical and social environment. They are less dependent on the concrete realities of the environment because they can utilize the symbolic representations.

The essence, then, of cybernetic psychology rests on its principle of sensory-oriented feedback which is intrinsic to individuals (they "feel" the effects of their decisions) and is the basis for self-corrective choices. Individuals can feel the effects of their decisions because the environment responds in full rather than, "You're right," or "Wrong! Try again." That is, the environmental consequences of one's choices are played back. Learning in cybernetic terms is sensorially experiencing the natural environmental consequences of one's behavior and engaging in self-corrective behavior; instruction concerns itself with creating for the learner an environment in which this full feedback takes place.

The application of cybernetic principles to educational procedures is perhaps most dramatically and clearly seen in the development of simulators as training devices. A simulator is a training device which represents reality very closely, but in which the complexity of events can be controlled. For example, a simulated automobile has been constructed in which a driver sees a road (through a motion picture film), has a wheel to turn, a clutch and brake to operate, a gear shift lever, turn signal indicator, and all the other devices of a contemporary automobile. The driver can start this simulated automobile and when she turns the key, she hears the noise of the motor running. When she presses the accelerator, the noise increases in volume, so that she has the sensation of having actually increased the flow of gas to a real engine. As she drives, the film can show her curves in the road, and as she turns the wheel, she can have the illusion that her automobile is turning. The system of the automobile on the road has been reproduced in a simulation. In the simulator, the student can be presented with learning tasks to which she can respond, but her responses do not have the same consequences that they would have in a real-life situation, that is, the student's simulated automobile does not crash into anything, although it looks like it is crashing from her point of view. Also, she can be presented with tasks (in the manner of training psychology) which are less complex than those she would have to execute in the real world, in order to help her acquire the skills she will later need for real world operation. She can also practice putting the brake on and turning the wheel, and get some sense of how the automobile responds when she does those things.

Simulators have several advantages for certain kinds of training. One is that things can be made much less complex than in the real world thus providing the student with the opportunity to master basic tasks that are extremely difficult when all the complexities of real-world operation impinge upon him. A very good example of this is flying an airplane. Learning how to fly an airplane without the aid of a simulator leaves very little room for error. A student pilot has to do everything adequately the first time, or the plane is in difficulty. By the use of a simulator, training can be staged. The trainee can be introduced to simple tasks, and then more complex ones until he builds up a repertoire adequate for piloting the craft. Also, difficulties of various kinds can be simulated, such as storms, mechanical difficulties, and so on, and he can learn how to cope with those kinds of things. Thus, when he comes to the real-world situation, he has built up the necessary repertoire.

Secondly, the use of a simulator permits the student to learn from self-generated feedback which he experiences himself. As he turns the wheel of the plane to the right, for example, he can feel the plane bank;

he can feel the loss of speed in some respects and he can learn what needs to be done in order to trim the craft during the turn. In other words, he can learn through his own senses, rather than simply through verbal descriptions, the corrective behaviors which are necessary. If in the driver simulation, he heads toward curves too rapidly and then has to jerk the wheel in order to avoid going off the simulated road, this feedback permits him to adjust his behavior, so that when he is on a real road, he will be more controlled as he approaches sharp turns. The cybernetic psychologist designs simulators in this way—so that by receiving feedback about the consequences of his behavior, the learner is able to modify his own responses, and develop a repertoire of appropriate behaviors.

Thus far, the applications within normal elementary and secondary education are somewhat less spectacular, although the Metropolitan Studies Center of Washington, D.C. has developed an urban simulator with which they are experimenting with children from the upper-elementary grades. Omar Khayyam Moore's famous talking typewriter really simulates a human being who talks back to the student as he presses typewriter keys representing particular words or letters. However, most applications to education up to this point are fairly simple. If we look at a number of them, the cybernetic principles will be made more explicit than we can make them didactically.

The Life Career Game.   The Life Career Game was developed to assist guidance counselors and students in their mutual task of planning for the future, a task which requires the student to take into account many factors such as job opportunities, labor market demands, social trends, and educational requirements (Boocock, 1968). Vocational and educational guidance attempts to assist students in becoming aware of these multiple factors, to evaluate their significance, and to generate alternative decisions.

In the Life Career Game the student is able to *interact* with these various components of the environment. He makes decisions about jobs, further education or training, family life, the use of leisure time, and receives feedback on the probable consequences of these decisions. The environment in this case is represented by other people or organizations. That is, the responses from the environment are determined by the probability of the responses from people in the actual roles of teachers, college admissions officers, employers, and marriage partners. As the player moves through the different environments of school work, family, and leisure, he is able to see the interrelationships among his decisions and among the components of his life. The game is played as follows:

The Life Career Game can be played by any number of teams, each consisting of two to four players. Each team works with a profile or case history of a fictitious person (a student about the age of the players).

The game is organized into rounds or decision periods, each of which represents one year in the life of this person. During each decision period, players plan their person's schedule of activities for a typical week, allocating his time among school, studying, job, family responsibilities, and leisure time activities. Most activities require certain investments of time, training, money and so on (for example, a full-time job takes a certain amount of time and often has some educational or experience prerequisites as well; similarly having a child requires considerable expenditure of time, in addition to financial expenses), and a person clearly cannot engage in all the available activities. Thus, the players' problem is to choose the combination of activities which they think will maximize their person's present satisfaction and his chances for a good life in the future. . . .

When players have made their decisions for a given year, scores are computed in four areas—education, occupation, family life, and leisure. Calculations use a set of tables and spinners—based upon U.S. Census and other national survey data which indicate the probability of certain things happening in a person's life, given his personal characteristics, past experiences, and present efforts. A chance or luck factor is built into the game by the use of spinners and dice.

A game usually runs for a designated number of rounds (usually 10 to 12) and the team with the highest total score at the end is the winner (Boocock, 1968, p. 108).

The variations of the Life Career Game serve to illustrate the educational features of a simulation game as well as the enormous potential of simulation for incorporating several educational objectives into the basic game design. For instance, every simulation implies a theory about behavior in the area of life being simulated. This is represented in the goal-achievement rules (the objectives of the game), and the rules governing the environmental responses.

One version of the Life Career Game assumes that every person receives a different amount of satisfaction from each of the several areas of life. Put another way, each person attaches a different amount of importance to the various areas of life. Following this assumption, players determine their own goals by weighing these areas in terms of importance to them. At the end of the game, the objective achievements in those areas are converted to subjective satisfaction according to the weighted conversion ratios selected by the players. Alternatively, if one of the processes being simulated is the selection and modification of goals contingent upon the consequences of one's actions, one may be asked to weigh these areas at various times during the course of play. In both cases, the student is playing against the environment according to a personal criterion rather than an externally determined goal (e.g., Do I have more points than someone else?).

The game may also be played to include certain requisite skills such as actually making formal applications for jobs, setting up interviews, selecting courses from the college catalog. It can also be conducted to allow group discussion at the end of rounds, analyzing and challenging each other's decisions and identifying the values underlying them.

Internation Simulation

Harold Guetzkow (1963) and his associates developed a very complex and interesting simulation for use at the high school and upper-secondary levels for teaching students principles of international relations. The internation simulation consists of five "nation" units, and the participants are grouped into these nations as the decisionmakers and "aspiring decisionmakers" within the countries. The development of the relations among the nations has been derived from the characteristics of nations and from principles which have been observed to operate among nations in the past. Each of the decision-making teams has available to it information about the country. This information includes the national economic systems' basic capability, the consumer capability, what is called "force" capability, or the ability of the nation to develop military goods and services, and trade and aid information. The nations play together an international relations game which involves trading and developing agreements of various kinds. International organizations can be established, for example, or mutual aid agreements, or trade agreements. The nations can even make war on one another, the outcome being determined by the relative force capability of one group of allies against another group. The simulation enables students to play the roles of national decision makers and to make the kinds of realistic negotiations diplomats and other representatives make as nations interact with one another. In the course of this simulation, students learn ways in which economic and other restraints operate on a country. For example, if a student is a member of the decision-making team of a small country and tries to engage in a trade agreement, the student finds that he has to give something in order to get something. If a student's country has a largely agricultural economy, and she is dealing with an industrialized nation, she finds that she is in a disadvantageous position unless that nation badly needs the product which she has to sell. By receiving feedback about the consequences of her decisions, therefore, the student and her fellow participants come to understand the kinds of principles which actually operate in international relations.

The possibility that curriculum renovation efforts will be successful depends, as we have said, on how well the Responsible Parties have prepared the school to accommodate necessary changes. If a social climate conducive to change has been established and the faculty accustomed to monitoring and improving their teaching repertoire, then the changes are good that desired curriculum changes can be successfully implemented. In the next chapter we will look at two schools trying to cope with federally mandated and supported mainstreaming programs. In one case the Responsible Parties had made the necessary preparations, while in the other, they had not. The contrasting results are striking.

12

Avoiding Disasters

This chapter is included to make vivid an obvious truth that usually is overlooked. It is simply that major curriculum innovations generally come to grief unless Stage Two is well-established. As we have seen, the entire Academic Report Movement foundered on the rocks of unprepared schools. Now that we have seen what Stages One and Two look like, let us examine some case studies of schools that attempted to "mainstream" students. One school was ready; the others were not.

MAINSTREAMING

In the middle 1970s Public Law 94–142 was passed and provided resources to schools designed to facilitate the provision of what came to be called the "least restrictive alternative" for children who were judged to have special needs. Included were children with various degrees of loss of sight, less than normal or loss of hearing, the orthopedically handicapped, and children with emotional and intellectual conditions that resulted in learning diabilies. Some of these students had been in separate schools or institutions for the handicapped and others had been in special classes in public schools where specialists worked with them. Schools were charged with making possible maximal integration of children with special needs into the regular environment of the school so that they would not be further disadvantaged by loss of social and intellectual contact with their peers. Schools varied widely in their responses to the mainstreaming initiative.

In the next few pages we will report case studies of schools attempting to implement Public Law 94–142 in a state which supplemented federal funds considerably. The case studies tell the story quite clearly.

DISTRICT A

A series of interviews were conducted with about 20 teachers in an elementary school and a high school in one county. Interviews were also conducted with staff development personnel and the principals of the schools.

The Elementary School

The elementary school has about 400 children in a neighborhood of comfortable, modest homes. The children are primarily white and about a third are Spanish. The school principal is quite clear about her position with respect to special education. She has a "personalization of education" perspective. She is hopeful that as mainstreaming is implemented she will get more resources to do the job that she wants to do. She is a fervent believer that students in special day classes should not spend all of their time in those classes. She has been badgering the district office to make the special day class teachers essentially resource teachers with the children's home base in the classroom. Special services and help for the classroom teachers would be provided by the specialists in special education. Essentially she sees categories of special needs to be important for diagnostic purposes, but she believes that *every* child is different and there's nothing really special about special education. She thinks it's natural for people to learn at different rates and with different styles, and believes that the school should make every effort to reach everybody on their own terms. The more special tutorial assistance the children can get, the better. She likes the idea of parental and student involvement in making educational plans for individual students but thinks that making very detailed and specific long-range plans is unrealistic. She believes that the most important job with respect to children with special needs is to try to help them grow in such a way that will eliminate those needs, and she believes an optimistic and supportive environment is essential to that. She does not particularly like the tendency of special education personnel to utilize highly specific sequenced instruction for almost every kind of disability. She believes there is no particular reason why children of less academic ability should be oriented more toward highly sequenced instruction than toward any other kind, and that a mixed diet is essential for every child.

The primary teachers generally agree with the principal. They seem very comfortable having children from the special day classes (there are two such classes in the school) in their classrooms. They are skeptical about the service offered by speech therapists, but they do not resist it. They are almost totally ignorant about the special education categories and need information badly. They know nothing about blindness, deafness, or orthopedic handicaps with respect to instruction, but most of them have confidence that the ways they teach probably are adequate to reach special needs. They would like to know more but are not sure what good it will do them. They are completely surprised that there are so many alternative teaching strategies available and wonder how those can be used for children with particular kinds of special needs.

The intermediate teachers are much more subject oriented and they are not nearly as much in tune with the principal's philosophy, although there are exceptions. They think that mainstreaming in the intermediate grades is relatively impractical but they are not certain just what kinds of handicaps they are talking about. However, their general view is that students who do not learn from the ordinary modes of instruction in the regular classroom should be tracked in some kind of way. They believe that special education sources should develop that track. They have no idea what will happen to the children later on and they are obviously compassionate about them. They simply don't seem to know what to do. On the whole they see the IEP as a paper exercise. Like the primary teachers they see nothing special about special education but think that putting the kids in small groups with specialists is probably a good idea because the children can get more attention than they can give them in the regular classroom situation. They do not object to having the children with them part of the day but profess that they are not sure how to handle the individual learning needs of slow children. On the other hand, they are equally unsure about what to do with students who learn more rapidly, although it bothers them less because those students at least cover the basic material. They seem to feel that at least the faster students are not deprived of a basic education, but how to enrich their education is not clear. As in the case of the primary teachers they are relatively ignorant of the categories for the handicapped and know almost nothing about special methods for taking care of the various categories of children of special needs.

The High School

The high school principal has a compliance perspective. He sees special education primarily from a mainstreaming point of view and he believes that as a child gets older and his deficit in education becomes larger mainstreaming in the high school setting is simply not very practical. He is very much concerned with the amount of paperwork that will accompany the Master Plan and believes that he will probably have a net loss of resources when it is implemented. On the whole he thinks that mainstreaming is probably destructive to the child who is mixed with students with whom he cannot compete and whom he holds back in discussions. "When a really slow kid asks a question the teacher can spend 10 or 15 minutes of a period trying to explain something to him while the other students just sit there and are uncomfortable and may actually ridicule the child. It is good for nobody."

He does not have a differentiated view of special needs. He sees blindness, deafness, and orthopedic handicaps as problems that should be handled by special institutions, although if the kids are bright he sees nothing wrong with their being in school. However, his concentration is on kids who are behavior problems or who are very slow at academic learning. Those are the problems which concern him most. He is in favor of a vocational education track for those kids. In his view the ones who simply will not cooperate should be dropped from the school, while the ones who are slow can at least learn some skills if vocational education is well implemented.

The counselor is the coordinator of special education for the school. She finds the categories confusing and nonfunctional. She is very good-hearted and took a special course on special education to help her understand how to do her job as mainstreaming occurs. She said that the course was compliance oriented and that most of the time was spent on ways to develop IEPs and avoid litigation. She came away fairly discouraged. Like the principal she simply doesn't know what you can do with uncooperative children or children who are slow at academic learning unless there is a vocational education option. She spends a good deal of her time counseling the students toward vocational options of one sort or another. Vocational education is very active in the area as is the Regional Occupation Program, and she uses those programs to a considerable extent.

The social studies teachers are divided. Some of them are subject oriented and maintain the general view of the principal. Others are student oriented and believe that the school has a responsibility for finding a way to serve all the children in its area. Whichever perspective they have, they all need information very badly. Most teachers have not had training in special needs, how to identify them or what is needed educationally. To some extent they have been involved in the development of IEPs and to a person they hate the process.

The math and science teachers believe there is a terrific problem helping kids to feel okay when they are not learning. They too feel that vocational education is the solution and generally favor a two-track educational system. They have not learned to think effectively about various kinds of special needs and how they can be handled in the school environment.

During the interviews the interviewers developed the impression that the combination of ignorance and confusion is serious in both schools. The connotation for a child with special needs is "an odd duck." Most of the secondary teachers have what appears to be a phobic reaction to peculiarities. The biggest exception is the primary team in the elementary school whose members are much less concerned and upset about the spectrum of individual differences.

There is something in the very designation of people as having special needs that appears to trigger in many of these teachers much of the emotional reaction that the old-fashioned categories used to bring about. The interviews left the feeling that we still have not come far from the Middle Ages in our views of normality and abnormality. Also, they left the impression that the feeling toward people manifesting considerable talent is very much the same as that manifested toward the students who display special needs.

These two schools manifest the need for comprehensive staff development if the Master Plan is to be implemented. The few workshops they have received do not by any means meet the considerable needs they have. It is hard to imagine that anything less than a regular, long-term, thoroughgoing program will bring about appropriate and beneficial use of the resources of Master Plan.

The Attitudinal Dimension

The differences between the two schools illustrate the effects of social climate and orientation within the school setting on the attitudes the people have toward children with special needs. In the elementary school the Master Plan is a welcome addition. In the secondary school it meshes awkwardly both with the structure of the school and the attitudes of the personnel. The kinds of technical assistance needed for the two schools are quite different. Complicating the picture is the fact that the elementary school which embraces differences between children is open to staff development and technical assistance. This particular secondary school is resistant to assistance from outside. The kinds of technical assistance to be rendered to the two different environments can only be perceived by and modulated by the local district administration.

The tasks of resource teachers and program specialists in the two schools will also be quite different. If the secondary school is to mesh comfortably with the Master Plan the principal needs to reorient his approach toward his faculty and help them understand the philosophy behind the Master Plan and the kinds of changes that have to be made if it is to operate productively. Unless he learns to exert strong and positive leadership the fate of the initiative will be in question.

DISTRICT B TRIES TO MAKE
AN ORDERLY TRANSITION

In this district there are 54 special education teachers and 300 regular classroom teachers. The staff, especially the special education staff person, believes that there will be few changes as the district moves under Master Plan, an event which will occur this year. A couple of years ago they organized a training program using a plan developed by a large nearby district. They sent about 10 people to that district who went through a five-day workshop. One day was spent on compliance aspects, three days on testing, and one day on the construction of educational plans.

Their task was then to train people in the school. They trained 10 people in each school in essentially the same pattern, and then the faculty of that school trained the other members, and so forth.

The substitute time was the primary cost of this and was paid for under Public Law 94–142.

They feel that because there has been a recent, substantial turnover of administrators in the district, considerable effort needs to be made to train them. They worked hard to recruit resource specialists. Their criteria require a person to have a special education certificate, an MA or close to it, and at least three years of experience in a special day class. They are providing training to those people to help them relate to the teachers. The cabinet is split over whether the resource specialist should come from the ranks of special education teachers (the position of the coordinator) or whether they should come from the ranks of experienced teachers and be chosen because it is highly probable that they will work effectively with other teachers (the position of the line administrator). They feel that in general there is a serious lack of training for resource specialists. They are working hard in this area. Most of the teachers, they feel, will attempt to persuade the resource teachers to put considerable energy on direct instruction. The superintendent is afraid that the function of the resource specialist will gradually accumulate into de facto special education day classes.

The superintendent also feels that most of the inservice that is available is on compliance, identification, and writing the educational plans, but that they literally do not know where to go to get good training on the actual meaning of a disability or how to treat it. That is, he feels that their profession as a whole my not have accumulated knowledge, and diagnosis may lead to frustration because they are relatively ignorant about many kinds of disabilities. Assuming there is a reasonable fund of knowledge, he literally does not know how to make that knowledge available to his staff in the sense that there is no known university, sets of centers, etc., which are offering solid inservice education in that particular substantive sense. He feels that the greatest amount of knowledge is known about the children who are intellectually slow to learn and that a fair amount is known about the deaf, but there are serious mysteries. Aphasic kids, for example, are simply mysterious to most people. When the term "severe delayed language development" is used children who are so identified are presented as mysteries. One of the cabinet members feels that a general personalization and individualization of instruction is the proper route to take and that probably the special education initiative is leading toward the world of the future. Before PL 94–142, in a school of 600 kids, perhaps one or two would be institutionalized for severe problems, about 20 would be in special education day classes, and about 25 would be receiving some kind of speech therapy or other specific motor therapy. As PL 94–142 occurred the number of day classes decreased to about 12 and a resource teacher program, as it was developed, picked up those children and about 18 others, making a total of about 24. The speech therapy situation did not change. Adaptive physical education classes are beginning to develop which represent a real difference for some children. The number of children qualifying for special education increased from 2 percent to about 8.9 percent after PL 94–142 was passed. About 65 percent were classified as learning handicapped.

The secondary school principal sees many of the requirements of Master Plan as an imposition without much help. She feels it was laid on without adequate coordination. Weekly referral meetings have been useful but meetings with parents and child advocates have been time consuming (she admitted that she has had only two such meetings during the last year). However, the bad taste remains. Interestingly enough, in terms of potential legal action, the district administrators reported that they are more likely be be approached by a child advocate who wants a child to be classified as having special needs so that they can receive special services, as contrasted with the period prior to PL 94–142, when they were more likely to be sued because they had, in fact, classified a child as having special needs.

The superintendent reported that he believes one of the problems in the implementation of Master Plan is that for many years teachers were told that they did not have the capability to handle special needs; now they're being told that they can and must, and are being required to relate to resource personnel that they are not comfortable using. Thus they must change their orientation. He feels there is a serious need to evaluate the content of staff development and to learn what can be offered and how. He feels that there should be strict honesty about what we know and don't know.

In one elementary school the investigator sat in the teachers' room and discussed special education with anybody who would participate. Most of the teachers were very curious and thought the investigator was probably there to provide information. They seemed to be quite confused about mainstreaming. One teacher voiced his concern about what he expected would be large numbers of physically handicapped children who would shortly inundate the school. Clearly the district has made the decision to mainstream every child possible, at least partly. They are using the familiar plan of a "special day class-only" option, "special day class with integrated recreational activities," "special day class plus the 'soft academic subjects' (art, music, physical education)," and "special day class plus some integration for the 'harder' academic areas." The main impression from the interview was that the district needs a very thorough course in what they are doing. The district administrator and special education director have a relatively clear idea about what *they* are doing, but there is an enormous need for clarification at the faculty level at that school.

When the investigator talked about time for in-service training, the teachers raised an objection to most options, ending up with the problem that they would like it in "prime" time but they don't want to leave their children.

The investigators spent much time in the faculty room of a junior high school and had lengthy interviews with the two resource specialists and the reading teacher.

The two resource specialists said that one of the problems facing them was that so many of the teachers in the school were new in their assignments. The district had closed a high school and transferred quite a number of teachers into the junior high where they are floundering around trying to get organized. Thus a child who has even mild special needs presents what seems to be an overwhelming problem to them. Both of these young teachers are extremely enthusiastic, feel that they know what they're doing, and believe that most of the children they are working with have either discipline problems or are relatively slow learners, but are not really that abnormal. The average IQ of the children in the special class is somewhere between 85 and 90. They use a modified "pull-out" program for some children but work the other way. Together they operate a day class. One of them teaches humanities and social studies and the other science and mathematics. The children take reading and history with regular students. Both of these teachers feel that the techniques that should be used with the special education children are fairly simple if people would only follow them, and add up to good teaching for everyone. That is, one needs to use multisensory approaches, be extremely careful in explaining directions, give plenty of time to complete assignments, and not make the assignments too big or confusing. They are very reluctant to approach other teachers to try to help them, partly because the teachers seem to be so overwhelmed by the problems they have, partly because they are unfamiliar with that type of role, and partly because they feel they are challenging the "whole-class bulk assignment" kind of procedure that characterizes the school. They are not about to take on their fellow teachers. The teachers tease them good naturedly about their apparently greater amounts of leisure time.

Here is an example of a relatively well-administered school with very good, young resource teachers trying to do their best and the school impacted by large numbers of new teachers who are in new roles (a problem which has come up persistently). It is a clear case of good effort with a lack of optimization of resources because of inadequate training.

Interviews in other schools resulted in a similar picture. In addition, the primary-grade teachers were comfortable with the special needs children in their classrooms but did not know what their special needs were. They were unsure why the children had been assigned to special day classes in the first case.

Here we have an example of a thoughtful district administration which is well aware of the needed training and coordination, which struggles with turnover of building administrators, and which would like a thoroughgoing, districtwide program of staff development in special education, but also does not know where to purchase the training. Because the district is so committed, they will probably gradually make things work out, but with much more struggle and pain and loss of efficiency than would be the case if the comprehensive training they want were readily available to them.

THE SOCIAL CLIMATE OF INNOVATION

These brief examples indicate very well the problem of bringing about a sensible change when the climate is not ripe for it. Clearly the most favorable climate was in the elementary school of District A, but even there it was not optimal and the implementation of the plans for mainstreaming in the upper grades are obviously falling short of the intentions. The illustrations also make clear the real importance of a well-defined and embedded staff development program and the difficulty of making adjustments in the school when inservice work is not in place.

The absence of a committee of Responsible Parties seriously hampers all of these schools. Even in the elementary school of District A, the provisions for mainstreaming are being wedged into the program rather than being part of an integrated plan.

Imagine the difference if each school was governed by a strong committee of Responsible Parties, if the entire program were under discussion, if the environments were accustomed to efforts at improvement and the appropriate inservice education was in place. There is no indication from these case studies that any of these schools are ready for anything beyond Stage One school improvement and the provisions for mainstreaming will fare badly unless the schools are well into Stage Two or beyond.

Part V

STAGE THREE: REDESIGNING THE SCHOOL

Once the process of school improvement has been established and the school meets basic effectiveness criteria and can improve its curriculum areas at will, the Responsible Parties are ready to examine the missions and means of the school, consider the possibilities in current technology, and examine social change. A number of very powerful options are available which involve changes more radical than specific improvements in the social system and the curriculum areas.

13

Alternative Forms
of Schooling

At this point the Responsible Parties are well established, the basic effectiveness criteria have been met, and improvements can be made regularly and systematically in each of the curriculum areas. It is now time to begin the arduous task of examining the overall mission of the school and the means that are used to achieve them.

Children who are entering school today can expect to be alive in 2060. The technological developments that so dazzle today's world by then will have been replaced by others that are only dimly conceived today. National and world societies will also change substantially: great nations are rising and the planet is becoming fully populated; colonies may well be established on other planets; life in cities will change even more radically than in the past, and in melting pot societies like the United States races and ethnic groups will have to come to new accommodations and live on more productive terms than they have. Confrontation politics will have too serious consequences to be sustained as a way of bringing about change, and new social orders will reshape governments. Thus as we enter Stage Three of school improvement, we are attempting to build a school that can prepare students to grow throughout their lives, students who can absorb and make productive the technological and social changes that lie before them. The solutions of today will have to be replaced by the solutions of tomorrow in order to retain our fundamental values about the quality of life and human dignity.

As we have seen, reformers have developed visions of schooling from a variety of perspectives. Also, within each of the curriculum areas (reading, arithmetic, social studies, science, the performing arts, physical education, etc.) research and development efforts have generated a vast number of alternative approaches. Educational technologists have labored to generate alternatives in the use of media and in the organization of schools. Architects have developed ways of matching physical plants to educational models and of developing facilities that are adaptable to a wide variety of ends and means.

In the next pages we will visit a teaching team in a mythical school of the future called Agapé. Our purpose is to look at schooling in terms of recent developments so that we may reach out to meet the basic needs of our society and its children. Also, because Agapé presents a number of ways of teaching it permits us to explore the various forms of effective schooling.

THE DIRECT INSTRUCTION TEAM

Harvey is the team leader of an elementary school direct instruction team that consists of eight members including an assistant to the team leader, named Marge (see Figure 13.1). Harvey and Marge are jointly responsible for the direction of the team and the continuing education of its members. She is a reading specialist and he is a science specialist. Every elementary school direct instruction team includes one reading specialist within the two leadership positions. This is because much reading instruction is done by the team, although, as we will see, it is not the only source of reading instruction. Harvey and Marge are responsible for creating and carrying out the operating curriculums for 200 children. These curriculums are tailored to the special characteristics of the children, the school community, and the subject matter. They are guided by curriculum plans created by the area curriculum council, which is composed of curriculum specialists from all subject areas plus representatives from each direct instruction team.

Two other members of the team have professional status. George is a young teacher with a strong background in the social sciences. He hopes to become a specialist in computer-assisted instruction, and Harvey and Marge arrange for him to work as much as possible with the computer support center. Florence is a middle-aged woman who is returning to teaching after an absence of several years. She expects to become a reading specialist and much of her in-service training is therefore Marge's responsibility. The remainder of the team includes four paraprofessionals. Two of these, Joan and Maureen, are college graduates, one with a degree in the social sciences and one in mathematics. They have both completed a special course to prepare them to work with a direct instruction team, and they expect to continue their professional preparation and become certified teachers. As part of this preparation they are assigned for one year to a direct instruction team, and in a succeeding year they will be rotated among the instructional support centers for further in-service preparation. Tommy is a high school graduate, 19 years old, who is unsure regarding his

FIGURE 13.1   The Direct Instruction Team.

Teacher Leaders

Harvey   Marge

Teachers

George   Florence

Paraprofessionals

Joan   Maureen   Tommy   Mary

future. He and many other youngsters like him are attached to direct
instruction teams and instructional support centers throughout the
school district where they work under close supervision. At the end of
each year, Tommy and his peers discuss with the personnel director
their future roles and educational plans. As long as they remain attached
to instruction teams, it is necessary for them to carry on programs to
further their education. Mary is also a high school graduate. She is
married and the mother of two, and is a warm, supportive person who
tends to gather around her the shy and lonely children. She takes
responsibility among other things for the orientation of the new children
who come under the guidance of the direct instruction team.

In one sense, about 25 parents are also members of the team. Several
serve part-time as volunteer (unpaid) aides to the team, and Harvey and
Marge operate a regular parent-tutoring series in which they explain the
children's educational program and inform parents about ways of
helping the children at home.

Harvey and his assistant deploy the direct instruction team as required by their plans. While certain kinds of teaching are done only by the
professionals within the team or the instructional support centers, all
team members, including the paraprofessionals, function in teaching
roles. The paraprofessionals, more often than the professionals, help the
children move from place to place, setting up equipment, and maintaining the environment as an attractive and efficient place. As they gain
experience and confidence, the paraprofessionals are able to carry on
more significant teaching.

SUPPORT CENTERS

Harvey's staff also includes professionals and paraprofessionals from six
instructional support centers. Together with parent volunteers they
form Harvey and Marge's extended staff. The staffs of each of these

FIGURE 13.2   Direct Instruction Teams and Support Centers.

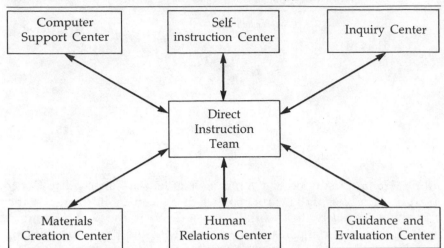

centers are specialists who create or organize instructional materials and programs and are available as consultants to members of the direct instruction teams. Let us look at the instructional support centers. (See Figure 13.2.)

Computer Support Center

In this center are specialists who apply computer technology to curriculum and instruction problems. They develop and adapt computer simulations and also automate programmed instructional materials created by others and used in the self-instruction center. They work with the diagnostic and counseling centers to automate diagnostic procedures and help the direct instruction team automate the scoring of objective tests in order to track the progress of the children. One computer support center serves about 20 direct instructional teams. For many applications, it uses a large computer which, in turn, is used by a great many computer support centers scattered throughout the region. The Agapé center includes two teachers who are specialists in computer-assisted instruction, several paraprofessionals, some of whom are computer programmers, and temporary personnel who are attached to the center for various purposes.

Self-Instruction Center

This center serves five or six direct instructional teams. It provides programmed materials and many self-instructional packets prepared by the staff in consultation with subject specialists and members of the direct instructional teams. It uses computer-based instruction for many purposes. These include self-instructional programs in mathematics and science that were purchased from commercial firms. It has developed packets of readings in various subject areas that are used in the nearby high school. Its staff is available to develop specialized materials for those direct instruction teams for which it is responsible, and its library is available for use by the direct instruction team. Sometimes children are taken there for extra work or special assignments and its staff helps monitor their progress. It is important that a self-instructional center has the capacity not only to adapt materials created by commercial firms and research agencies, but also to develop materials that serve the particular needs of the direct instructional team.

Inquiry Center

The inquiry center is a library in the most advanced sense of the word. It provides films, tape recordings, and other materials that children can use as they carry out their personal inquiry. It contains facilities for listening to tapes and records, for viewing motion pictures, film strips, and slide collections, and for retrieving data stored in the computer. The inquiry center staff contains professionals and paraprofessionals who help children use the facilities, who help shape their inquiry, and who are responsible for stocking adequate materials in each subject area. The staff also consults with members of the direct instruction teams in the development of instructional units and they sometimes participate as teachers. They give lectures and demonstrations to large groups and work with the team leaders to carry on inservice training programs for team members.

Materials Creation Center

The materials creation center is staffed by professional writers, artists, and audiovisual specialists responsible for creating visual and written materials tailored to the learning needs of the students in·the area. They work with the staffs of both the direct instructional teams and the independent inquiry centers. A direct instruction team together with a social studies specialist for example, may desire to create materials for a unit on one of the new nations of the world. They consult with the staff of the materials creation center to produce readable, new materials for all the children, including those with special needs. The materials creation center might develop projects on its own, but its primary purpose is to serve the needs of the direct instruction teams and the specialists in the independent inquiry centers. In so doing they free the school from dependence on commercial firms whose materials cannot be specifically keyed to local needs and interests.

TABLE 13.1
Instructional Support Centers

	Function	Staff	Serves
Materials Creation	Create visual/written materials Work with DIT Develop material for Inquiry Assist self-instruction center specialists Film preparation, e.g., current events newscast	2 media specialists 6 professional writers, artists, musicians (part-time)	20 DIT 3 self-instruction centers
Inquiry	Library/media center with books, tapes, records, film strips, slides Data storage and retrieval terminals Consult with DIT on resource units Large-group instruction assistance Assist in staff development Professional library	2 librarian/media specialists 2 specialists in humanities sciences 6 paraprofessionals	6–7 DIT
Self-instruction	Prepare self-instruction units in math, science, social studies, spelling, grammar, and high school science,	6 specialists in math science social science art	5–6 DIT elementary and high school specialists help in inquiry

Center	Functions	Staff	DIT
	mathematics, and social studies Assist DIT in unit development presentation	music children's literature 6 paraprofessionals 20 volunteers	10 DIT
Human Relations	Counseling Human relations training Diagnosing problems in social system in DITs Small-group organization Develop staff development programs Organizational development Quality Circles Problem solving	6 counselors 2 paraprofessionals	
Guidance and Evaluation	Diagnosis/prescription Create special tests and assessment devices Career charting (teachers, aides, interns)	4 counselor/evaluators 2 psychometrists 1 statistician	5–6 DIT
Computer Support	Computer simulations Programmed instruction Diagnostic development testing automation Support for all other centers	2 CAI specialists 2 programmers 2 paraprofessionals	20 DIT 5 inquiry centers 5 self-instruction centers 10 guidance centers 20 materials creation

Direct Instruction Term (DIT) = 200 students

Human Relations Center

The human relations center is staffed by professionals and paraprofessionals whose assignment is to provide counseling and human relations training to students and staff. For example, direct instruction teams might call on the human relations center to help diagnose and correct a cooperative learning problem within their student groups. A human relations expert might then be dispatched to work with a small group of children helping them to organize and work together more efficiently. Other children might be sent to the human relations center to work in a special program designed to increase their capacity and flexibility for interpersonal relations. The human relations center, however, is not a "life adjustment" factory, devoted to subordinating individuals to the interests of the group. On the contrary, it exists to help in human relations situations so that both group and individual learning needs are satisfied.

Guidance and Evaluation Center

This center works both with the computer support staff and with the human relations staff to help the direct instruction team diagnose and make prescriptions for individual progress. It creates special tests and other assessment devices. Their counselors work with children to identify intellectual growth, and to make prescriptions pertaining thereto. The guidance and evaluation staff does the test making for most direct instruction teams, although some teams prefer to make their own and rely on the center primarily for advice and technical assistance. (See Table 13.1.)

A DAY WITH A TEACHER

8 A.M., Oct. 22, some year in the future: Harvey convenes the meeting of his direct instruction staff to discuss two aspects of the educational program. One project involves the computer support center whose technicians have developed a model store in which the economic activities of the store are simulated. Harvey, his staff, and the computer staff are all engaged in creating a simulation that will teach their students the economic principles that operate as a store purchases goods, sets prices, creates advertising programs, and organizes its personnel. The students are to learn these principles by making decisions in a game-type situation. As they make decisions about the price of a product, they will receive feedback on sales and will be able to adjust prices, advertising, and other factors to see if they can increase the product's profit. While the program has been used successfully with older children, this is the first attempt to apply the technique to the seven-to-nine age bracket within this school district. Hence, one member of the evaluation center is observing the process and offering advice about the testing program. Also, the social science specialist from the independent inquiry center is working as an observer and consultant, because if the experiment works the material may have use there. During their meeting, Harvey and his staff selects 20 children for their trial run. If all goes well, the number of students who participate will gradually be increased. Although the instructional team has much help from the computer personnel, Harvey wants to proceed slowly so that his own team can train themselves to use the simulation effectively and to follow it up with other instruction outside the center. He also wants to give George some practice and a chance to explore further his interest in becoming a specialist in computer applications.

The other project that the direct instructional team discusses is their fine arts program. Using visitors, the local art museum, and specialists from the creative arts and humanities staffs of the high school, they have developed a unit on Renaissance art within the social studies program. Some of the staff have reported a total lack of interest in Renaissance art among the students. They arrange for one of the museum specialists, who believes she is having great success with the children, to hold a demonstration later that day so the staff can observe how she treats the content. Some of the team are dubious about the value of the unit in general, and Mary is assigned to discuss with the children their reactions to the program.

The meeting ends at 8:40 A.M. and Harvey prepares for a science discussion that he will lead at 9:00 A.M. Marge gathers Maureen, Tommy, and Joan about her and until 9 A.M. they discuss some of the problems they are having in the reading program.

9:00 A.M.: Harvey leads a discussion by 10 children of a science project. This group has built a static electricity generator and is conducting a set of experiments with it. Science is Harvey's own subject specialty, and he handles two project groups like this regularly, an advanced group (this one), and a group of rather difficult children whom he hopes to reach through their interest in science. Tommy observes Harvey during the discussion because he will be following up on what Harvey does during the rest of the week.

While Harvey's discussion goes on the rest of the team is deployed variously. Mary and Maureen lead a number of children to the independent inquiry center, where they help the children select books. Joan and Laura accompany another group of children to the self-instruction center, where the children are working through self-instructional materials to develop reading skills. This program was set up by Marge in consultation with the self-instruction support center. It is Joan and Laura's job to administer the program and to give such personal help as the students need. At the same time, Marge is working with a group of slow readers who have not been responding to self-instructional materials. She has developed an experience approach for them which tailors their activities to their specific needs.

George watches as the computer-assisted instruction technicians prepare the simulated store. Before the hour is over, Tommy leaves Harvey's discussion and sets up a large-group instruction room for a current events film which will be shown during the next hour to many of the children. This film has been created by the materials creation center in response to requests from several teams who were concerned that there were not sufficient materials available for current events instruction for children from seven to nine. They were concerned that many of the children of that age did not benefit either from commercial television newscasts or the weekly films prepared by local news agencies. Consequently, during this year the materials creation specialists are filming a short newscast each week and distributing it to the various direct instruction teams.

10:00 A.M.: Harvey and George are in the computer support center, watching their students operate the simulated store. The operation goes well. The children are able to cope with the problems they are given and are excited with the work. The experience is so positive that the decision is made to continue with that group on a regular basis and then expand its use to another group. Harvey makes arrangements to brief the computer staff on the social studies program that is the basis of the simulation. Harvey and George discuss ways of establishing relationships between the store game and the rest of the program. It is George's task to see that there is follow-up when the children get back under the wing of the direct instruction team.

Harvey also makes arrangements for two members of the computer support staff to bring the simulated store directly into the team suite after the trial period is over. He thinks the trials should be held in the center area, where he and the computer support staff can review and revise the materials. But when they are to be made a part of the social studies program and used on a regular basis, the simulation will be moved into the team suite.

Also, while he is there, Harvey discusses with the center director some new individualized developmental spelling programs that the director says have just come on the market. Harvey's students have been doing very well with these programs, and the director has informed him that if computer assistance is added to the program it could be used with teams throughout the school district. However, until computer assistance is obtained, the program is restricted to the use of Harvey's team and perhaps one other because evaluation of student progress is so laborious.

10:50 A.M.: Harvey watches the end of the discussions of the current events films being conducted by Laura, Marge, Joan, and Maureen. Joan has made a tape recording of her session so that Harvey or Marge can help her analyze and improve her teaching. It is a matter of team routine that each week members tape or videotape a lesson and then review it with another team member. Also, the team routinely makes videotape recordings of large-group presentations and then determines whether to place them in the file at the inquiry center for later use. Often, the team prefers to use videotape lectures or demonstrations because the same presentation can then be simultaneously used with different groups in various ways.

11:00 A.M.: Harvey spends most of the hour preparing a set of creative writing activities which will be used with most of the children in the instructional group. He and the team have decided that there has been too little spontaneous writing coming from the group, so they intend to try a set of stimulator activities to involve the children in creative writing. Harvey designs the activities so that all 200 children will be grouped into teams writing collections of poems, stories, plays, radio dramas, and a newspaper. Different members of the team will act as consultants for the various groups. The work of each student team will be used to stimulate the members of the other teams.

While Harvey prepares this unit, Marge and Maureen work with a small group of children making a videotape which will be used in the arithmetic program. The other members of the direct instruction team have children variously in the self-instruction center working on arithmetic programs, and in the independent inquiry center working on projects in the social studies. Four children have gone with Tommy to the human relations center where they have a session one day each week with one of the counselors.

12:00 noon: Harvey eats lunch with Mary and a small group of children. He and Marge have lunch with a different group of children each day so that every other week each child has an intimate and informal half-hour with one of the two team leaders. Mary accompanies Harvey because these children have recently transferred to the team from another school district. Her job is to make them comfortable and welcome, to get to know them, and to transmit any important personal information to Harvey and Marge. One of the girls was in the group which operated the simulated store that morning, and Harvey persuades her to describe to the others what she did and to tell them how she felt about it. This of course provides him with a child's-eye view of the simulation activity and as he listens he notes that she has not yet connected the work of the store with the remainder of the social studies program. After only one experience with the store, it is natural that gadgetry and its operation will fill her mind, but he thinks to himself that he must be careful to keep track of that aspect of the situation.

1:00 P.M.: Nearly all the children are engaged in small-group or individual activities. Many of them are in the self-instruction center, some are in the independent inquiry center. Marge and Laura each have a small remedial reading group gathered around them. Harvey and Tommy take this morning's science group with them to the independent inquiry center, where the children are hunting for materials for their next set of experiments. When he is satisfied that Tommy can handle the situation, Harvey returns to the team suite and prepares the large-group instruction area, where a member of the art staff will work during the next hour. He explains to the art consultant that the team has been having great difficulty with the Renaissance art unit. The art consultant agrees to make a demonstration tape of his discussion with a small group of children so that the staff can examine it. Also, since some of the staff's problems may be caused by their own inadequate knowledge of art, the consultant calls his office and arranges for another art specialist to observe during the small-group discussion period to see if he can get some idea whether the problem is with the teachers or with the choice of subject matter.

2:00 P.M.: Harvey listens to the art lecture and prepares to follow up with his small group. At the beginning of the unit, they used videotapes for the large-group meetings, but since the children did not respond actively, they decided to use live speakers for short periods of time followed by discussions, some of which would be held by the art consultants. Today, the art consultant has brought along a suit of armor and a set of weapons from the medieval period. Many of the boys in the group are enthusiastic. As Harvey observes the children's reactions he wonders whether it might not be best to concentrate more on the social life of the times, integrating art units like this with the social studies units, rather than treating the art by itself as they have attempted to do in this unit.

In the conference afterwards Harvey and the art consultants discover that they have simultaneously come to the conclusion that the Renaissance art unit is going extremely well with the older, more verbal students and not well at all with the others. With Marge, they come to a rapid decision to continue the program for one or two more days, and then, if their feelings are confirmed, to extend the unit with the students for whom it seems to be productive and create a completely different type of activity for the other students.

3:00 P.M.: For 20 minutes, half the team listens to and criticizes tapes or videotapes of lessons with the other half of the team. Harvey plays a tape of his morning science discussion, and Marge critiques it for him. They both notice that one child has contributed very heavily to the discussion session. Marge also questions whether the hypotheses the group set up were as well worded and explicit as they might have been. Harvey feels that their criticism is accurate, and they discuss ways that they can help sharpen their thinking.

3:30 P.M.: Over coffee, Marge conducts a meeting with the entire staff about the reading program. She has some suggestions for individual conferences, and has a report from the self-instruction center about the student's progress with word-attack skills. The team's objective is to get the children to teach themselves everything possible, thus freeing the instructional time for things they have difficulty teaching themselves. Marge has set up the reading programs so that nearly all of it takes place in individual conferences during which the children discuss their progress in using self-instructional materials and identify projects and readings for independent inquiry. Small groups are formed for remedial work and for the children who do not seem to work well by themselves. Mary's role is with the children who have trouble keeping themselves at individual learning tasks. Her tactics are motherly and supportive, whereas Marge is rather brisk and direct, and they try to plan so that they work with the children for whom their styles are most effective.

4:00 P.M.: All the team members are working independently, preparing for the next day. Harvey prepares the agenda for the meeting next morning when he will explain the creative writing unit and the staff will discuss it. He also prepares a mathematics lesson for one group of the older children. Marge finishes up correspondence for the team, (they share a secretary with another team) and George spends the hour with the computer support center planning the use of the simulated store the next day. Laura matches self-instructional reading units to student's needs during the next few days. Each day she does this for a certain number of children, so that each child's progress is revised by her or by Marge at least once every two weeks. Joan, Maureen, and Tommy are in the independent inquiry center, developing resource units to be used with the next set of social studies programs.

The Team and the Teacher

Harvey is a teacher with a large and complex staff of people who can do many things. He is not simply a master teacher—one who works better with children than anyone else or who knows his subject better than anyone else. Harvey is also a master at coordinating the work of other people and at developing curricular patterns that are tailored to the kinds of children he has, the community where they live, the requirements of the subject matter, and the large variety of instructional materials available. His staff includes the seven members of his direct instruction team plus the specialists within the various support centers. Harvey's staff provide an individualized education which blends each child's interests, needs, and personal problems with the best the age can provide by way of educational technologies. The direct instruction team members are the final decision makers in the educational process, so judgments about what each child will do and learn are made by the people who know him or her best.

KINDS OF LEARNING

Harvey and his team orchestrate an environment that uses three separate learning modes: (1) *personal inquiry*, where they pursue an interest of their own; (2) *independent study*, where they work with materials geared to their ability levels, and through the use of these materials learn to teach themselves; and (3) *group inquiry*, where they inquire into problems that are important to them and appear significant to their teachers. Let us look more closely at these three kinds of learning.

Personal Inquiry

Harvey and his staff help the children arrange their time so that a good proportion of each week is spent pursuing projects the children select and carry out alone or in small groups with help provided, as needed, by the teachers. For example, the students select books to read for pleasure but consult with the teachers about these. The teachers try to persuade each student to write or record something of personal significance every week, whether it be a story, essay, something dictated into a tape recorder, or something written for production by a group. The children pursue topics that interest them: one month they may study snails in great depth; another month they may read the poems of Robert Frost; yet another month they may study the history of baseball. Several times each week the students meet with one teacher and discuss their personal inquiry program and the resources needed to carry it out. If they need a book or a telescope, these can be found in the independent inquiry center. If they have trouble finding clay for a sculpture, the teacher will help them find it. Harvey's direct instruction team makes sure that each child has a well-developed inquiry program.

They try to build a social climate which encourages and supports individual inquiry of many kinds into many areas of life. Their role is to act as academic counselor to the children. Although the teachers have opinions about what would be productive for each child's personal inquiry, their teaching behavior is modulated to the students' frame of reference.

Independent Study

The student's independent study is at her own pace but toward goals she has in common with other children in the group. For example, each student needs to learn word-attack skills in reading and in spelling and the conventions of the standard grammar of her time. In the self-instruction center there are many programs and materials that each student can use independently as she works toward common goals at her own pace. She may learn spelling through programmed instruction, arithmetic with the help of a teacher through a basal text, phonics skills in a language laboratory. Progress will be monitored through tests which are imbedded in the instructional materials and scored by computers many miles from the school. The scores are interpreted by the teachers who have direct contact with her and adjust her program according to her progress and learning style. Because some students have difficulty teaching themselves, the teachers stand ready to help them directly. For example, Marge met with several small groups in reading. Some of these groups have difficulty learning to read by any means. Others are readers of considerable capacity but find it difficult to learn through programmed or other self-instruction materials. One of Harvey's abilities is the diagnosis of learning style and the arrangement of environment so that the independent study programs are matched to the learner.

Each instruction team, however, tries to promote a climate in which each student will take responsibility for her own learning. If a student has difficulty, the knowledge of that difficulty is shared with her and she is helped to develop and independent study program designed to meet her problem.

Group Inquiry

There are many things a person can teach himself if he has a guide and a friend and the assistance of good books and other study materials. But there are some things that are difficult to learn alone. It is no fun to debate the outcome of an election with yourself. Setting up hypotheses for an experiment is often better when they must stand up against competition. Putting on a play is rarely a solitary endeavor. The discussion of important ideas is necessary if your own understanding is to be improved. So, part of each student's day is spent working with a reasonably small group, usually from 5 to 10 children. These inquiry groups are formed at the beginning of the school year and changed as the year goes on. Their task is to determine things of common interest. Teachers make many suggestions. For example, each year there is an inquiry about something political because such inquiry is essential to the education of each student. Some of the inquiries take only a few days; some take weeks or months.

The student also studies as a member of a large group—through lectures, simulations, films. The purpose of such large-group study is to stimulate small-group inquiry, as in the case of the Renaissance unit that does not seem to be going well. The direct instruction team avoids large-group study for its own sake. If possible, a lecture is videotaped so that small groups or individuals can observe it. Similarly with demonstrations. Resource visitors are brought in for open questioning rather than for lecturing. If there is to be an information-giving session, the direct instruction team tries to get the visitor to tape record or videotape it.

Students do not engage in the same amount of personal inquiry, individual study, and group inquiry. Some individuals have such well-developed personal inquiry skills and individual study programs that the group part of their education is rather small. The opposite is true for others. However, the direct instruction team tries to keep some balance in the life of each learner among all three modes of learning. Even a student who is having difficulty with personal inquiry may develop that skill if he has sufficient exposure and counseling. Every child can be taught to learn some things through individual study. The fact that they have difficulty with group inquiry does not mean that they should be withdrawn from it entirely. It may mean that they need special instruction in handling themselves as members of a group.

The child, then, lives a balanced life as a learner. For personal inquiry he studies things that he selects and that are important to him, but with assistance from his teachers. In independent study he studies things that he understands will help him to develop in skill and in intellect. In group inquiry he works with his peers, thrashing out what is significant and how to learn it.

Harvey does not work alone. He has staff support and the best technological aids the age can provide. In addition, he is in a position to control technology—*he is not controlled by it*. And because his support centers have the capacity to create materials, Harvey is able to tailor the educational program to the needs of the child, the conditions in the community, and the nature of the academic disciplines.

MAKING THE DIMENSIONS OF EDUCATION EFFECTIVE

The students who relate to Harvey Thompson's team in the Agapé school are engaged in a variety of learning experiences that affect both the rate and quality of their learning. First, the overall social climate of the school supports:

1. *An orientation toward achievement.* Each student is expected to work hard and push toward their highest level of achievement.
2. *Cooperation.* Students are expected to help one another and to value one another's differences as well as similarities.
3. *Individual effort.* The school values each person's talents and generates a "you can do it" climate.
4. *Clarity of goals.* Each activity is explained to the children—they know what they are trying to learn and the entire staff works together to keep the goals clear.

Second, the school organization provides for individual differences. Students who are having difficulty receive personal attention. Students who are developing rapidly are given the opportunity to exploit their talents and to cover material quickly.

Third, each kind of instruction is carefully managed to ensure that:

1. Diagnosis is linked to instruction. Every effort is made to teach students "where they are."
2. Activities build on one another to bring about cumulative effect.
3. Student work is monitored closely and students receive regular information about their achievement.
4. Students are related to in a positive way.

These are the elements that ensure student learning whether we are creating new schools or tightening up the familiar old school around the corner.

DESIGNING SCHOOLS AROUND
DISTINCTIVE LEARNING EXPERIENCES

Let us stretch our imaginations a bit more as we attempt to combine our vast repertoire of teaching models with the power of multimedia informational and teaching systems. To sharpen the issue, let us visit another school of the future, this time a secondary school. Our school is not housed within a single building but is organized as a series of learning centers that occupy a variety of physical locations. These centers, which reflect the primary models of learning, are independently organized although they share some technical support systems. In fact, a general storage and retrieval system is designed so that students can retrieve information and engage instructional systems in several media both from their homes and from the learning centers.

The learning centers are designed to serve several major purposes which give their names to the respective centers as follows: *skills centers, academic centers, performing arts centers, social ecology centers,* and *idiosyncratic centers.* Let us consider these centers in turn. (See Table 13.2.)

1. *The skills center.* The skills center employs diagnosticians who assess a variety of basic skills (e.g. communications, mathematics, etc.) and then refer students to appropriate instructional systems and tutors. Whereas the younger students spend considerable time in the skills center, people of all ages periodically return to improve skills or learn new ones.

Media skills such as making and viewing films are as prominent in the center as are basic communication skills like reading and writing. Training in the use of multimedia instructional systems, information storage and retrieval systems, and diagnostic and management systems is also embedded in the center. The acquisition of these skills facilitates self-education and thereby complements the function of the idiosyncratic center. At the advanced levels seminars on form and substance, as well as training in the comparative analysis of media and symbol systems and their role in the culture, are pursued.

2. *Academic centers.* The academic learning centers are devoted to the humanities, aesthetics, sciences, and mathematics. Student groups join these for three types of courses. First are the survey courses in specific content areas, conducted by teachers with support from the instructional systems center. These are followed by inquiry courses in which students try out the specific modes of inquiry of the various disciplines. Finally advanced students work with academic tutors who help them construct plans of personal study and relate to groups of similarly advanced students. These centers are housed in laboratories that are especially constructed for the disciplines (as physics laboratories, art workshops, and so on) and are supported by the library and instructional systems centers in the same way as are the other centers.

3. *The performing arts centers.* Music, drama, television and film production, dance, athletics, and the other performing arts are housed in a network of laboratories, workshops, and little theaters throughout the community. Students use the performing arts centers in a variety of

ways, some for an initial survey experience, others for recreation, some for skill development, and others as a long-term expressive venture.

4. *The social ecology centers.* Social improvement is the objective of the social ecology center. It is organized to facilitate problem-solving groups who study social issues and problems, examine and improve their own interpersonal behavior, and learn to generate social action of various kinds. The library, data bank, instructional systems centers, and the academic center all provide support. The social ecology center employs a series of simulators and an information retrieval system based on the "social situation of planet Earth." An urban simulator supports the study of community problems, an international simulator aids the study of international problems, and an "earth resources" simulator is used to study biological support systems.

The teachers in the social ecology centers are group leaders skilled in human relations training and the use of teaching models that facilitate dialogue on social problems and the organization of social action. Students use of the social ecology center begins with neighborhood problems and face-to-face human relations and gradually expands into the study of ecology, urbanization, government, and the creation of an international community. The simulators enable them to study social processes and to try alternative modes of social behavior. Human relations exercises help them to explore ways of reaching out to one another and organizing themselves to improve day-to-day social life.

5. *Idiosyncratic centers.* These centers serve the students on their own terms. They are staffed with counselors who relate to students as equals, helping them formulate their goals and procedures. They help the students relate to a wide variety of part-time teachers—members of the community who serve largely on a voluntary basis as tutors, advisors, and teachers of short courses. In addition they help students relate to the other centers where other teachers and tutors can serve them.

The idiosyncratic centers are also supported by a multimedia library and data bank, most of which is automated. It employs microfiche and microfiche copying units that access virtually all the material available in the Library of Congress. This library also supports the activities of the other centers.

An instructional systems bank, comprised of various self-administering, multimedia instructional systems, also serves the centers. A modular plan permits students to select among the offerings and assemble sequences to serve specific purposes.

Thus, the idiosyncratic centers consist of counseling areas where students of all ages contact with counselors who help them define their

TABLE 13.2
Kinds of Learning Conditions and Purposes

	Interface	Content	Mode
Skills	Diagnosticians Tutors	Basic skills Communication skills: 　Media 　Viewing film 　Writing 　Reading	Tutorials Seminars Self-instruction Systems
Academic	Teachers Academic specialists Academic tutors	Humanities Aesthetics Sciences Mathematics	Survey courses Modes of inquiry/discipline 　courses Personal, self-guided study
Performing Arts	Teachers Coaches Critics Demonstrators	Skill development Music Drama Recreation Personal expression	Laboratories Workshops Little theatres Studios Playing fields

Social Ecology

Simulators
  Urban
  Internation
  Earth Resources
Retrieval systems
Social simulation

Television film production
Dance
Athletics

Social issues/problems,
  interpersonal skills
Generate social action
Biological support systems
Human relations exercises

Survey courses

Problem-solving groups

Library
Teaching strategies
Seminar groups

Idiosyncratic

Teachers/full- or part-time as
  counselors and facilitators
Community volunteers
  Tutors
  Resources
  Advisors
Short-course instructors
Librarians
Clerks

Personal goals & procedures
Relate to educational resources
  & support services
Modular offerings
Personal growth
Enhance individuality

Counseling areas
Library
Data bank
Tutorial services
Counseling
Evaluation

own goals and procedures and help them use the support services they need to achieve personal growth and enhanced individuality.

The school contains other learning centers, but those described thus far provide a sufficient idea of the concept behind the school. The primary goal of such centers is the student's acquisition of a variety of learning models that enhance further self-education. Learning centers and their support systems would always be changing to meet emerging educational needs while maintaining the supportive social system needed to provide stability for students. Although a comprehensive design is still in the future, we have discussed some of the elements needed in any flexible learning system of the future.

Distance Education

In addition to these local centers (other local centers could be devoted to the study of vocations, etc.), courses could be prepared by education centers at a great distance. Instruction could be accomplished by combinations of books, study packets, and broadcast and taped materials (TV lectures, demonstrations, documentaries, etc). The staff of the idiosyncratic center either provide or arrange for tutorial services and counseling and they administer evaluation.

Courses far beyond the capability of small local education agencies are thus made available to students. The best scholars provide instruction backed up by taped examples appropriate to each field (science experiments, plays, documentary films, etc.). Students can explore their interests and progress to very high levels in specialized areas, as well as gain exposure to a broad range of fields.

In our present schools, the teacher selects and implements the major learning experiences. In the kinds of school we have described here the teaching role is adjusted to fit particular educational goals and the teaching models and technology appropriate to them. Such an educational design is rarely encountered in this country.

Although we have had innovative schools, most of them have been build around particular philosophies and goals. An educational system in a pluralistic society requires a more complex view of schooling. Research theory and the development of instructional technology have given us the tools for improving and diversifying the learning experiences we offer. If we can learn to plan schools around learning centers tailored for particular educational missions, we will have reached a new level of educational technology. Until then we can improve the quality of our schools by helping educators expand their teaching repertoire through clinical training. In so doing, we can boost the probability that effective learning will take place.

It is well within our capacity to develop all the learning options described here and more. This compressed account is just a taste of what we can do.

We have presented these ideas not only to emphasize that the familiar form of the school is not our only option for deploying people and resources, but also to make as vivid as we can the specificity of purpose and method that makes for effectiveness in every school. Clear goals, a forceful social climate, careful diagnosis and provision for individual differences, the use of methods appropriate to the goals, and the enlistment of the students around the mission of the schools are essentials whatever educational philosophy dominates or however the school is organized.

14

Technology-Based Education Comes of Age

We continue our excursion into the school of the future, for that is what Stage Three school improvement is all about, with a brief look at some of the technological possibilities—what we will call *resource-based education*. Contemporary media and communication technology are expanding our educational possibilities and, potentially, the structure of our educational institutions, for example the open universities in England and Europe. The Responsible Parties need to know what technology is available and how it can be productively used. The massive impact of media in out-of-school applications make it an unavoidable fact of life for children and youth. Currently its greatest use is for entertainment rather than formal education, and unless its undeniable power is harnessed for education we are in danger of seeing a world in which the trivial, magnified by technology, may overwhelm the substantive which lives in out-of-date scholastic environments.

We have emphasized that school improvement can focus on (1) making current educational programs more effective, (2) bringing new content or teaching processes into the school, and (3) creating new institutional forms for education built around recent and emerging media.

In this chapter we will consider briefly the various media and technological forms that can be brought to bear on all of these levels of school improvement. Designers of better education have to reckon with them—*and* consider their weaknesses—and search for the most productive ways of combining them with human resources. For the solution is not to pit people against machines, but to use them in productive combination.

A century devoted to the rationale of technique was also a century so irrational as to open in every mind the real possibility of global destruction. It was the first century in history which presented to sane and sober minds the fair chance that

236

the century might not reach the end of its span. It was a world half convinced of the future death of our species, yet half aroused by the apocalyptic notion that an exceptional future still lay before us. So it was a century which moved with the most magnificent display of power into directions it could not comprehend. The itch was to accelerate—the metaphysical direction unknown. (Mailer, 1971)

Mailer's statement captures the paradox of our times. Technology, including our media of communication, teases us with the possibility of creating new and more satisfying ways of life. It promises to stretch our possibilities for personal growth and common action. As we seek to solve the problems of our cities, computer simulation helps us comprehend complex processes and reduce them to manageable terms. Concurrently, it frightens us by increasing our potential for violence and social control. The tendency to violence, for example, is magnified by broadcast television as it indiscriminately searches for plot lines and dramatic episodes. In education, technology increases the potential for both good and bad schooling. Trivial content, taught in a more powerful way, becomes menacing. Unfair testing practices—standardized, automated, and authoritatively administered—become nightmarish.

To find ways in which communication and technology can enhance society rather than exaggerating its defects is one of the major tasks in education. The fact that we have developed powerful communications media that can affect all aspects of our lives is not at issue. We have only scratched the surface in applying communications media to education. Media technologists in education generally feel that early efforts to use media in the classroom have been relatively unsuccessful. Experimenters, however, have continued to expand our educational possibilities through the development of open- and closed-circuit television, the creation of multimedia instructional systems, and the expansion of libraries into multimedia information storage and retrieval systems.

Many of these newer media developments have yet to touch the lives of the majority of students inside schools. One reason for this is that school environments have generally not been conducive to such developments. For example, most secondary schools are organized into sets of 45- to 50-minute time periods. Thus, educational films have generally been held to between 10 and 20 minutes, which barely leaves time to orient the students to the film, show it to them, and then have discussion afterward. Such constraint not only affects the kinds of topics that can be treated but also results in superficial treatment of complex topics. Despite some successes, closed circuit television has been very difficult to use in the classroom. As Guba and Snyder (1965) pointed out, broadcast television paces instruction, requiring teacher and students to accept the flow of the broadcast medium. Teachers, however, had their own flow of instruction and never learned to incorporate the mediated episodes into their curricular patterns. More exotic uses of the media, in which constraints of time and organization are ignored, have been infrequent. Elaborate game-type simulation, for example, is barely used at all, although wonderful simulations are available. Effective use, however, requires schools to change.

The application of communications media to education requires a general school design that both guides the development of alternative educational forms and creates a congenial institutional framework in which these forms can be applied. *The structure of the school is in many senses the medium of instruction*—it facilitates certain kinds of learning modes and inhibits others. The home, for example, has turned out to be a most suitable place for broadcast television at the nursery school level, as exemplified by the programs from the Children's Television Workshop (Palmer, 1974). Programs such as "Sesame Street" would not have nearly the effect they are having if there were not television sets in most homes and if parents were not delighted to have them occupy their children. The same programs have been used successfully in schools willing to put aside the time and to manage the pupils while they watch the programs.

Far and away the greatest application of media to education has been at the post-secondary level where complex skills such as those used in piloting airplanes, or in trades, or in graduate study are taught. However, enormous potential exists for resource-based learning at all levels of education. The only barrier is a lack of understanding about such resources and how they can be used. Among the topics that should be examined by the Responsible Parties are the following:

Categorizing learning resources

Organizing learning resources

Locus of control

Learner preparation

Tutorial support

Regulating attendance

Where resources can be used

Sponsors of resource-based learning

These concepts will provide us with a basis for examining alternative uses of resources within educational programs.

CATEGORIES OF LEARNING RESOURCES

As modern technology has concerned itself with the storage of information and the provision of instruction, the kinds of learning resources which have become available have increased considerably. Their function, however, is the same as the first set of written words or collection of cultural artifacts; that is, to provide information and instructions to the learner. As we consider the following resources it is important to remember that they can be brought together in various combinations to fit particular functions.

- Textbooks
- Workbooks
- Data storage and retrieval systems
- Audiotapes
- Videotapes
- Computer terminals and computers
- Broadcast and closed-circuit television.

Textbooks

Textbooks are the printed embodiment of a course. Students who have mastered a good textbook have "had" a course, although we would not want that to be their only experience with a curriculum area. However, if properly constructed a textbook can provide an orientation to a field, encompass basic information, suggest additional readings, and suggest activities to enrich the content. Textbooks provide guidelines for teachers as well as students, and structure many teacher-administered courses. From studies of teaching in the United States it is probably fair to say that nearly 90 percent of all instruction is guided by textbooks.

Workbooks

Most workbooks are produced in conjunction with textbooks although a well-constructed workbook can function independently. Workbooks are essentially guides to activities which the student can use to explore an area. In the laboratory sciences they direct the experiments and demonstrations which illustrate basic concepts. In other areas they are guides to projects and exercises which can be used to obtain information and skills.

Documents

Documents are sources of information. They can be organized in data storage and retrieval systems which students can use to find information. As indexes are prepared and microfilm and other devices for storing information are perfected, students can have access to enormous quantities of information about almost any conceivable topic. Encyclopedias provide summaries of information. Document storage systems provide raw data. Data storage and retrieval systems can be arranged for general use; that is, to provide the kind of information which in limited forms has been available in encyclopedias; or they can be specific to the needs of particular courses or topic areas. An elaborate set of storage and retrieval systems on social studies topics is described below.

Audiotapes

Audiotapes, with or without accompanying slides, filmstrips, or other audiovisual materials can provide most of the information which can be contained in textbooks or workbooks as well as original information in document form. Audiotapes can be used as supplements to workbooks and textbooks, or as the primary source of information within a course. It is possible, for example, to build a language laboratory around a storage and retrieval system of audiotapes or they can serve as learning resources in literature or drama courses. Cassettes can provide detailed instruction for laboratory experiments, can contain lectures, and, of course, can store the musical heritage of the society.

Videotape and Videodiscs

Videotape is an even more powerful learning resource than audiotape. Videotape libraries can provide students with sets of lectures and plays, concerts, laboratory and skill demonstrations, artistic and sport performances, and documentation of political, social, and economic events. Virtually our entire heritage of film is currently available on videotape. Mediated courses can now be made available to learners of every age who have available to them video cassette machines to use in conjunction with their television sets.

The newest addition to the technology in this area is the videodisc. The disc looks something like a record and can be produced relatively inexpensively. An interesting collaborative effort between the American Broadcasting Company and The National Education Association has produced 20 hours of programming for middle-grade students. These "schooldiscs" include segments focusing on language arts, social studies, the sciences, and the arts, interweaving basic skills with selected themes or concepts such as cause and effect, stereotypes, or careers.

Both videotapes and videodiscs offer a level of accessibility that broadcast television does not because they can be placed in random access systems for student use or can be used by teachers at times that are convenient to them.

Computers and Terminals

Using silicon chips, floppy discs, and audio-video cassettes, computers can now bring students a wide variety of media options. Textbook, workbook, document, audiotape, and videotape capability can be made available through computer terminals. In addition, computers can provide the management of instruction and simulations. A computer can guide students through a course or through units of a course, suggesting activities and providing feedback about performance. In the literature on computers, the terms *computer-assisted instruction* (CAI) and *computer-managed instruction* (CMI) are frequently used. Computer-managed instruction entails the use of a computer to lead the student through a course, coordinating textbooks, workbooks, documents, audiotapes, videotapes, and simulations with accompanying tests and feedback. Computer-assisted instruction utilizes the same type of capability but the student remains the manager of his instruction and the other media are coordinated at the student's option or programmed by the student's learning rate.

Broadcast and Closed-Circuit Television

The primary difference between the use of broadcast and closed-circuit television and videotape is in the timing and the possibilities for interaction between an instructor and students. Broadcast or closed-circuit television courses, for example, have to be given within relatively fixed schedules. With respect to lectures and demonstrations, virtually the same course can be stored on videotape for control by the student. Through telephone communication, however, it is possible for students to be linked to an instructor in a distant classroom who can answer questions or provide exercises to be done. An outstanding example of interactive communication use with broadcast television occurred in the "Cabinets in Crisis" experiment done by the Twenty-one Inch Classroom in Boston a few years ago. Programs such as "Inside/Out" and others from the Agency for Instructional Television have been used quite successfully as part of a regular classroom schedule, with the teacher using a guidebook to facilitate classroom previewing and follow-up activities.

These learning resources can be combined in various fashions. A course delivered over broadcast television can include the use of textbooks, workbooks, and documents; and sections of the course can be administered through computer control with audiotape or videotape components. Textbooks and workbooks can be supplemented by documents, audiotapes, and videotapes. A computer-managed course can use any of the other kinds of resources.

Word Processors

The editing capability of word processors can speed up and clarify certain aspects of writing instruction. For example, students can produce a writing sample, the teacher can make editorial suggestions, and the students can try to implement them, all on word-processing equipment. Because the word processor saves the time of copying over, the pace of instruction can be accelerated.

ORGANIZING LEARNING RESOURCES

With such an array of learning resources, information and instruction can be organized in a variety of ways.

The Course

Courses can be constructed with either fixed or flexible options for activities. For example, programs like "Sesame Street" and "The Electric Company" are designed primarily for use over broadcast television to large audiences whose only requirement for participation is access to a television set. A different kind of televised course can be provided through videotapes and accompanying reading materials that extend or enrich the course. Similarly a course could be organized around a textbook which the student administers to himself with accompanying workbooks and laboratory exercises, backed up by a storage and retrieval system of documents, audiotapes, and videotapes.

Modular Instruction

Instructional resources can also be organized in modular units, which permits students to obtain instruction on specific topics according to his or her needs. For example, many software packages for miniature computers contain a variety of instructional programs on financial, statistical, and mathematical operations. A student of statistics could select the particular modules (e.g., calculating averages) that he or she needs. In most curriculum areas a set of core modules dealing with basic concepts needs to be mastered before advanced concepts can be profitably studied.

Random Access

Perhaps the most striking feature of current media capability is that of organization into random access units of varying sizes. The data bases of various scholarly areas such as ERIC system for storing documents in education provide an example. It provided students in education access to research and descriptive documents. Except for broadcast of close-circuit television and for books, most learning resources can be organized for random access. Documents, audiotapes, audiotape and slide combinations, and videotapes can be organized as vast libraries to support independent study or to supplement courses. For example, at the University of California in Los Angeles students who explore film have available to them on film and videotape a library of more than 4,000 titles. Instructors can assign those films and the students can obtain the film and view them on their own time. Or, a student wishing to explore a certain aspect of film can call up relevant films, see them, and control the tape in order to study particular sections. In addition, videotapes and films are available to provide instruction in various aspects of film technology. Thus it is conceivable either to have an elaborate set of exercises accompanying an instructor-controlled course or for students to engage in equally elaborate individual exploration of the area.

LOCUS OF CONTROL

Learning resources can be controlled by students, teachers, or by the institution. In the ultimate student-controlled situation sets of courses are arranged, appropriate modules are organized, and information, demonstrations, films, etc. are made available so that students can assemble their own education. Nearly all well-developed individuals have engaged in large amounts of independent study, teaching themselves about complex areas without the aid of preorganized courses and units. The most important aspects of doctoral study have involved independent research using libraries and other sources of document. Doctoral students prepare themselves to a point of competence in their areas of specialty. Young students are also capable of considerable independent study. Ultimately students must educate themselves, and the media simply provides them with vastly greater resources than has ever been available before.

Learning resources can also be controlled by the teacher or a combination of teacher and student. The teacher can organize a course using textbooks, workbooks, documents, audio and visual tapes, and computer exercises, or can choose to work over broadcast or closed-circuit television. Written materials, audiotapes, videotapes, and broadcast television can provide the material which has ordinarily been contained in face-to-face lectures with the other media providing group and independent study and skill training. For example, a statistics course could be organized in the following manner. There could be a series of lectures contained in videotapes supplemented by workbooks that lead students through exercises with raw data. Data storage and retrieval systems could provide them with access to additional data bases for further practice. Videotapes could be used to provide discussions by statisticians about alternative ways of approaching problems and computer terminals could provide much of the skill training.

In some personal computer systems a single silicon chip contains the instructions necessary to learn most of the basic statistical techniques which are used in the social sciences. This chip can cost as little as $40 and provides more instruction than was available to any but the most advanced students only 20 years ago.

Also, institutions can provide mediated programs leading to vocational qualification or to university degrees. Perhaps the most outstanding example of institutional control of learning resources is the Open University of Great Britain.

LEARNER PREPARATION

A vital component of any education program is preparing students to use learning resources. A few years ago it would have sufficed to provide the secondary or college student with a tour of the library that included an introduction to the Dewey Decimal System and the Reader's Guide to Periodic Literature. Currently, if students are to use the resources available to them they need to learn not only how to use textbooks, workbooks, and traditional libraries, but also how to use data storage and retrieval systems, audiotapes, videotapes, and computer terminals, as well as how to relate to broadcast and closed-circuit television. Even very young students learn to use all of these resources. A student can receive instruction in reading through broadcasts like "Sesame Street," relate to a computer terminal to learn mathematics, use a videotape machine to see films of her own and foreign cultures, and explore essential documents. However, the learner must be prepared to use these learning resources effectively. In such a rich learning environment roles inevitably change. The teacher becomes an orchestrator and guide and the student becomes an organizer and synthesizer. The preparation of learners needs to be a gradual, thoughtful process that helps them not only manage the hardware but make increasingly wise decisions about their use.

TUTORIAL SUPPORT

Depending on the complexity of the learning task and the learner's readiness to engage in it, tutorial support is needed. Consider for example, a case in which a secondary student is taking a course in statistics. Through the extension services of a university the student has been given a textbook, a workbook, a data base of experimental findings, and a schedule of broadcast lectures and demonstrations. What are the ways that tutorial support can be provided? One is through the media itself. If the student completes exercises on a computer terminal, feedback can be received about the adequacy of the performance and additional instruction can be given. However, mediated instruction has its limitations. A human tutor can read and understand the problem better than any machine, and can provide specific assistance.

A second possibility for contact is through the mails. A student can mail in both completed exercises and questions in areas where help is needed, and a tutor can respond by return mail. A third possibility is to have tutors available for telephone interaction about critical points. Or, having created a test for a distant student, a tutor can call to provide advice and information.

Fourth, opportunities for face-to-face tutoring can be provided. The Open University identified tutors in various sections of the United Kingdom who could be contacted either at tutorial centers or by appointment in other places. At specified intervals students could come to the tutorial centers to discuss their problems and the tests that they had taken. In a school setting, face-to-face support is relatively easy to arrange. For example, in the skills center described earlier, primary and intermediate students can make appointments to receive assistance. In traditional classrooms, teachers provide tutorial support en masse and by appointment. The importance of the tutorial function is indicated by the finding that elementary school teachers provide such support in more than 50 percent of their activities. More often than not students come to them for help with assignments or they circulate among the students doing assignments. Providing tutorial support while students work with textbooks or workbooks is a familiar activity in schools.

Thus if we think of students working with a variety of learning resources within a core structure, it is possible for them to get support by mail, by telephone, or face-to-face, either in tutorial centers set up for that purpose or within traditional schools organized with that function in mind.

REGULATING ATTENDANCE FOR SUPPORT

How does the student make contact with tutorial services? One way is by appointment, a second is by class schedule, and a third is on demand within learning centers.

Attendance by Appointment

In one community people interested in learning how to pilot small sailboats have available to them a series of instructional modules. Modules familiarize them with the terminology of sailboating, impact the ability to read maps, are designed around navigation skills, and provide an understanding of the basic principles of piloting itself. Each of these modules utilizes textbooks, workbooks, and videotapes. An initial course is offered to orient students to the learning tasks required if they are to receive a pilot's license. They then have the option of attending classes in which instructors go over the materials, use boats to demonstrate the skills which are required, and provide supervision. Tutoring is available immediately after the regularly scheduled classes. Students who choose to study mainly on an independent basis can make appointments with tutors employed by the yacht club. These students are expected to master the material in the textbooks, workbooks, and videotapes as best they can and then to make appointments regarding questions they need to have clarified. In addition, tests of knowledge and performance are scheduled periodically so that students can obtain feedback about their progress and obtain assistance as it is required. In addition, there are several hours a week when instructors are in the yacht club area and students can get help on demand provided a tutor is available.

The same kinds of options can obtain within a school setting such as a language laboratory. A student wishing an introduction to the French language may elect to take a course. They then become responsible for reading the text, completing workbook activities, using the language laboratory which employs audiotapes, attending lectures and drill and practice sessions, and obtaining tutorial support during or after the sessions. Students opting to study primarily on their own with the aid of a study guide that coordinates the textbook, workbooks, and audiocassette materials, can obtain tutorial service in specified hours by appointment or on demand during scheduled periods.

Nearly all students find some need for tutorial services and it is important that technical support systems include provision for that. The sailboating example is a particularly clarifying one. Students may study terminology, and read about and see videotapes explaining how to operate a sailboat. The learning problem, then, is to transfer that information to the real sailboat. Most of us, either because we are insecure or because we cannot make the transfer from instruction to the demands of the sailing situation, will require the assistance of a tutor. It is important not to create instructional resources in an environment totally removed from human interaction. Even the most sophisticated computers cannot lead every person faultlessly through complex operations, and it is probably not desirable to attempt to stretch the computer to such capability.

WHERE DOES THE LEARNING TAKE PLACE?

Students can learn in a variety of locations: at home, in the classroom, in the library, in a resource center, or in a learning laboratory. In this chapter we are concerned with how to make learning effective in each of these environments. Let us consider the example of a student who wishes to complete a high school requirement. One option is to take a class at the local high school and another is to take a home-study course. In each case a library is made available as is a general resource center, one which provides multimedia learning resources. Clearly, the library and resource center can be one, but for purposes of analysis it is useful to consider them separately. Also, a learning laboratory can be set up in areas such as language study.

A broadcast course can be received over the home television, and at-home tutoring is possible via the telephone and the mail. Imagine a home equipped with audiocassette and videocassette play-back machines and a microcomputer. The student thus equipped can utilize audiotapes, videotapes, slides, and filmstrips, and thereby experience computer-assisted instruction, computer-managed instruction, and game-type simulations mediated through the computer in addition to the usual textbook and workbook assignments. If a course includes an elaborate package of all of those materials, then the home environment can be very rich indeed. Under such circumstances a well-developed, self-directed learner can go a long way toward self-instruction. In addition, tutorial support can be provided by appointment or on demand through the mail, over the telephone, or face-to-face.

Home and classroom instruction can also be combined. The student may go to class for lectures and demonstrations, and engage in independent home study using all of the above options. The student could add tutorial support with face-to-face interviews with tutor or instructor. In technical areas it is usually worthwhile for students to work in learning laboratories. Language laboratories, for example, can provide more detailed instruction and explicit feedback than is possible through microprocessors, and at advanced levels of the hard sciences laboratory equipment is essential.

CABLE-BASED NETWORKS

Forward-looking communities are exploring the potential for cable television to generate new educational opportunities. Consider the following plan by one city of about 60,000 population to install two coaxial cable systems, one with 108 home channels, some of which provide two-way communication, the second with 54 two-way channels connected to government, civic groups, businesses, and industries.

This system will be able to offer courses, informational programs, and continuing education from all the sources we have been discussing, including schools and colleges. In addition, subscribers will be connected to data storage and retrieval systems, to news services, and to specialized staffs providing up-to-date information on areas as diverse as stock prices and airline reservations. It will make possible the development of information systems using videotext (printed information on the screen) and will provide access to large computers for subscribers who have their own terminals.

Potentially such networks provide numerous ways that schooling can be improved. Much wider ranges of courses can be provided than the traditional elementary or high school can offer, and many traditional offerings can be improved in many ways.

1. English courses can be augmented with drama presentations, readings, and lectures on special topics. Students can read assignments and ask for tests when they are ready.

2. Science courses can be augmented with lectures, demonstrations, and tests. The student can see experiments beyond the scope of those possible in the traditional school laboratory. Presently very few elementary teachers are competent to teach science. Upgrading in this area could be significant.

3. Social Studies students can study city government as it happens as well as having available vast numbers of documentary films correlated with their curriculum.

4. Athletic instruction can be augmented by expert coaches demonstrating techniques and explaining how to acquire them.

5. In the arts, the possibilities are extensive. Ballet, modern dance, architecture, sculpture, and painting can all be studied in community workshops and galleries. In addition, it will be possible to design courses with in-school and out-of-school components each using media

as appropriate. For example, students could see a writing technique demonstrated and explained via television at home and then practice the technique in school with direction and tutoring by the instructor. Similar applications could be made in painting, sculpture, dance, etc.

As the Responsible Parties consider future goals, strategies, and resources for their schools, they will see that institutions other than schools can also sponsor learning activities. Today many states provide self-instructional courses that students can use to prepare themselves for high school diplomas. Industries offer in-service education through mediated courses. State universities offer courses for college credit. Obviously schools have many options. A high school student may take a course developed by a community college or university far from where he lives, using their resources. The student would thus be connected with his local institution only insofar as he wished to have the credit accepted for a diploma or other credential. These services can be used quite satisfactorily to provide advanced courses for gifted students.

Accrediting agencies and trade organizations may also offer courses. An example is the set of courses in sailboating which we described earlier in which a local yacht club assembled courses developed by others and offered them as part of the club's licensing function. Private agencies are also increasingly turning to resource-based learning. Students preparing to be artisans or accountants may go to schools where varying degrees of the learning is resource based.

What the Responsible Parties will do with the array of possibilities depends largely on their social vision. That we have such alternatives is itself a product of committed persons with vigorous and clear notions of what our social life should be and what the role of education should be in that society.

15

The Spectrum of School Missions

Schools like Agapé discussed in Chapter 13 are not made casually. They come into existence only after careful consideration of the various purposes the school might seek, of available technologies, and most important, of alternative approaches to teaching and staffing. As the Responsible Parties mature they increasingly reflect on alternative school missions and the means of achieving them. In this chapter we provide a framework from which to begin that considerable task.

The possible functions of education are so numerous that the task of identifying them can be bewildering without some form of analytical structure. This structure should enable us to generate the central, unifying objectives the school will strive for—it is those central objectives that focus the efforts of the school and, hence, form its mission.

The mission of the school can be defined in terms of how it enters into the lives of students. Formal education is an organized attempt to enter into and change students' lives to help them develop the capacity to respond to reality in new ways. The primary task in selecting the mission of the school is to identify how the school can enter the lives of students in order to change their responses to living in the world.

We begin our analysis by identifying the following three areas or domains of student development, each of which can be greatly enhanced by organized schooling.

1. *The personal domain*—involves such personal capabilities as intelligence, creativity, and motivation.
2. *The social domain*—involves interactive social and economic skills.
3. *The academic domain*—involves the skills that comprise an academic subject area such as mathematics or English.

Let us now use these three categories to sort out the various functions of the school, and to generate combinations of functions that can serve as the missions or guiding objectives of school programs. We begin by looking a little more closely at each of these domains.

THE PERSONAL DOMAIN

The human organism is equipped in various ways to respond to its environment. It has intelligence, including the ability to solve problems, to analyze and synthesize information, and to build new ideas. It has creativity, or the capacity to do new and interesting things with its environment. It has an organized inner self with feelings of adequacy and openness and with the ability to grow and to face complexity. There is independence or autonomy, the capacity to respond fearlessly and on one's own terms. There are feelings of affiliation and warmth that permit comfortable and nonthreatening responses.

A school can direct its functioning at one or more of these human capacities. It may emphasize creativity, for example, and shape itself so as to promote a creative, aesthetic response to life. It may organize itself around the attempt to increase intelligence and rationality or it may seek ways of increasing the personality development of the individual.

A school that sees its mission as the development of personal capacity will emphasize the individual in everything it does. It will try to challenge students, to free them, to teach them how to teach themselves. Such a school will pay attention to social and academic demands, but it will concentrate on the personal capacity of the individual.

Various educational theorists have advocated interesting ways of improving the learner's general capacity to deal with the world. Let us look briefly at six types of functions that have been advocated within the personal domain together with the names of leading theorists.

Alternate Functions within the Personal Domain

1. Develop the self. There are various views of this; see Fromm (1956), Rogers (1951), Maslow (1962), and Combs (1949).
2. Develop productive thinking capacity, including creativity flexibility, ability to produce alternatives. See D. Hunt (1971), Torrance (1965), Rokeach (1960).
3. Develop a personal meaning. See Fromm (1956), Phenix (1964), Dewey (1916).
4. Develop problem-solving ability and flexibility. See Thelen (1961), Bruner (1955), Hullfish and Smith (1961), D. Hunt (1971).

5. Develop aesthetic capacity. See Santayana, Ducasse, Dewey (1916), Eisner (1982).
6. Develop motivation to achieve. See Atkinson (1966), Hansen (1962), Bloom (1971).

1. *Develop the self.* In recent years a large number of educators and psychologists, many of them from the phenomenalist school of personal psychology, have stated that a central mission of education should be the development of a strong self—the creation of a person who feels adequate and who reaches out warmly to others. These theorists believe that the principal function of the school lies in helping the child find and develop a healthy self—one with great capacity for personal and social development. Education should help students find direction rather than impose it on them.

2. *Develop productive thinking capacity.* Creative problem-solving, the ability to produce alternatives, the capacity to integrate material into new forms—these are seen by some as the primary mission of the school. Theorists like Torrance, Taylor, and Thelen view creative thinking as the school's primary goal and psychologists like Hunt, Rokeach, and Wertheimer have studied the characteristics of creativity and the kinds of environments that stimulate it.

3. *Develop a personal meaning.* Other theorists have emphasized the capacity to respond to others—to seek the common cause and to avoid alienation. Writers like Fromm and Phenix have described the process by which people discover themselves and find meaning in a social world. In so doing, they have defined another possible focus for the school.

4. *Develop problem-solving ability and flexibility.* Another possible focus is the student's capacity to solve problems and to plan and organize independent lines of inquiry. We find this emphasis in the writing of Dewey, Holt, Hullfish and Smith, and Neill, among others. The view of intelligence as problem-solving ability has been spread through recent popularizations of Piaget's work. The view that intelligence is malleable rather than fixed has increased the plausibility of focusing directly on intelligence as a primary mission of the school.

5. *Develop aesthetic capacity.* Quite a different approach is to focus on the aesthetic capacity of students to change their perception of beauty and their motivation to create beauty in their physical and social environments. In the works of Ducasse, Eisner, Santayana, and again, Dewey, we can find this type of approach.

6. *Develop motivation to achieve.* Another distinctive approach is to arouse students' desire to improve themselves—to master knowledge and skills. Described by the psychologists McClellan and Atkinson

among others, we find this approach recommended by educators like Hanson (1962). We can also see it in the philosophy behind many compensatory education programs which frequently arouse the desire of the inner-city children to develop themselves more fully.

We have identified six types of personal development that can give focus to a school program and, in each case, some of the supporting theorists or researchers. All six probably sound worthwhile to the reader, and any one of them could serve nobly as the driving mission of a vigorous school. Yet, they represent only a few of the possible focuses of a school program and only one or two of them have actually been the focus of more than a handful of school programs.

Next we shall consider a different set of school functions, this time focusing on the interaction of learners with their society.

THE SOCIAL DOMAIN

There are as many ways to structure schooling toward social objectives as there are toward personal objectives. And, of course, personal and social development can be seen together. The attempt, for example, to develop creative thinking might be done with respect to social improvement. Similarly, the attempt to focus on personal problem-solving ability might be combined with a focus on cooperative problem solving. The approach to personality development outlined by the psychologists Harvey, Hunt, and Schroder (1961) describes the intellectual capacity to deal with complexity while simultaneously dealing with interpersonal relations integratively. Hence, their structure provides a way of looking at intellectual and interpersonal complexity together.

The following list outlines six approaches to social intervention. As with our previous list of personal objectives, they represent only a few of the possibilities, and when combined with those personal objectives, just begin to describe the alternatives a school can seek.

Alternative Functions within the Social Domain

1. Enculturation—socializing students to their culture and transmitting their cultural heritage.
2. Develop internationalism and social activism.
3. Develop cooperative problem-solving—democratic-scientific approach, political and social activism.
4. Develop economic competence and social mobility.
5. Promote nationism.
6. Improve human relations—increasing affiliation and decreasing alienation.

A brief description of each of these options follows.

1. *Enculturation.* Schools do this, of course, when they consciously teach students society's dominant norms and values and the meaning of their cultural heritage. This is the most common way in which schools try to affect social relations. By inculcating a common set of norms and values they reduce cultural diversity and thereby the potential for social conflict.

2. *Develop internationalism and social activism.* Schools can direct students toward a life of service and social activism. For instance, in one school the children are continually involved in social work from the middle elementary years, and many of them take part in political activities, including those of international organizations. This, of course, reflects the focus of that particular school. In the work of Kenworthy (1955), Preston (1956), and Becker (1979) we can see such a determination.

3. *Develop cooperative problem solving.* Yet another societal focus sees the school directing students toward cooperative problem solving. Schools were to be operated as a miniature democracy in which young citizens would learn the arts of cooperative inquiry and how to apply the scientific method to social problems that interested them. John Dewey was the formal spokesman of this view. Today we find it, in quite different forms, in the work of Thelen (1962) and others. This view has recently emerged in schools with an emphasis on social activism as in some of the experimental schools of Washington, D.C. and other cities.

4. *Develop economic competence and social mobility.* Still another objective might be the development of economic independence. Schools with this view emphasize skills and knowledge that are essential for economic survival and development. This is a more common mission for technical middle schools and high schools than it is for elementary schools, although many people see reading and arithmetic as the central elementary school subjects because of their potential economic usefulness.

5. *Promote nationalism.* The schools of many nations attempt to direct the education of students toward nationalistic ends. In William L. Shirer's *The Third Reich* (1960) we have an excellent description of the program to induct the youth of Germany during the 1930s into the service of the state. Today we can see the emphasis in less extreme forms in the schools of many nations.

6. *Improve human relations.* Social education can also be directed at the improvement of human relations. Such a mission characterized the school improvement program of the Wilmington, Delaware public schools in the late 1950s and early 1960s under the direction of Muriel Crosby (1965). The philosophy of the Bank Street School (1950) reflected

this same emphasis, and we can see it in the work of Shaftel (1967) and Taba (1966), among others.

Many people feel today that one of the central missions of urban schools should be to combat the alienation of mass society and to help people find meaning and affiliation within the emerging "brave new world." Although there is still no powerful theoretical statement on this position, the work of Durkheim (1896), Jackson (1966) and Kenniston (1963) are worth consulting.

THE ACADEMIC DOMAIN

We turn now to focuses that have their origins in the academic disciplines. These are characterized by the attempt to teach students ideas and techniques that have been developed by scholars. This is the predominant focus in most contemporary schools. Mathematics is taught with the belief that the mathematicians' way of thinking and calculating will be useful in the life of the learner. The same can be said about history and historical thinking. Science content is taught and, less frequently, the systems of thinking employed by scientists. Foreign languages, literature, and social science are sometimes taught, and in rare instances, aesthetics, ethics, and humanitarian philosophies.

The accumulated knowledge of the human race is increasingly concentrated in the hands of professional scholars. Not only in the humanities, sciences, and social sciences is knowledge systematically produced at an explosive rate, but many pursuits that were at first the result of practical imagination (such as marine architecture and agriculture) have become the objects of systematic scholarship. The larger universities presently provide offices for people studying just about every conceivable human activity. The elementary school is the student's first formal link with this scholarly activity. It can consciously function to make the scholarly world accessible to them and to prepare them for a life-long relationship with scholarly material.

Many people share the view that the elementary school should find its primary functions in the academic domain. Some see academic learning as the route to all development in all domains—they tend to brand any other function as anti-intellectual and therefore bad. Others, however, are increasingly concerned with the complexity of the modern world and see the scholarly disciplines as the key to handling it conceptually.

Increasingly, we find the view that there is nothing fundamentally incompatible among the personal, social, and academic domains. Before considering a reconciliation of the three domains, however, we should discuss a few alternative academic missions available to schools. The following list contains five possible academic objectives.

Alternate Functions within the Academic Domain

1. Emphasize general symbolic proficiency—reading, writing, arithmetic, technical methods.
2. Emphasize information from selected disciplines—history, geography, literature, etc.
3. Emphasize major concepts from the disciplines.
   a. treat broad, related fields together (social studies, language, arts, science).
   b. treat a few disciplines separately (i.e., economics, physics, history, music).
4. Emphasize modes of inquiry.
   a. treat theory building and scientific method.
   b. treat knowledge creation within a few, selected disciplines.
5. Emphasize broad, philosophical schools or problems— aesthetics, humanitarian issues, ethics.

Let us now examine each of these in turn.

1. *Emphasize general symbolic proficiency.* By far the most common academic mission is to transmit the technical and symbolic systems that we use to communicate. That is to say, reading, writing, and arithmetic receive the greatest emphasis in today's elementary schools, especially in nursery, kindergarten, and primary school years. In the middle grades map skills, study skills, information-location techniques, summary writing, and other skills are added.

In recent years there has been a resurgence of interest in foreign languages for elementary school children—not as literature and rarely (in practice) to develop cross-cultural understanding, but chiefly for oral and sometimes written proficiency. Usually this is simply an extension of the popular symbolic-systems mission of the school, although the matter is confused by the fact that achievement of a foreign tongue confers certain kinds of prestige in America.

The fact that the technical-symbolic mission is so well established and is so likely to be accepted as one of the primary missions of the school encourages us to minimize its discussion. However the importance of academic objectives both in today's schools and in those of the future should not be underestimated.

2. *Emphasize information from selected disciplines.* A less dominant, but equally common approach to elementary education has been the attempt to present a broad overview of many fields. If one examines middle-grade science textbooks, for example, one finds small sections

introducing an enormous quantity of topics. Or, in the social studies, the common practice is to hit the high spots of the political history of the United States or the Western world, and the general economic geography of the contemporary world. In mathematics, the tradition has been to cover the fundamental processes and related ideas.

The justification for this broad approach has been that elementary students need a store of background information into which they can delve in later years. The school functions to provide them with the basic information and skills that they will use later when their study becomes more deeply academic. Hence, by acquainting them with the broad outlines of governmental functioning, we prepare them for the serious study of political behavior during high school. In a sense, therefore, the broad approach is seen as preparation for later academic study.

3. *Emphasize major concepts from the disciplines.* Since the publication of Jerome Bruner's influential book (1961) much emphasis has been placed on the organizing concepts within academic disciplines. Bruner's thesis is that within each discipline there is a network of ideas that contain the major relationships within the field. For example, sociologists use ideas like *norms, sanctions,* and *roles* to describe what has been learned about small groups. Hence, if we were to follow Bruner's structural principle, we would build a course on small groups around these ideas. In mathematics, one would teach the fundamental operations (addition, subtraction, multiplication, division) in such a way that the ideas or principles that control those operations were revealed and used to organize the material. In science, biology courses would be organized around ideas like *structure* and *function* that unify the content, whereas units on machines would be held together with ideas like *force, mechanical advantage,* and so on.

Bruner's statement of the advantages of the structures' principle has been taken seriously by many of the leaders of the academic reform movement. Following Bruner's lead, curriculum developers in several areas are using the structural principle. For example, grammar and spelling courses are organizing around principles from linguistics. Even reading programs are being developed using phonetics, linguistics, and semantics as the source of unifying ideas. Bruner sees four advantages in this approach:

1. The structural ideas provide a conceptual map of the field that aids memory. The learner, in a sense, has an organizing structure on which to hang incoming information.
2. The student who masters the structural ideas has a sense of control over the discipline that is not yielded by factual coverage alone.

3. Organizing concepts provide a basis for applying learning to practical situations. One has the ideas needed to manipulate information in problem-solving situations.
4. Organizing concepts are what the scholar uses. By teaching them to students, we enable them to think using the same tools that the advanced scholar employs. This will undoubtably lead to more scholarly careers.

These ideas are so attractive that they have dominated much of the academic reform movement of the last 25 years. To summarize things three types of missions are available that involve teaching the organizing ideas of disciplines: to develop cognitive complexity; to provide cognitive maps, and to induce scholarly careers. For the Responsible Parties, the question is how much emphasis should be placed on teaching the organizing concepts of the various disciplines because of some intended effect on the students.

4. *Emphasize modes of inquiry.* A discipline can be conceived as a community of discourse, a place where a community of scholars explores some domain and builds, expands, and revises knowledge about that domain. On the growing edge of the disciplines, knowledge is being revised and reconceptualized at a rapid rate. It is here that the methods of the real scholars are being employed in the struggle to increase knowledge and understanding or to create something new. Many people feel that the methods used to create new knowledge, what we term the *modes of inquiry,* provide the most useful content for students. For as students learn how knowledge is produced, they will learn what knowledge is—they will grasp the revisionary character of the constructs that scholars create in order to understand and manipulate the world.

Also, it is argued, present information and concepts are rapidly going out of date. What we teach students now may well be seen as untrue by the time they reach maturity. But the ways in which scholars work are more durable, and they enable one to keep up better with what is going on. Further, if students are led into the experimental edge of a discipline they will learn its most fundamental ideas—the ones that are used to guide current inquiry—and they will be led into the discourse by which knowledge is held and revised. They will, in a sense, be made a part of the community of scholars. Also, it is argued, the methods of scholarship are problem-solving methods of high utility. If one learns how to develop, revise, and check out hypotheses, then one has a tool to apply to all problems throughout one's life. Hence, the most valuable part of the disciplines (viewed this way) is the part that deals with inquiry.

Several experimental curriculum projects have employed this approach in developing their materials. For example, the American Association for the Advancement of Science has developed procedures that introduce primary-grade children to the processes by which scientists collect and organize data, build ideas, and revise them. In a University of Illinois project, one elementary school has selected a single science, astronomy, and developed an extensive set of units designed to teach students how the astronomer works. The child is taught much geometry, for example, in order to apply it to investigations like those the astronomer performs.

In the social sciences, Lippitt and Fox (1969) of the University of Michigan have developed programs that introduce students to social science. Students learn to make observations, to organize them, and to build concepts from them. They learn how to make inferences and to distinguish inferences from value judgments. They are presented with scientific reports that are written from accounts of real experiments in social science.

So far, there have been a great many attempts to teach the organizing concepts of the disciplines, but very few attempts to teach the processes involved in developing and revising knowledge. It should be noted, however, that the theory of the Progressive Movement emphasized students learning the scientific method by carrying out projects and solving problems that they were interested in. Throughout the writings of Dewey, Kilpatrick, and Counts, and, more recently, in the writings of Thelen, and Miel, we find the assumption that the child learns the disciplines through practicing them. Practicing them means engaging in the activities the scholar uses when attempting to solve problems. The progressives, however, permitted students to develop their own problems. The teacher, knowing the discipline, would lead the child to develop control over scientific or scholarly processes and knowledge while pursuing the problem.

Many current curriculum reformers seem to be unaware of this aspect of the Progressive Movement and dismiss it as one devoted entirely to the individual and societal domains. The reason for this is to be found partly in the political aspects of the Progressive Reform Movement, which so often involved an attempt to make education more relevant to the child and the needs of society, that the academic issues were often eclipsed.

5. *Emphasize broad philosophical schools or problems.* A possible but little-used mission of the school would be to help children approach the aesthetic, ethical, and humanitarian philosophies of the time. We see this approach recommended for higher education, as in the writings of Robert Hutchins, Harold Taylor, and others, but it has never caught on

as a central focus of our elementary and secondary schools. Religious schools, of course, have attempted to inculcate particular philosophical positions, but a general philosophical approach in public education is rare. Some of the flavor is present in the Quaker Schools of Philadelphia and in a few of the old English schools, but we still know very little about it as a possible approach to education.

SELECTING THE MISSION OF THE SCHOOL

As indicated in the introduction to this book, the ordinary patterns of schooling seem so obvious and normal that consciously developing strong, well-thought-out missions for each school is a task that has not come naturally to the Responsible Parties. Hence, among the multitude of schools in this country today there is relatively little diversity.

Creating a sense of mission for a school, however, is a complex and difficult task. It involves answering serious questions regarding the school's general focus and specific objectives.

- Which of the personal capacities of the individual will be focused on?
- How much emphasis will be given to social considerations and human relations?
- What will be the emphasis within the academic domain?

For a fully rational approach to these questions, the position of Ralph W. Tyler (1950) has much to recommend it. Tyler suggests that the selection of school objectives should be made only after serious study of the students, the society, and the academic sources of content. The recent volumes of the Project on Instruction (1963) of the National Education Association have taken much the same position, recommending that the Responsible Parties engage in a continuous study of student, society, and subject matter and continually revise and refocus the objectives of the school.

For the Responsible Parties to do this effectively, they must augment themselves with specialists on child development, societal analysis, and the academic disciplines. They need to provide themselves with expert advice on the various ways that these domains can be analyzed, and as the school matures it needs to develop ongoing procedures for continuing and deepening the study of relevant factors.

If this is not done the school will tend to drift with the winds of educational fads. For an example of this, let us look at recent developments within the academic disciplines. For many years science teaching within the school was of the "kitchen cabinet" variety, with children and teachers experimenting with materials and phenomena that were near at hand. Most science teaching experts felt that the student gradually exploring his environment should be helped to employ the scientific method, that is, to build theories and discover the concepts of the sciences inductively. In actuality, very few teachers felt competent to teach science, and consequently, the area languished in most schools. In recent years, academic scholars have begun to recommend that the methods of the scientists—their modes of inquiry into phenomena—be made the center of the curriculum and that science instruction be rather formal and direct in teaching inductive and deductive procedures. Recognizing the lack of teacher preparation in science, these scientists are attempting to build *teacher proof* teaching materials that even poorly prepared teachers can easily administer. Throughout the nation, schools are adopting these materials because it is the current doctrine to do so. Now, the materials may have a beneficial effect on the students—that is not the question at issue here. The point is that faddism is not a proper basis on which to make a serious curriculum change. To avoid faddism, however, the Responsible Parties need to be quite sophisticated about the alternatives that are available to them.

When developing the central mission of the school, the Responsible Parties will want to take into account the conditions of the local community and the characteristics of the children who are likely to make up the school population. The mission for a Bohemian, intellectual community might be very different than that for a middle-class suburb, for example, and the task of the school for a foreign-speaking population in a rural area would likely be different than that for a polyglot urban community. A school for the gifted might seek different ends than a school for the culturally disadvantaged, and so on.

The mission of the school might be defined in terms of only one function, as in the case of Summerville. Or, it might be quite eclectic and seek to include functions from all three domains. In any event, the educational purpose of the school should be sharply etched and strong. It should select from the thousands of desirable objectives the few that are to give focus and character to the local school program. A realistic, well-defined focus will support the development of educational means that are coherent and strong and are likely to generate a momentum that will accomplish many other objectives as well. The example of the traditional English public schools is instructive. Drawing as they did from the upper classes, they made character, honor, and self-reliance their watchwords. These schools came to stand for those objectives. A new student was quickly swept up in them and in turn passed them on to younger students. Put pedantically, the schools had a clear function around which it was relatively easy to develop a coherent program.

SCHOOLS WITH ASSIGNED MISSIONS

For many years the organizers of large urban school districts have experimented with the deliberate creation of secondary schools that have a special mission in addition to their responsibilty for general education. Some schools have specialized in science and technology, others in the visual and performing arts, and so on. Students with a special interest can attend the school whose mission fits their preferences.

The development of *magnet schools* arises from a variety of political and social concerns that we will not explore here (see Estes, 1977, for a rationale). What concerns us is that the magnet school concept clarifies the opportunity that Responsible Parties have to examine the purpose of their school and the shape of its environment. To simply assign some cultural or vocational area as the special focus of the school does not by any means complete the job of identifying its mission. Many possible emphases should be considered within each curriculum area, whether the sciences, the arts, or a vocational cluster. There are also many possible means to consider—in content, teaching strategies, technologies, evaluation, and so on.

What is different about a magnet school is that it serves a large area. The community and administrative representatives within the Responsible Parties organization need to relate to the community and school district as a whole and to reflect its diversity. Also, the district administration needs to ensure that several groups of planners are in close communication with one another. A very complex organizational process will result, but one with exciting potential. The technical procedures for selecting missions and means is the same as for planning a new school, but must be "floated" in an intricate political context.

ALTERNATIVE SCHOOLS AT ALL LEVELS

Magnet schools provide one way of providing alternatives within large school districts. In recent years a number of other methods have also been used in large and small school districts, even within schools, to accommodate different visions of education and different student populations. For example, some parents wish their schools to be highly disciplined with tightly controlled curriculums and evaluation plans. Some of these wish to promote a basic education with no frills. Other parents wish their school environment to be student centered, open-ended, and to nurture the students' creativity. Sometimes the preferences are a matter of goals (basic skills *or* creativity) and sometimes a matter of means. Some school districts have responded by providing alternative models of schooling in separate schools or even under the same roof.

Similarly, alternatives have been generated because students are different. Some have a preference for highly structured tasks. Some require considerable independence. Others are disinterested in school, except for their areas of personal interest. As in the case of magnet schools, alternative schools have been developed seeking a variety of missions and employing a variety of approaches to education.

The legitimization of the idea that there *are* viable alternatives is an opportunity that should be capitalized on to bring more people into the decision-making process. Again, it requires intricate planning to organize decision-making groups to think out a variety of missions and clarify preferences for means as well as to implement them. But the effort, properly managed, should increase the vitality of the decision-making process. Also, many current decisions are made on the basis of unexamined opinions—some people "know" what they like, but have not really considered the alternatives. Many are unaware that different methods are good for different purposes, or that the student may thrive best in a school that provides a variety of environments. The reflective analysis of alternative missions and means may help many people develop a more balanced perspective and a deeper understanding of their intuitive preferences.

Epilogue: Social Vision and the Improvement of Schools

This book is classically American in the down-home, fundamental sense of the term. Its ideas reflect our style, the idealistic side of our heritage and the dilemmas of our urges to change and yet remain the same. It is built on the outrageous assumption that we can actually study a basic social institution, make improvements in it despite habit and tradition, and even change it radically when needed. This optimism flies in the face of much that we know about the difficulties of cultural change and our past failure to bring about lasting innovations in curriculum and teaching.

The ideas presented in this book are not new, merely a new blend of the ideas and beliefs that Americans have produced over the past two centuries as we have sought for a powerful and humane education that will preserve our society, make it better, and free the energy of our children. Whatever the arguments about the specific elements of his educational methods, the spirit is clearly captured by Dewey's understanding that if we are to have a democracy we must educate ourselves for it; that education makes a difference in the conduct of social and personal life and must reflect our ideals rather than our defects.

Also typically American is our belief that the schools belong to the people, an ownership that finds its most powerful expression in the local community. The reciprocal of this belief is the obligation that local citizens have to become active and thoughtful participants in the overall governance of their schools and in the educational process within them. The home, the school, and the student must march together. We are distressed by the glassy homogeneity of our schools and think we can express our diversity in educational alternatives that lie within the common ground of our heritage.

We believe in strength through diversity, expressed around a common cultural core. We do not fear social division along cultural lines

264

but reaffirm the tradition that seeks to draw the best from all our heritages and integrate them for the common good. Cultural difference enhances us and does not endanger us. We believe we are committed and flexible enough to embrace variety and be strengthened by it.

Our belief in planning is another part of our ideational armament. Part of the vision is that vigorous local planning prevents domination by any central core, however wise and benevolent. Planning is our unique genre, the expression of our pragmatism. We do not like to leave things to change but believe that we can select goals and find means of achieving them. We resist automatic solutions to problems in the belief that we can create options beyond the reach of present practice.

However, even the most carefully planned change is difficult. We recognize that we have to earn every small increment of improvement in education. We are our own worst enemies in the battle for effective schools, for habit and traditional practice become ingrained and threaten to submerge any innovation, however sensibly it is presented. Implementation of even small improvements requires intensive effort.

Although we are often accused of being excessively pragmatic, of being interested only in the efficient means to immediate goals, we have an abiding love of knowledge and a belief that education enhances the quality of human existence. Our society has a love-hate relationship with intellectuals, alternating between a suspicion of the "ivory tower" and a near-reverence of the scholarly. The tie is inescapable, however, and schooling is the channel not only to advanced inquiry, but to a balanced understanding of the role of scholarly knowledge in the life of everyone. The love of learning is what is central—reaching beyond our present conceptions.

A corollary is an appreciation of talent, an understanding that interesting minds bring us new creations and understandings, and richer aspirations as well. Along with that, we have an appreciation of the handicapped—a belief that all children have the talent and the right to live productive lives.

We believe in teachers and refuse to be intimidated by talk of burnout and retrenchment. We value the lives of teachers both for their own sake and because the lives of our children depend so much on the growth of their mentors.

All of this leads those of us who labor in education to continue our struggle for schools that will be more effective. We believe that we already possess a rich heritage of alternative models of curriculum and teaching and that we can become effective users of them as well as the inventers of new ones. In short, we are infected with the "can do" attitude of the cockeyed optimist.

BIBLIOGRAPHY

Adams, R. S., and B. J. Biddle. 1970. *Realities of Teaching: Explorations with Video Tape*. New York: Holt, Rinehart & Winston.

Allen, D., and F. T. McDonald. 1967. *Training Effects of Feedback and Modeling Procedures on Teaching Performance*. Report (OE–6–10–078) to the United States Office of Education, Stanford University.

Allen, D., and K. Ryan. 1969. *Microteaching*. Reading, Mass.: Addison-Wesley.

American Association for the Advancement of Science. 1963. *The New School Science; A Report to School Administrators on Regional Orientation Conferences in Science*. Washington, D.C.: American Association for the Advancement of Science.

Amidon, T., and J. Hough. 1967. *Interaction Analysis*. Reading, Mass.: Addison-Wesley.

Ammons, Margaret. 1961. "Educational Objectives: The Relation between the Process Used in Their Development and Their Quality." Unpublished doctoral dissertation, University of Chicago.

Anderson, Digby C. 1981. *Evaluating Curriculum Proposals*. New York: Wiley.

Anderson, Harold H., and Helen M. Brewer. 1939. "Domination and Social Integration in the Behavior of Kindergarten Children and Teachers." *Genetic Psychology Monograph*, 21:287–385.

Anderson, Harold H., and J. E. Brewer. 1946. *Studies of Teacher Classroom Personality II*. Stanford, Calif.: Stanford University Press.

Anderson, R. B. 1977. "The Effectiveness of Follow Through: What Have We Learned?" Paper presented at the annual meeting of the American Educational Research Association, New York.

Anderson, R. B., R. G. St. Pierre, E. C. Proper, and L. B. Stebbins. 1978. "Pardon Us, But What Was the Question Again?: A Response to the Critique of the Follow Through Evaluation." *Harvard Educational Review*, 48:161–170.

Anderson, Ronald H. 1976. *Selecting and Developing Media for Instruction*. Madison, Wisc.: American Society for Education and Development.

Anderson, Scarvia, ed. 1972. *Sex Differences and Discrimination in Education*. Worthington, Ohio: Charles A. Jones.

Airasian, Peter W., Thomas Kellaghan, and George F. Madaus. 1979. "Concepts of School Effectiveness as Derived from Research Strategies: Differences in the Findings." ED 192 456.

Apple, Michael. 1979. *Ideology and Curriculum*. London: Routledge & Kegan Paul.

Argyris, Chris. 1957. *Personality and Organization*. New York: Harper & Row.

———. 1960. *Understanding Organizational Behavior*. Homewood, Ill.: Dorsey Irwin.

———. 1971. *Management and Organizational Development: The Path from XA to YB*. New York: McGraw-Hill.

Argyris, Chris, and D. Schon. 1974. *Theory into Practice: Increasing Professional Effectiveness*. San Francisco: Jossey-Bass.

Arnheim, Rudolf. 1974. "Virtues and Vices of the Visual Media," in *Media and Symbols: The Forms of Expression, Communication and Education*. The Seventy-third Yearbook of the National Society for the Study of Education. David R. Olson, ed. Chicago: University of Chicago Press, 180–210.

Asch, S. E. 1952. "Effects of Group Pressure on the Modification or Distortion of Judgments" in *Readings in Social Psychology*. Guy F. Swanson, Theodore M. Newcomb, and Eugene L. Hartley, eds. New York: Holt, Rinehart & Winston.

Atkinson, John. 1966. *Achievement Motivation*. New York: Wiley.

Austin, Gilbert R. 1979. "Exemplary Schools and the Search for Effectiveness." *Educational Leadership*, 37(1):10–12.

Ausubel, D. 1963. *The Psychology of Meaningful Verbal Learning*. New York: Grune & Stratton.

Averch, Harvey A., Stephen S. Carroll, Theodore S. Donaldson, Herbert J. Kiesling, and John Pincus. 1971. "How Effective is Schooling? A Critical Review and Synthesis of Research Findings." Santa Monica, Calif.: Rand.

Baldridge, J. Victor, and Terrence E. Deal. 1975. *Managing Change in Educational Organizations*. Berkeley: McCutchan.

Ball, Samuel, and Gerry Ann Bogatz. 1970. *The First Year of Sesame Street: An Evaluation*. Princeton, N.J.: Educational Testing Service.

Bandura, Albert, and Richard H. Walters. 1963. *Social Learning and Personality Development*. New York: Holt, Rinehart & Winston.

Banks, James A. 1981. *Multiethnic Education: Theory and Practice*. Boston: Allyn & Bacon.

Barron, Frank. 1963. *Creativity and Psychological Health: Origins of Personal Vitality and Creative Freedom*. Princeton, N.J.: Van Nostrand.

Bates, Tony. 1980. "Applying New Technology to Distance Education: A Case Study from the Open University." *Educational Broadcasting International*, 13(3):110–114.

Becker, James M., ed. 1979. *Schooling for a Global Age*. New York: McGraw-Hill.

Becker, W. C. 1977. "Teaching Reading and Language to the Disadvantaged— What We Have Learned from Field Research." *Harvard Educational Review*, 47:518–543.

Becker, Wesley, and Douglas Carnine. 1980. "Direct Instruction: An Effective Approach for Educational Intervention with the Disadvantaged and Low Performers," in *Advances in Clinical Child Psychology*. B. J. Lahey and A. E. Kazdin, eds. New York: Plenum.

Becker, Wesley, Siegfried Endlemann, Douglas W. Carnine, and W. Ray Rhine. 1981. "Direct Instructional Model," in *Making Schools More Effective: New Directions from Follow Through*. Ray Rhine, ed. New York: Academic.

Bellack, Arno A., and Herbert M. Kliebard, eds. 1977. *Curriculum and Evaluation*. Berkeley, Calif.: McCutchan.

Bellack, Arno, Herbert Kliebard, Ronald Hyman, and Frank Smith. 1965. *The Language of the Classroom*. New York: Teachers College Press.

Ben-Peretz, M. 1975. "The Concept of Curriculum Potential." *Curriculum Theory Network*, 5(2):151–59.

Bereiter, C., and S. Engelmann. 1966. *Teaching Disadvantaged Children in the Preschool.* Englewood Cliffs, N.J.: Prentice-Hall.

Bereiter, C., and M. Kurland. 1978. "Were Some Follow Through Models More Effective Than Others?" Paper presented at the annual meeting of the American Educational Research Association, Toronto. Ontario, Canada.

Berliner, David C. 1975. *Federal Programs Supporting Educational Change: A Model of Educational Change,* 1, #41589/1. Santa Monica, Calif.: Rand.

———. 1979. "Tempus Educare," in *Research on Teaching: Concepts, Findings and Implications.* Penelope L. Peterson and Herbert J. Walberg, eds. Berkeley, Calif.: McCutchan.

Berman, Paul, and Milbrey McLaughlin. 1978. *Federal Programs Supporting Educational Change: A Model of Educational Change, Vol. VIII: Implementing and Sustaining Innovations.* Santa Monica, Calif.: Rand.

———. 1976a. *Federal Programs Supporting Educational Change: The Process of Change,* 3, #R1589/3. Peter W. Greenwood and Dale Mann. Santa Monica, Calif.: Rand.

———. 1976b. *Federal Programs Supporting Educational Change: The Findings in Review,* 4, #R1589/4. Santa Monica, Calif.: Rand.

———. N.d. *Federal Programs Supporting Educational Change, Vol. X: Executive Summary.* Santa Monica, Calif.: Rand.

Berman, Paul, and E. Pauly. 1975. *Federal Programs Supporting Educational Change, Vol. II: Factors Affecting Change Agent Projects.* Santa Monica, Calif.: Rand.

Bernstein, B. 1970. "Education Cannot Compensate for Society." *New Society,* 26:344–347.

Bettelheim, Bruno. 1982. *On Learning to Read: The Child's Fascination with Meaning.* New York: Knopf.

Beauchamp, George A. 1975. *Curriculum Theory.* Wilmette, Ill.: Kagg.

Bissel, J. S. 1973. "Planned Variation in Head Start and Follow Through," in *Compensatory Education for Children, Ages 2 to 8.* J. S. Stanley, ed. Baltimore: Johns Hopkins University Press, 63–101.

Bloom, B. S. 1976. *Human Characteristics and School Learning.* New York: McGraw-Hill.

———. 1971. "Mastery Learning," in *Mastery Learning: Theory and Practice,* James H. Block, ed. New York: Holt, Rinehart & Winston.

———. 1981. "The New Direction in Educational Research and Measurement: Alterable Variables." Paper presented at the annual meeting of the American Educational Research Association, Los Angeles.

———, et al. 1956. *Taxonomy of Educational Objectives, Handbook, I: Cognitive Domain.* New York: David McKay.

Boocock, Sarane, and E. O. Schild. 1968. *Simulation Games in Learning.* Beverly Hills, Calif.: Sage.

Borg, W. R. 1970. *The Mini Course.* Beverley Hills, Calif.: Macmillan Educational Services.

———. 1973. "Research and Development as a Vehicle for Improving Teacher Competence." Paper presented at the annual meeting of the American Educational Research Association, New Orleans, ED 076 584.

————, and Marjorie Kelley, Philip Langer, and Meredith Gall. 1970. *The Minicourse.* Beverley Hills, Calif.: Collier-Macmillan.

Boud, David, ed. 1981. *Developing Student Autonomy in Learning.* London: Kogan Page.

Bradford, L. P., J. R. Gibb, and K. D. Benne. 1964. *T-group Theory and Laboratory Method.* New York: Wiley.

Brandwein, Paul F. 1981. *Memorandum: On Reviewing Schooling and Education.* New York: Harcourt, Brace Jovanovich.

Brookover, W., et al. 1977. *Schools Can Make A Difference.* College of Urban Development: Michigan State University.

Brookover, W., John H. Schwitzer, Jeffrey M. Schneider, Charles H. Beady, Patricia K. Flood, and Joseph M. Wisenbaker. 1978. "Elementary School Social Climate and School Achievement." *American Educational Research Journal,* 15(2):301–318.

Brophy, J. E. 1979a. "Advances in Teacher Effectiveness Research." Paper presented at the annual meeting of the American Association of Colleges of Teacher Education, Chicago.

————. 1979b. "Teacher Behavior and Its Effects." *Journal of Teacher Education,* 71:733–750.

————. 1979c. "Advances in Teacher Research." *The Journal of Classroom Interaction,* 15(1):1–7.

————. 1982. "Successful Teaching Strategies for the Inner-city Child." *Phi Delta Kappan,* April:527–529.

Brophy, J. E., and C. Evertson. 1981. *Student Characteristics and Teaching.* New York: Longman.

Brophy, J. E., and T. Good. 1970. "Teachers' Communication of Differential Expectations for Children's Classroom Performance: Some Behavioral Data." *Journal of Educational Psychology,* 61:365–374.

————. 1974. *Teacher-Student Relationships: Causes and Consequences.* New York: Holt, Rinehart & Winston.

Broudy, H. S., and J. R. Palmer. 1965. *Exemplars of Teaching Method.* Chicago: Rand McNally.

Brown, George I. 1964. "An Experiment in the Teaching of Creativity." *School Review,* 72:437–50.

Brown, Mary, and Norman Precious. 1968. *The Integrated Day in the Primary School.* London: Ward Lock International.

Bruner, Jerome S. 1961. *The Process of Education.* Cambridge, Mass.: Harvard University Press.

————. 1966. *Toward a Theory of Instruction.* New York: Norton.

————. 1980. *Under Five in Britain.* London: Grant McIntyre.

Bruner, Jerome S., Jacqueline J. Goodnow, and George A. Austin. 1967. *A Study of Thinking.* New York: Science Editions.

Buber, Martin. 1958. *I and Thou.* New York: Scribner's.

Campbell, Roald F., Luverne L. Cunningham, and Roderick F. McPhee. 1965. *The Organization and Control of American Schools.* Columbus, Ohio: C. E. Merrill.

Cantor, Nathaniel. 1956. *The Dynamics of Learning.* Buffalo, N.Y.: Henry Stewart.

Cates, C. S., and S. Ward, eds. 1979. *Dissemination and the Improvement of Practice: Cooperation and Support in the School Improvement Process.* San Francisco, Calif.: Far West Laboratory for Educational Research and Development.

Cates, C. S., P. D. Hood, and S. McKibbin. 1981. *An Exploratory Study of Interorganizational Arrangements that Support Improvement.* San Francisco, Calif.: Far West Laboratory for Educational Research and Development.

Chamberlin, Charles Dean, and Enid Straw Chamberlin. 1942. *Did They Succeed in College?* New York: Harper & Row.

Charters, W. W., Jr., et al. 1973. "The Process of Planned Change in the School's Instructional Organization." Center for the Advanced Study of Educational Administration, University of Oregon, Eugene, CASEA Monograph, no. 25.

Charters, W. W., Jr., and J. Jones. 1973. "On the Risk of Appraising Non-Events in Program Evaluation," *Educational Researcher,* 2(11):5–7.

Charters, W. W., Jr., and R. Pellegrin. 1973. "Barriers to the Innovation Process: Four Case Studies of Differentiated Staffing." *Administrative Science Quarterly,* 1:3–14.

Clark, D. L., and E. G. Guba. 1977. *A Study of Teacher Education Institutions as Innovators, Knowledge Producers, and Change Agents.* Bloomington, Ind.: Indiana University. ERIC (ED 139 805).

Clark, D. L., S. McKibbin, and M. Malkas, eds. 1980. *New Perspectives on Planning in Educational Organizations.* San Francisco, Calif.: Far West Laboratory for Educational Research and Development.

Cline, M. G. 1974. *Education as Experimentation: Evaluation of the Follow Through Planned Variation Model: Early Effects of Follow Through.* Cambridge, Mass.: Abt Associates.

Cohen, M., V. Koehler, L. Datta, and M. Timpane. 1981. *Instructionally Effective Schools* (Research Area Plan). Washington, D.C.: National Institute of Education.

Coladarci, T., and N. L. Gage. 1981. "Minimal Teacher Training Based on Correlational Findings: Effects on Teaching and Achievement." Paper presented at the annual meeting of the American Educational Research Association, Los Angeles.

Coleman, James S. 1963. *The Adolescent Society.* Glencoe, Ill.: The Free Press.

Combs, A. W. 1965. *The Professional Education of Teachers: A Perceptual View of Teacher Education.* Boston: Allyn & Bacon.

Combs, A., and D. Snygg. 1949. *Individual Behavior.* New York: Harper & Row.

Connelly, F. M., and M. Ben-Peretz. 1980. "Teachers' Roles in the Using and Doing of Research and Curriculum Development," *Journal of Curriculum Studies,* 12(2):95–103.

Connelly, F. M., and F. Elbaz. 1980. "Conceptual Bases for Curriculum Thought: A Teacher's Perspective," in *1980 Yearbook, Association for Supervision and Curriculum Development.* A. Foshay, ed. Alexandria, Va.: ASCD: 95–119.

Connelly, F. M., and R. Enns. 1978. *Shaping the Contracting Curriculum:*

Principles, Problems and Solutions. Report of the Task Force on Curriculum, Commission on Declining School Enrollment, Ministry of Education, Toronto.

Coombs, Philip H. 1968. *The World Educational Crisis.* New York: Oxford University Press.

Corey, Stephen M. 1953. *Action Research to Improve School Practices.* New York: Teachers College, Columbia University Press.

Coulson, John E., ed. 1962. *Programmed Learning and Computer-Based Instruction.* New York: Wiley.

Counts, George S. 1932. *Dare the School Build a New Social Order?* New York: John Day.

Cremin, L. 1961. *The Transformation of the School.* New York: Knopf.

———. 1965. *The Genius of American Education.* Pittsburgh: University of Pittsburgh Press.

Crosby, Muriel. 1965. *An Adventure in Human Relations.* Chicago: Follett.

Crowther, F. 1972. "Factors Affecting the Rate of Adoption of the 1971 Alberta Social Studies Curriculum for Elementary Schools." Unpublished master's thesis, University of Alberta.

Cumming, John, and Elaine Cumming. 1962. *Ego and Milieu.* New York: Atherton.

Cyert, Richard M., and James G. March. 1963. *A Behavioral Theory of the Firm.* Englewood Cliffs, N.J.: Prentice-Hall.

Davis, James E., and Frances Haley. 1978. *Planning a Social Studies Program: Activities, Guidelines, and Resources.* Boulder, Colo.: Social Science Education Consortium.

Denham, C., and A. Lieberman, eds. 1980. *Time to Learn: A Review of the Beginning Teacher Evaluation Study.* Washington, D.C.: National Institute of Education.

Dewey, John. 1910. *How We Think.* Boston: D.C. Heath.

———. 1916. *Democracy and Education: An Introduction to the Philosophy of Education.* New York: Macmillan.

———. 1920. *Reconstruction in Philosophy.* New York: Henry Holt.

———. 1960. *The Child and the Curriculum.* Chicago: University of Chicago Press.

Dickerson, Laurel, and William H. Pritchard, Jr. 1981. "Microcomputers and Education: Planning for the Coming Revolution in The Classroom." *Educational Technology,* January:7–12.

Dienzeide, H. 1974. "Educational Technology for Developing Countries," in *Media and Symbols: The Forms of Expression, Communication and Education.* The Seventy-third Yearbook of the National Society for the Study of Education. David R. Olson, ed. Chicago: University of Chicago Press, 429–469.

Dillon-Peterson, B., ed. 1981. *Staff Development/Organization Development.* Alexandria, Va.: Association for Supervision and Curriculum Development.

Dornbusch, S. M., and W. R. Scott. 1975. *Evaluation and the Exercise of Authority.* San Francisco: Jossey-Bass.

Dow, I., and R. Whitehead. 1980. *Curriculum Implementation Study.* Funded by Ontario Public School Men Teachers' Federation.

————. 1981. *New Perspectives on Curriculum Implementation*, Ontario Secondary School Teachers' Federation.

Downey, Lawrence. 1966. *The Secondary Phase of Education*. Waltham, Mass.: Blaisdell.

————, and Associates. 1975. *The Social Studies in Alberta-1975*. Edmonton, Alberta: L. Downey Research Associates.

Doyle, Walter. 1977. "Paradigms for Research on Teacher Effectiveness," in *Review of Research on Education, Volume 5*. L. Schulman, ed. Itasca, Ill.: F. E. Peacock, 163–198.

————. 1979. "Making Managerial Decisions in Classrooms," in the *78th Yearbook of the National Society for the Study of Education*. Daniel Duke, ed. Chicago: University of Chicago Press, 42–74.

Doyle, Walter, and G. Ponder. 1977–78. "The Practicality Ethic in Teacher Decision-Making." *Interchange*, 8:1–12.

Dreeben, Robert. 1968. *On What Is Learned in School*. Reading, Mass.: Addison-Wesley.

————. 1973. "The School as a Workplace," in *Second Handbook of Research on Teaching*. R. M. W. Travers, ed. Chicago: Rand McNally.

————. 1978. "The Collective Character of Instruction." Invited address to the annual meeting of the American Educational Research Association.

Ducasse, Curt John. 1944. *Art, the Critics, and You*. New York: O. Priest.

Duckworth, K. 1981. *Linking Educational Policy and Management with Student Achievement*. Eugene, Ore.: Center for Educational Policy and Management, University of Oregon.

Duke, D. L., B. K. Showers, and M. Imber. 1980. "Teachers and Shared Decision Making: The Costs and Benefits of Involvement." *Educational Administration Quarterly*, 16:93–106.

Duncan, M. J., and B. F. Biddle. 1974. *The Study of Teaching*. New York: Holt, Rinehart & Winston.

Dunnette, M. D. 1976. *Handbook of Industrial and Organizational Psychology*. Chicago: Rand McNally.

Durant, Will, and Ariel Durant. 1968. *The Lessons of History*. New York: Simon & Schuster.

Edmonds, Ronald. 1979a. "Effective Schools for the Urban Poor." *Educational Leadership*, 37(1):15–18, 20–24. EJ 208 051.

————. 1979b. "Some Schools Work and More Can." *Social Policy*, 9(5):28–32.

Edwards, J. A. 1959. *A Treatise Concerning Religious Affections*. John E. Smith, ed. New Haven: Yale University Press.

Eisner, Elliot W. 1979. *The Educational Imagination: On the Design and Evaluation of School Programs*. New York: Macmillan.

Elmore, R. 1980. *Complexity and Control: What Legislators and Administrators Can Do about Implementing Public Policy*. Washington, D.C.: National Institute of Education.

Emmer, E. T., and C. M. Evertson. 1981. "Synthesis of Research on Classroom Management." *Educational Leadership*, January: 342–346.

Erikson, Erik. 1950. *Childhood and Society*. New York: W. W. Norton.

Estes, Nolan, and Donald R. Waldrip, eds. 1977. *Magnet Schools: Legal and Practical Implications*. Piscataway, N.J.: New Century.

Fantini, M. D. 1973. *Public Schools of Choice.* New York: Simon & Schuster.

Fenton, Edwin. 1967. *The New Social Studies.* New York: Holt, Rinehart & Winston.

Fetts, Paul M. 1962. "Factors in Complex Skill Training," in *Training Research and Education.* Robert Glaser, ed. Pittsburgh: University of Pittsburgh Press, 172–98.

Fisher, Charles, and David Berliner, et al. 1980. "Teaching Behaviors, Academic Learning Time, and Student Achievement: An Overview," in *Time to Learn.* D. Denham and A. Liebermann, eds. California Commission for Teacher Preparation and Licensing, 7–32.

Flanders, N. 1970. *Analyzing Teacher Behavior.* Reading, Mass.: Addison-Wesley.

Flesch, Rudolph. 1955. *Why Johnny Can't Read—And What You Can Do about It.* New York: Harper & Row.

Foltz, Karl, and Margaret Foltz. 1966. *Cybernetic Principles of Learning and Educational Design.* New York: Holt, Rinehart & Winston.

Foshay, Arthur Wells, ed. 1980. *Considered Action for Curriculum Improvement.* Washington, D.C.: Association for Supervision and Curriculum Development.

Freire, P. 1970. *Pedagogy of the Oppressed.* New York: Herder & Herder.

Friedenberg, Edgar B. 1965. *Coming of Age in America: Conformity and Acquiescence.* New York: Random House.

Fromm, Erich. 1941. *Escape from Freedom.* New York: Farrar & Rinehart.

———. 1955. *The Sane Society.* New York: Rinehart.

———. 1956. *The Art of Loving.* New York: Harper & Row.

Fullan, Michael. 1980a. "Evaluation and Implementation," in *Evaluation Roles.* A. Lewy, ed. Gordon Breach.

———. 1980b. "School Focussed In-Service Education." Centre for Educational Research on Innovation, Organization for Economic Cooperation and Development (OECD), Paris, France.

———. 1981. "School District and School Personnel in Knowledge Utilization," in *Improving Schools: Using What We Know.* Rolf Lehming and Michael Kane, eds. Beverly Hills: Sage.

Fullan, Michael, and K. Leithwood. 1980. *Guidelines for Planning and Evaluating Program Implementation.* Prepared for the Ministry of Education, British Columbia, Canada.

Fullan, Michael, and P. Park. 1980. *Curriculum Implementation: A Resource Guide.* Ontario Ministry of Education, Ontario, Canada.

———. 1981. *Ontario Curriculum: 1981,* Ontario Teacher's Federation, Ontario, Canada.

Fullan, Michael, and Alan Pomfret. 1977. "Research on Curriculum and Instructional Implementation. *Review of Educational Research,* 47(1):335–397.

Fullan, Michael, ed. 1972. "Innovations in Learning and Processes of Educational Change." *Interchange,* 3:23. The Ontario Institute for Studies in Education. Ontario, Canada.

Fund for the Advancement of Education. 1967. *Profiles of Significant Schools.* New York: The Ford Foundation.

Gage, N. L., 1970. *Teacher Effectiveness and Teacher Education.* Palo Alto, Calif. Pacific Books.

————, et al. 1974. "Teacher Training Products: The State of the Field." Research and Development Memorandum, Stanford Center for Research and Development in Teaching. Stanford University.

————. 1979. *The Scientific Basis for the Art of Teaching.* New York: Teachers College Press.

Gage, N. L., ed. 1963. *Handbook of Research on Teaching.* Chicago: Rand McNally.

Gagné, Robert, et al. 1962. *Psychological Principles in System Development.* New York: Holt, Rinehart & Winston.

Gall, M. D. 1970. "The Use of Questions in Teaching." *Review of Educational Research,* 40:707–721.

Gall, M. D., and K. A. Crown. 1973. Research Design—Questioning Study (Minicourse H9). San Francisco, Calif. Far West Laboratory for Educational Research and Development.

Gilkeson, Elizabeth C., et al. 1981. "Bank Street Model: A Developmental-Interaction Approach," in *Making Schools More Effective: New Directions from Follow Through.* W. Ray Rhine, editor. New York: Academic.

Giroux, Henry A., Anthony N. Pena, and William F. Penir. 1981. *Curriculum and Instruction: Alternatives in Education.* Berkeley: McCutchan.

Getzels, Jacob W., and Herbert Thelen. 1960. "The Classroom Group as a Unique Social System," in *The Dynamics of Instructional Groups.* Nelson B. Henry, editor. The Fifty-ninth Yearbook of the National Society for the Study of Education. Chicago: The University of Chicago Press, 53–82.

Giacquinta, Joseph B. 1973. "The Process of Organizational Change in Schools." *Review of Research in Education, Vol. 1,* Fred N. Kerlinger, ed. Itasca, Ill.: F. E. Peacock, 178–208.

Glass, Gene. 1981. "Effectiveness of Special Education." Paper presented at the Wingspread Conference, Racine, Wisconsin, September 1981.

Glasser, William, 1965. *Reality Therapy.* New York: Harper & Row.

————. 1968. *Schools Without Failure.* New York: Harper & Row.

Goffman, Erving. 1961. *Asylums.* Garden City, N.Y.: Doubleday Anchor Books.

Good, T. L. 1979. "Teacher Effectiveness in the Elementary School: What We Know about it Now." *Journal of Teacher Education,* 30:52–64.

————. 1981. "Teacher Expectations and Student Perceptions: A Decade of Research." *Educational Leadership,* February: 415–422.

Goodlad, John I. 1967. *School Curriculum Reform.* New York: The Fund for the Advancement of Education.

————. 1975. *The Dynamics of Educational Change.* New York: McGraw-Hill.

————. 1979. *Curriculum Inquiry: The Study of Curriculum Practice.* New York: McGraw-Hill.

Goodlad, John I., and Robert Anderson. 1965. *The Nongraded Elementary School.* New York: Harcourt, Brace & World.

Goodlad, John I., and M. Francis Klein. 1970 *Looking Behind the Classroom Door.* Worthington, Ohio: Charles E. Jones.

Goodlad, John I., et al. 1974. *Toward a Mankind School: An Adventure in Humanistic Education.* New York: McGraw-Hill.

Gordon, Calvin Wayne. 1963. *Dimensions of Teacher Leadership in Classroom Social Systems: Pupil Effects on Productivity, Morality, and Compliance.* Los Angeles

Program on the Education of Teachers, Dept. of Education: University of California.

Gordon, William J. 1961. *Synectics*. New York: Harper & Row.

Green, P. S., ed. 1975. *The Language Laboratory in School*. New York: Oliver & Boyd.

Greene, M. 1973. *Teacher as Stranger*. New York Bureau of Publications, Teachers College, Columbia University Press.

Greenwood, Gordon, William B. Ware, Ira J. Gordon, and W. Ray Rhine. 1981. "Parent Education Model," in *Making Schools More Effective: New Directions from Follow Through*. W. Ray Rhine, ed. New York: Academic.

Gross, N., J. Giacquinta, and M. Bernstein. 1971. *Implementing Organizational Innovations: A Sociological Analysis of Planned Educational Change*. New York: Basic Books.

Guba, E. G., and C. A. Snyder. 1965. "Instructional Television and the Classroom Teacher." *AV Communication Review*, 13:5–26.

Guetzkow, Harold, et al. 1963. *Simulation in International Relations*. Englewood Cliffs, N.J.: Prentice-Hall.

Halfiker, Leo R. 1971. *A Profile of Innovative School Systems*. Center for Cognitive Learning, Wisconsin Research and Development, University of Wisconsin, Madison.

Hall, Gene E. 1977. "A Longitudinal Investigation of Individual Implications of Educational Innovations." Paper presented at the annual meeting of the American Educational Research Association. The R & D Center for Teacher Education, University of Texas, Austin, Texas.

———, et al. 1976. "Levels of Use of the Innovation: A Framework for Analyzing Innovation Adoption." *Journal of Teacher Education*, 26:52–56.

———, et al. 1980. "Implementation at the School Building Level: The Development and Analysis of Nine Mini Case Studies." Paper presented at the annual meeting of the American Educational Research Organization.

Hall, Gena E., and Susan F. Loucks. 1977. "A Developmental Model for Determining Whether the Treatment Is Actually Implemented." *American Educational Research Journal*, 14(3):263–76.

———. 1982. "Bridging the Gap: Policy Research Rooted in Practice," in *Policy Making in Education*. Ann Lieberman and Milbrey McLaughlin, eds. Chicago: University of Chicago Press.

Hamingson, D., ed. 1973. *Toward Judgment*. The Publications of the Evaluation Unit of the Humanities Curriculum Project, 1970–72. Norwich, United Kingdom: University of East Anglia.

Hansen, Carl. 1962. *Amidon*. Englewood Cliffs, N.J.: Prentice-Hall.

Hanson, R. A., and R. E. Schutz. 1978. "A New Look at Schooling Effects from Programmatic Research and Development," in *Making Change Happen?* Dale Mann, ed. New York: Teachers College Press.

Harnischfeger, Annegret, and D. E. Wiley. 1976. "The Teaching-Learning Process in Elementary Schools: A Synoptic View." *Curriculum Inquiry*, 6:5–43.

———.1975. *Achievement Test Score Decline: Do We Need to Worry?* Chicago: CEMREL.

Harvey, O. J., David E. Hunt, and Harold N. Schroder. 1961. *Conceptual Systems and Personality Organization*. New York: Wiley.

Hawley, Willis D., ed. 1981. *Effective School Desegregation*. Beverly Hills: Sage.

Heath, Robert W., ed. 1964. *The New Curricula*. New York: Harper & Row.

Herman, M. 1975. *Male-Female Achievement in Eight Learning Areas*. Denver, Colo.: Education Commission of the States.

Hernick, R., M. Molanda, and J. D. Russell. 1982. *Instructional Media and the New Technologies of Instruction*. New York: Wiley.

Herriott, N., and N. Gross. 1978. *The Dynamics of Planned Educational Change*. Berkeley: McCutchan.

Hersen, Michael, Richard M. Eisler, and Peter M. Miller. 1981. *Progress in Behavior Modification*. New York: Academic.

Hersh, R., "What Makes Some Schools and Teachers More Effective?," in *Nexus* 4(2):19–23.

Hocking, Elton. 1967. *Language Laboratory and Language Learning*. Department of Audiovisual Instruction, National Education Association of the United States.

Hoetker, James, and William Ahlbrand. 1969. "The Persistence of the Recitation." *American Educational Research Journal*, 6 (March):145–167.

Hofstadter, R. 1963. *Anti-Intellectualism in America*. New York: Knopf.

Holt, John. 1964. *How Children Fail*. New York: Pitman.

Homans, George C. 1950. *The Human Group*. Boston: Harcourt, Brace & World.

House, Ernest. 1974. *The Politics of Educational Innovation*. Berkeley: McCutchan.

———. 1981. "Three Perspectives on Innovation: Technologies, Political and Cultural," in *Improving Schools: Using What We Know*. Rolf Lehming and Michael Kane, eds. Beverly Hills: Sage.

House, Ernest, G. V. Glass, L. D. McLean, and D. F. Walker. 1978. "No Simple Answer: Critique of the Follow Through Evaluation." *Harvard Educational Review*, 48:128–160.

Howey, Kenneth. 1980. "Successful Schooling Practices: Perceptions of a Total School Faculty." San Francisco, Calif.: Far West Laboratory for Educational Research and Development.

Howey, Kenneth R., Sam Yarger, and Bruce Joyce. 1978. *Improving Teacher Education*. Washington, D.C.: Association of Teacher Educators.

Hullfish, Henry G., and Philip G. Smith. 1961. *Reflective Thinking: The Method of Education*. New York: Dodd, Mead.

Hunt, David E. 1970. "A Conceptual Level Matching Model for Coordinating Learner Characteristics with Educational Approaches." *Interchange*, 1(2):1–31.

———. 1970. "Matching Models in Education," in *Moral Education*. C. Beck, et al., eds. Toronto: University of Toronto Press.

———. 1971. *Matching Models in Education*. Toronto: Ontario Institute for Studies in Education.

Hunt, David E., B. R. Joyce, J. Greenwood, J. E. Noy, R. Reid, and M. Weil. 1974. "Student Conceptual Level and Models of Teaching: Theoretical and Empirical Coordination of Two Models." *Interchange*, 5:19–30.

Hunt, David E., and E. W. Sullivan. 1974. *Between Psychology and Education*. Hinsdale, Ill.: Dryden.

Hunt, Maurice P., and Lawrence E. Metcalf. 1955. *High School Social Studies: Problems in Reflective Thinking and Social Understanding.* New York: Harper & Row.

Hunt, J. McVey. 1963. *Intelligence and Experience.* New York: Ronald.

Hunter, Madeline. 1967. *Motivation Theory for Teachers.* El Segundo, Calif.: TIP Publications.

———. 1971. "The Learning Process," in *Handbook for Teachers.* Eli Seifman and Dweight Allen, eds. Glenview, Ill.: Scott-Foresman.

———. 1980. "Six Types of Supervisory Conferences." *Educational Leadership,* 37:408–412.

Hussén, Torsten, ed. 1967. *International Study of Achievement in Mathematics: Comparison of Twelve Countries, Vol. I and II.* New York: Wiley.

Hyreman, Charles S. 1959. *The Study of Politics: The Present State of American Political Science.* Urbana, Ill.: University of Illinois Press.

Ide, T. R. 1974. "The Potentials and Limitations of Television as an Educational Medium" in *Media and Symbols: The Forms of Expression, Communication and Education.* The Seventy-third Yearbook of the National Society for the Study of Education. David R. Olson, ed. Chicago: University of Chicago Press, 330–356.

Information Futures. 1977. *Educational Technology: The Alternative Futures.* Pullman, Wash.: Information Futures.

Institute for Research on Teaching. 1980. *Communication Quarterly,* vol. III, no. 2. East Lansing, Mich.: Michigan State University.

IPI. 1966. *Individually Prescribed Instruction: Mathematics Continuum.* Pittsburgh: University of Pittsburgh, Learning Research and Development Center.

Ivins, W. 1953. *Print and Visual Communication.* Cambridge, Mass.: Harvard University Press.

Jackson, Philip. 1966. *Life in Classrooms.* New York: Holt, Rinehart & Winston.

Jacob, Philip. 1956. *Changing Values in College.* New York: Harper & Row.

James, W. 1889. *Talks to Teachers on Psychology and to Students on Some of Life's Ideals.* New York: Holt.

———. 1939. Talks to Teachers on Psychology. New York: Holt.

Joyce, Bruce R. 1965. *Strategies for Elementary Social Science Education.* Chicago: Science Research Associates.

———. 1967. "Staff Utilization." *Review of Educational Research,* 37 (3):323–336.

———. 1972a. *New Strategies for Social Education.* Chicago: Science Research Associations.

———. 1972b. "Variations on a Systems Theme," in *Perspectives on Reform in Teacher Education.* Bruce Joyce and Marsha Weill, eds. Englewood Cliffs, N.J.: Prentice-Hall.

———. 1974. "Listening to Different Drummers: The Effect of Teaching on Learners," in *Assessment in Competency-Based Teacher Education.* R. Houston, ed. Berkeley: McCutchan.

———. 1978. *Involvement: A Study of Shared Governance of Teacher Education.* Washington, DC: ERIC Clearinghouse on Teacher Education.

———. 1980. "The Ecology of Staff Development." Paper presented to the annual meeting of the American Educational Research Association.

———. 1980. "The Social Ecology of the School: Dynamics of the Internal/External Systems." Paper presented to the annual meeting of the American Educational Research Association.

Joyce, Bruce R., Robert Bush, and Michael McKibbin. 1981a. "Information and Opinion from the California Staff Development Study: The Compact Report," Sacramento, Calif.: California State Department of Education.

———. 1981b. "Information and Opinion from the California Staff Development Study." Sacramento, Calif.: State Department of Education.

Joyce, Bruce R., et al. 1969. *The Teacher-Innovator*. A Report to the U.S. Office of Education, New York: Teachers College Press.

———. 1972. "Teacher Innovator System for Analyzing Skills and Strategies." Unpublished paper, Teachers College, Columbia University.

Joyce, Bruce R., and Berj Harootunian. 1967. *The Structure of Teaching*. Chicago: Science Research Associates.

Joyce, Bruce R., and E. Joyce. 1970. "The Creation of Information Systems for Children." *Interchange,* 7(2):111–12.

Joyce, Bruce R., and Michael McKibbin. 1980. "The Social Ecology of the South Bay School." Paper presented to the annual meeting of the American Educational Research Association, Boston.

———. 1982. "The Inner Curriculum of Staff Development," *Educational Leadership,* in press.

Joyce, Bruce R., and Greta Morine. 1976. *Creating the School*. Boston: Little, Brown.

Joyce, Bruce R., G. Morine, M. Weil, and R. Wald, eds. 1971. *Materials for Modules: A Classification of Competency-Oriented Tools for Teacher Education.* U.S. Office of Education.

Joyce, Bruce R., and B. Showers. 1980. "Improving Inservice Training: The Message of Research." *Educational Leadership,* 37(5):379–385.

———. 1981. Teacher Training Research: Working Hypothesis for Program Design and Directions for Further Study. Paper presented at the annual meeting of the American Educational Research Association, Los Angeles.

———.1982. "The Coaching of Teaching." *Educational Leadership,* vol. 40, no. 1.

Joyce, Bruce R., and Marsha Weil. 1972. *Perspectives for Reform in Teacher Education.* Englewood Cliffs, N.J.: Prentice-Hall.

———. 1980. *Models of Teaching,* 2d ed. Englewood Cliffs, N.J.: Prentice-Hall.

Joyce, Bruce R., M. Weil, and R. Wald. 1972. "The Training of Educators: A Structure for Pluralism." *Teachers College Record,* 73:371–91.

———. 1973. "The Teacher Innovator: Models of Teaching as the Core of Teacher Education." *Interchange* 4:27–60.

Joyce, Bruce R., Sam Yarger, and Kenneth Howey. 1977. *Preservice Teacher Education.* Palo Alto, Calif.: Consolidated Publications.

Karwelt, Nancy. 1976. "A Reanalysis of the Effect of Quantity of Schooling on Achievement." *Sociology of Education,* 49:236–246.

Katz, Daniel, and R. L. Kahn. 1966. *The Social Psychology of Organizations.* New York: Wiley.

Katz, Michael B. 1971. *Class, Bureaucracy and Schools.* New York: Praeger.

Kelly, G. A. 1955. *The Psychology of Personal Constructs.* New York: Norton.

Keniston, Kenneth. 1963. *The Uncommitted: Alienated Youth in American Society.* New York: Harcourt, Brace & World.

Kenworthy, Leonard S. 1955. *Introducing Children to the World.* New York: Harper & Row.

Kersh, B. Y. 1963. *Classroom Simulation.* Monmouth, Ore.: Teacher Research of the Oregon State System of Higher Education.

Kilpatrick, William Heard. 1951. *The Philosophy of Education.* New York: Macmillan.

Kimball, Solon T., and James E. McClellan, Jr. 1964. *Education and the New America.* New York: Vintage.

King, Arthur R., Jr., and John A. Brownell. 1966. *The Curriculum and the Disciplines of Knowledge.* New York: Wiley.

Kircher, S. E. 1975. "The Effectiveness of a Training Package on ESL Teachers in A B E Programs." MA Thesis, Colorado State University. ED 110 739.

Kirman, Joseph M., and Jack Goldberg. 1981. "Distance Education: Teacher Training via Live Television and Concurrent Group Telephone Conferencing." *Educational Technology*, April: 41.

Knapper, Christopher Kay. 1980. *Evaluating Instructional Technology.* New York: Wiley.

Knott, J., and A. Wildavsky. 1980. "If Dissemination is the Solution, What is the Problem? *Knowledge,* 1(4):537–78.

Kohlberg, Lawrence. 1966. "Moral Education in the Schools." *School Review,* 74:1–30.

———. 1976. "The Cognitive Developmental Approach to Moral Education," in *Moral Education. . .It Comes with the Territory.* David Purpel and Kevin Ryan, eds. Berkeley, Calif.: McCutchan.

Kormos, J. 1978. "Educator and Publisher Perceptions of Quality Curriculum and Instructional Materials during Declining Enrolments." Information Bulletin 18, Commision on Declining School Enrolment, Ministry of Education, Toronto, Canada.

Kozol, Jonathan. 1967. *Death at an Early Age.* Boston: Houghton Mifflin.

Leenders, M., and J. Erskine. 1978. *Case Research: The Case Writing Process.* School of Business, University of Western Ontario.

Lehming, Rolf, and Michael Kane. 1981. *Improving School: Using What We Know.* Beverly Hills: Sage.

Leithwood, K. 1980. "Alternative Procedures for Assessing the Nature and Degree of Program Implementation." Paper presented at the annual meeting of the Canadian Society for Studies in Education.

———. 1980. *Implementation Handbook.* Ontario Association of Education Administrative Officials.

———. 1981. "Dimensions of Curriculum Innovation." *Journal of Curriculum Studies,* 13(1):25–36.

Leithwood, K., and D. Montgomery. 1980. "Assumptions and Uses of a Procedure for Evaluating the Nature and Degree of Program Implementation." Paper presented at the Annual Meeting of the American Education Research Association.

————. 1980. "Evaluating Program Implementation." *Evaluation Review*, April.

Leonard, George B. 1966. "California: A New Game with New Rules." *Look*, 30(13):28–33.

Lewy, Arieh, ed. 1977. *Handbook of Curriculum Evaluation*. New York: Longman.

Lieberman, Ann, and Milbrey W. McLaughlin, eds. 1982. *Policy Making in Education*. Eighty-first Yearbook of the National Society for the Study of Education. Chicago: University of Chicago Press.

Lindner, Robert. 1954. *Rebel without a Cause.* New York: Grune & Stratton.

Lindvall, C. M., and John O. Bolvin. 1966. "The Project for Individually Prescribed Instruction." Oakleaf Project, unpublished manuscript. Pittsburgh: University of Pittsburgh: Learning Research and Development Center.

Lipham, James M. 1981. *Effective Principal, Effective School*. Reston, Va.: National Association of Secondary School Principals.

Lippitt, Ronald, and Robert Fox, directors. 1969. *Social Studies in the Elementary School*. Project supported by the United States Office of Education. Ann Arbor: University of Michigan.

Lorayne, Harry, and Jerry Lucas. 1974. *The Memory Book*. New York: Ballantine Books.

Lortie, Dan. 1975. *Schoolteacher*. Chicago: University of Chicago Press.

Loucks, S., and M. Melle. 1980. "District Wide Implementation of an Elementary School Science Curriculum: A Three Year Effort." Paper presented at the annual meeting of the American Education Research Association.

Lukas, C., and C. Wohlleb. 1970–71. *Implementation of Head Start Planned Variation: Part 1 & 2*. Cambridge, Mass.: Huron Institute.

Maccoby, E. E., and C. N. Jacklin. 1974. *The Psychology of Sex Differences*. Palo Alto, Calif.: Stanford University Press.

Madaus, George F., Peter W. Arasian, and Thomas Kellaghan. 1980. *School Effectiveness: A Reassessment of the Evidence*. New York: McGraw-Hill.

McClure, Robert, ed. 1971. *The Curriculum: Retrospect and Prospect*. The 70th Yearbook of the National Society for the Study of Education. Chicago: University of Chicago Press.

McDonald, B., and R. Walker, eds. 1974. *Innovation Evaluation, Research and the Problem of Control*. Norwich, United Kingdom: SAFARI-PROJECT, University of East Anglia.

McDonald, Frederick, 1976. *Beginning Teacher Evaluation Study: Phase II, 1973–74. Executive Summary Report*. Princeton, N.J.: Educational Testing Service.

McKibbin, Michael. 1982. *One Hundred Principals: Roles and Role Perceptions*. Palo Alto, Calif.: Booksend Laboratories.

McKibbin, Michael, and Bruce Joyce. 1980. "Psychological States and Staff Development." *Theory Into Practice*, 19(4):248–255.

McKibbin, S., A. Lieberman, and D. Degener, eds. 1981. *Using Knowledge for School Improvement: A Guide for Educators*. San Francisco, Calif.: Far West Laboratory for Educational Research and Development.

McLaughlin, M., and P. Marsh. 1978. "Staff Development and School Change." *Teachers College Record*, 86(1):69–94.

McLuhan, Marshall. 1964. *Understanding Media: The Extensions of Man.* New York: McGraw-Hill.

McNeil, John D. 1977. *Curriculum: A Comprehensive Introduction.* Boston: Little, Brown.

———. 1977. *Designing Curriculum: Self-Instructional Modules.* Boston: Little, Brown.

Mager, Robert F. 1962. *Preparing Objectives for Programmed Instruction.* Palo Alto, Calif.: Fearon.

Mailer, Norman. 1971. *Of a Fire on the Moon.* Boston: Little, Brown, 47–48.

Man: A Course of Study: Talks to Teachers. 1968. Cambridge, Mass: Education Development Center.

March, James G., ed. 1965. *Handbook of Organizations.* Chicago: Rand McNally.

Maslow, Abraham. 1962. *Toward a Psychology of Being.* Princeton: Van Nostrand.

Massialas, Byron, and Benjamin Cox. 1966. *Inquiry in Social Studies.* New York: McGraw-Hill.

Maxim, George W. 1977. *Learning Centers for Young Children.* New York: Hart.

Medley, D. 1977. *Teacher Competence and Teacher Effectiveness.* Washington, D.C.: AACTE.

Mertens, S. K., and S. J. Yarger. 1981. *Teacher Centers in Action.* Syracuse: Syracuse Area Teacher Center.

Meyer, H. H. 1975. "The Pay-for-Performance Dilemma." *Organizational Dynamics,* 3(3):39–50.

Miles, Matthew, ed. 1963. *Innovation in Education.* New York: Teachers College Press, Columbia University.

———. 1981. "Mapping the Common Properties of Schools," in *Improving Schools: Using What We Know.* Rolf Lehming and Michael Kane, eds. Beverly Hills: Sage.

Mill, John Stuart. 1947. *On Liberty.* New York: Appleton-Century-Crofts.

Mitchell, Lucy Sprague. 1950. *Our Children and Our Schools.* New York: Simon & Schuster.

Mohlman, G. G. 1982. "Assessing the Impact of Three Inservice Teacher Training Models." Paper presented at the annual meeting of the American Educational Research Association, New York.

Mohlman, G. G., T. Coladarci, and N. L. Gage. 1982. "Comprehension and Attitude as Predictors of Implementation of Teacher Training." *Journal of Teacher Education,* 33(1):31–36.

Murnane, R. J. 1980. "Interpreting the Evidence on School Effectiveness." Unpublished manuscript, Economics Department and Institution for Social Policy Studies, Yale University.

Murphy, Patricia D., and Marjorie M. Brown. 1970. "Conceptual Systems and Teaching Styles." *American Educational Research Journal,* 7, November:519–540.

Muth, John W., and Lawrence Senesh. 1977. *Constructing a Community System-Based Social Science Curriculum.* Boulder, Colo.: Social Science Education Consortium.

Myrdal, Gunnar. 1944. *The American Dilemma.* New York: Harper & Row.

National Education Association Project on the Instructional Program of the Public Schools. 1963. *Deciding What To Teach*. Ole Sand, director. Washington, D.C.: National Education Association.

Naumann, Etienne M. 1974. "Bringing about Open Education: Strategies for Innovation." Unpublished doctoral dissertation, University of Michigan.

Neill, A. S. 1960. *Summerhill*. New York: Holt, Rinehart & Winston.

Newcomb, Theodore. 1947. *Personality and Social Change*. New York: Harper & Row.

Noble, Pat. 1980. *Resource-Based Learning in Post-Compulsory Education*. London: Kegan Page.

Novotney, Jerrold M., and Kenneth A. Tye. 1973. *The Dynamics of Educational Leadership*, 2d ed. Los Angeles, Educational Resource Associates.

Oliver, Donald, and James P. Shaver. 1966. *Teaching Public Issues in the High School*. Boston: Houghton-Mifflin.

Olson, David R., ed. 1974. *Media and Symbols: The Forms of Expression, Communication and Education*. Seventy-third Yearbook of the National Society for the Study of Education. Chicago: University of Chicago Press.

Ontario Association of Education Administrative Officials. 1980. *Handbook on Implementation for Supervisory Officials*. OAEAO, Toronto.

Ontario Ministry of Education. 1979. "The Ontario Assessment Instrument Pool: A Curriculum-based Aid to Evaluation." *Review and Evaluation Bulletins*, 1(1).

Overly, Norman. 1970. *The Unstudied Curriculum*. Washington D.C.: Association for Supervision and Curriculum Development.

Palmer, Edward L. "Formative Research in the Production of Television for Children," in *Media and Symbols*, the seventy-third yearbook of the National Society for the Study of Education. David R. Olson, ed. Chicago: University of Chicago Press.

Parsons, Talcott. 1951. *The Social System*. Glencoe, Ill.: The Free Press.

Perls, Frederick. 1968. *Gestalt Therapy Verbatim*. Lafayette, Calif.: Real People.

Perls, Frederick, Ralph Hefferline, and Paul Goodman. 1968. *Gestalt Therapy*. New York: Julian.

Phenix, Philip. 1961. *Education and the Common Good*. New York: Harper & Row.

———. 1964. *Realms of Meaning: A Philosophy of the Curriculum for General Education*. New York: McGraw-Hill.

Piaget, Jean. 1952. *The Origins of Intelligence in Children*. New York: International Universities Press.

Pinar, Williams. 1974. *Heightened Consciousness, Cultural Revolution, and Curriculum Theory*. Berkeley: McCutchan.

———. 1975. *Curricular Theorizing: The Reconceptualists*. Berkeley: McCutchan.

Plato. 1945. *The Republic*. Frances MacDonald Cornford, trans. New York: Oxford University Press.

Podrebarac, G. R. 1981. "Establishing Future Educational Priorities." Address at the Canadian Association for Curriculum Studies, unpublished.

Popham, James W. 1975. *Educational Evaluation*. Englewood Cliffs, N.J.: Prentice-Hall.

Popham, James W., and E. L. Baker. 1970. *Systematic Instruction.* Englewood Cliffs, N.J.: Prentice-Hall.

Popham, James W., and John D. McNeil. 1965. "The Influence of Taped Instructional Programs on Certain Cognitive and Affective Behavior of Teachers." Paper presented to the annual meeting of the American Educational Research Association, Chicago.

Posner, George, and Alan N. Rudnitsky. 1978. *Course Design.* New York: Longman.

Pratt, David. 1980. *Curriculum: Design and Development.* New York: Harcourt Brace Jovanovich.

Preston, Ralph C. 1956. *Improving the Teaching of World Affairs.* Englewood Cliffs, N.J.: Prentice-Hall.

Ramp, Eugene A., and W. Ray Phine. 1981. "Behavior Analysis Model," in *Making Schools More Effective: New Directions from Follow Through.* W. Ray Rhine, ed. New York: Academic.

Reid, William A., and Decker F. Walker, eds. 1975. *Case Studies in Curriculum Change: Great Britain and the United States.* London: Routledge & Kegan Paul.

Resnick, Lauren, and Phyllis A. Weaver, eds. 1980. *Theory and Practice of Early Reading, Vols. 1, 2, 3.* Hillsdale, N.J.: Lawrence Erlbaum.

Rhine, W. Ray, ed. 1981. *Making Schools More Effective: New Directions from Follow Through.* New York: Academic.

Rimm, David C., and John C. Masters. 1974. *Behavior Therapy: Techniques and Empirical Findings.* New York: Academic.

Rist, R. 1970. "Student Social Class and Teacher Expectations: The Self-fulfilling Prophecy in Ghetto Education." *Harvard Educational Review,* 40:411–451.

Roberts, Arthur D., ed. 1975. *Educational Innovation: Alternatives in Curriculum and Instruction.* Boston: Allyn & Bacon.

Roberts, D. 1980. "Theory, Curriculum Development and the Unique Events of Practice," in *Seeing Curriculum in a New Light: Essays From Science Education.* H. Munby, G. Orphwood, and T. Russell, eds. Toronto, OISE.

Robinson, F. N.d. "Superordinate Curriculum Guidelines as Guides to Local Curriculum Decision-Making: An Ontario Case Study," in *Studies in Curriculum Decision-Making.* K. Leithwood, ed., forthcoming. Toronto, OISE.

———. 1978. "The Scope of Guideline Aims and Objectives." Information Bulletin 12, Commission on Declining School Enrolment, Ministry of Education, Toronto, Canada.

Rogers, Carl R. 1951. *Client-Centered Therapy: Its Current Practice.* Boston: Houghton Mifflin.

———. 1961. *On Becoming a Person.* Boston: Houghton Mifflin.

Rogers, Colin. 1982. *A Social Psychology of Schooling.* London: Routledge & Kegan Paul.

Rokeach, Milton S. 1960. *The Open and Closed Mind: Investigations into the Nature of Belief Systems and Personality Systems.* New York: Basic Books.

Rosenshine, B. V. 1971. *Teaching Behaviors and Student Achievement.* London: N.F.E.R.

————. 1976. "Recent Research on Teaching Behaviors and Student Achievement." *Journal of Teacher Education*, 27:61–65.

Rosenthal, R., and L. Jacobson. 1968. *Pygmalion in the Classroom*. New York: Holt, Rinehart & Winston.

Rousseau, Jean Jacques. 1933. *Emile*. New York: E. P. Dutton.

Rowe, Mary Budd. 1978. *Teaching Science as Continuous Inquiry*. New York: McGraw-Hill.

Rowntree, Derek. 1979. *Educational Technology in Curriculum Development*. New York: Harper & Row.

Rubin, Louis, ed. 1977. *Curriculum Handbook*. Boston: Allyn & Bacon.

Rugg, Harold, ed. 1927. *The Foundations and Technique of Curriculum Construction*. Twenty-sixth Yearbook of the National Society for the Study of Education. Chicago: University of Chicago Press.

Rushby, Nicholas, Jr. 1979. *Computers in the Teaching Process*. New York: Wiley.

Rutter, M., B. Maughan, P. Mortimore, J. Ouston, and A. Smith. 1979. *Fifteen Thousand Hours: Secondary Schools and Their Effects on Children*. Cambridge, Mass.: Harvard University Press.

Salter, A. 1949. "The Theory and Practice of Conditioned Reflex Therapy," in *Conditioning Therapies: The Challenge in Psychotherapy*. A. Salter, J. Wolpe, and L. J. Reyna, eds. New York: Holt, Rinehart & Winston.

Sampson, Anthony. 1965. *Anatomy of Britain Today*. New York: Harper & Row.

Santayana, George. 1896. *The Sense of Beauty: Being the Outlines of Aesthetic Theory*. New York: Scribner's.

Sarason, Seymour B. 1972. *Creation of Settings and the Future Societies*. San Francisco: Jossey-Bass.

Scanlon, Robert. 1966. *Individually Prescribed Instruction*. Philadelphia, Pa.: Research for Better Schools.

Scanlon, Robert, and Mary Brown. 1966. "In-Service Education for Individualized Instruction." Unpublished manuscript. Philadelphia. Pa.: Research for Better Schools.

Schaefer, Robert J. 1967. *The School as a Center of Inquiry*. New York: Harper & Row.

Schaffarzick, Jan, and David H. Hampson, eds. 1975. *Strategies for Curriculum Development*. Berkeley: McCutchan.

Schmuck, Richard, Philip Runkel, Jane Arends, and Richard Arends. 1977. *The Second Handbook of Organizational Development in Schools*. Palo Alto, Calif.: Mayfield.

Schramm, Wilbur. 1977. *Big Media, Little Media: Tools and Technology for Instruction*. Beverly Hills: Sage.

Schroder, Harold M., Marvin Driver, and Sigmund Streufert. 1967. *Information Processing in Individuals and Groups*. New York: Holt, Rinehart & Winston.

Schutz, William. 1958. *FIRO: A Three-Dimensional Theory of Interpersonal Behavior*. New York: Holt, Rinehart & Winston.

————. 1967. *Joy: Expanding Human Awareness*. New York: Grove.

Schwab, Joseph, and Paul Brandwein. 1962. *The Teaching of Science*. Cambridge, Mass.: Harvard University Press.

Schwab, Joseph, ed. 1963. *The Biology Teachers Handbook*. New York: Wiley.

Sealey, Leonard. 1977. *Open Education: A Study*. New Haven, Conn.: The Edward W. Hazen Foundation.

Shaftel, Fannie R., and George Shaftel. 1967. Role-Playing for Social Values: Decision Making in the Social Studies. Englewood Cliffs, N.J.: Prentice-Hall.

Shane, Harold G., ed. 1977. *Curriculum Change Toward the 21st Century*. Washington, D.C.: National Education Association.

Sherif, Muzafer. 1952. "Group Influences upon the Formation of Norms and Attitudes," in *Readings in Social Psychology*. George Swanson, Theodore Newcomb, and Eugene L. Hartley, eds. New York: Holt, Rinehart & Winston.

Shirer, William L. 1960. *The Rise and Fall of the Third Reich*. New York: Simon & Schuster.

Sigel, Irving E. 1969. "The Piagetian System and the World of Education," in *Studies in Cognitive Development*. David Elkind and John Flavell, eds. New York: Oxford University Press.

Skinner, B. F. 1953. *Science and Human Behavior*. New York: Macmillan.

———. 1957. *Verbal Behavior*. New York: Appleton-Century-Crofts.

———. 1968. *The Technology of Teaching*. New York: Appleton-Century-Crofts.

Smith, B. O. 1969. *Teachers for the Real World* (Task Force reprint). Washington, D.C.: American Association of Colleges for Teacher Education.

Smith, Karl U., and Margaret Foltz Smith. 1966. *Cybernetic Principles of Learning and Educational Design*. New York: Holt, Rinehart & Winston.

Smith, Louis. 1967. *Social Psychological Aspects of School Building Design*. A report to the United States Office of Education. St. Louis, Mo.: Washington University.

Smith, Louis, and William Geoffrey. 1968. *The Complexities of the Urban Classroom*. New York: Wiley.

Smith, Louis, and Pat M. Keith. 1971. *Anatomy of Educational Innovation: An Organizational Analysis of an Elementary School*. New York: Wiley.

Snyder, Benson. 1971. *The Hidden Curriculum*. New York: Knopf.

Sprague-Mitchell, Lucy. 1950. *Our Children and Our Schools*. New York: Simon & Schuster.

Squires, David A. 1980. *Characteristics of Effective Schools: The Importance of School Processes*. Philadelphia: Research for Better Schools. ED 197 486.

Stallings, Jane. 1979. "How to Change the Process of Teaching Reading in Secondary Schools." Menlo Park, Calif.: SRI International.

———. 1979. "How to Change the Process of Teaching Basic Reading Skills in Secondary Schools: Executive Summary." Menlo Park, Calif.: SRI International.

———. 1980. "Allocated Academic Learning Time Revisited or beyond Time on Task." *Educational Researcher*, 9:11–16.

Stallings, Jane, and D. H. Kaskowitz. *Follow Through Classroom Observation Evaluation, 1972–1973*. Menlo Park, Calif.: Stanford Research Institute.

Stauffer, Russell G. 1970. *The Language-Experience Approach to the Teaching of Reading*. New York: Harper & Row.

Stollard, George W. 1961. *The Dual Progress Plan*. New York: Harper & Row.

Suchman, Richard. 1962. "The Elementary School Training Program in Scientific Inquiry." Report of the U.S. Office of Education Project title VIII, Project 216. Urbana, Ill.: University of Illinois.

Sullivan, Edmund. 1967. "Piaget and the School Curriculum: A Critical Appraisal," Bulletin No. 2 Toronto: Ontario Institute for Studies in Education.

Taba, Hilda. 1952. *Intergroup Education in Public Schools*. Washington, D.C.: American Council on Education.

———. 1962. *Curriculum Development*. New York: Harcourt, Brace & World.

———. 1964. *Thinking in Elementary School Children*. San Francisco: San Francisco State College.

———. 1966. *Teaching Strategies and Cognitive Functioning in Elementary School Children*. Cooperative Research Project 2404. San Francisco: San Francisco State College.

———. 1967. *Teachers Handbook for Elementary Social Studies*. Palo Alto, Calif.: Addison-Wesley.

Taba, Hilda, S. Levine, and F. Ellzey. 1964. *Thinking in Elementary School*. Cooperative Research Project No. 1574. San Francisco: San Francisco State College.

Tanner, Daniel, and Laurel N. Tanner. 1980. *Curriculum Development: Theory into Practice*. New York: Macmillan.

Taylor, Calvin, ed. 1964. *Creativity: Progress and Potential*. New York: McGraw-Hill.

Temkin, Sanford, ed. 1974. *What Do Research Findings Say about Getting Innovations into Schools: A Symposium*. Philadelphia: Research for Better Schools.

Terry, James V., and Robert D. Hess. 1975. *The Urban/Rural School Development Program: An Examination of a Federal Model for Achieving Parity between Schools and Community*. Stanford, Calif.: Stanford University.

Thelen, Herbert A. 1967. *Classroom Grouping for Teachability*. New York: Wiley.

———. 1981. *The Classroom Society*. New York: Wiley.

———. 1954. *Dynamics of Groups at Work*. Chicago: University of Chicago Press.

———. 1960. *Education and the Human Quest*. New York: Harper & Row.

Thoresen, C. ed. 1973. *Behavior Modification in Education*. Chicago: NSSE Yearbook, University of Chicago Press.

Toffler, Alvin. 1970. *Future Shock*. New York: Random House.

Tomlinson, Tommy M. May 1980. "Student Ability, Student Background and Student Achievement: Another Look at Life in Effective Schools." Paper presented at Conference on Effective Schools, Educational Testing Service, New York, May 1980.

Torrance, E. Paul. 1965. *Gifted Children in the Classroom*. New York: Macmillan.

———. 1962. *Guiding Creative Talent*. Englewood Cliffs, N.J.: Prentice-Hall.

Tye, Kenneth A., and Jerrold M. Novotney. 1975. *Schools in Transition: The Practitioner as Change Agent*. I/D/E/A Reports on Schooling. New York: McGraw-Hill.

Tyler, Ralph W. 1950. *Basic Principles of Curriculum and Instruction*. Chicago: University of Chicago Press.

Waller, Willard. 1965. *The Sociology of Teaching.* New York: Wiley. Originally published in 1932.

Watson, Goodwin, ed. 1967. *Change in School Systems.* Washington, D.C.: National Education Association.

Weatherley, R. 1979. *Reforming Special Education: Policy Implementation from State Level to Street Level.* Cambridge Mass.: MIT Press.

Weber, G. 1971. "Inner City Children can be Taught to Read: Four Successful Schools." Occasional Papers, No. 18 Washington, D.C.: Council for Basic Education.

Weber, Max. 1947. *The Theory of Social and Economic Organization.* New York: Oxford University Press.

Weikart, David P., Charles F. Hohmann, and W. Ray Rhine. 1981. "High/Scope Cognitively-Oriented Curriculum Model," in *Making Schools More Effective: New Directions from Follow Through.* W. Ray Rhine, ed. New York: Academic.

Weiss, Iris R. 1978. "1977 National Survey of Science, Mathematics, and Social Studies Education." Washington, D.C.: United States Government Printing Office.

Werner, W. 1980. "Implementation as Belief." Faculty of Education, University of British Columbia.

———. 1981. "An Interpretive Approach to Curriculum Implementation," Unpublished paper, Vancouver, B.C.: University of British Columbia, Canada.

Wertheimer, Max. 1945. *Productive Thinking.* New York: Harper & Row.

Wheeler, R. F. 1981. *Rethinking Mathematical Concepts.* New York: Wiley.

White, Leslie. 1949. *The Science of Culture.* New York: Farrar, Straus.

Williams, Richard C., Charles C. Wall, W. Michael Martin, and Arthur Berchin. 1974. "Effecting Organizational Renewal in Schools: A Social Systems Perspective." IDEA Reports on Schooling. New York: McGraw-Hill.

Willis, Charles L. 1974. "What We Have Learned about the IDEA Change Program for Individually Guided Education: An Interim Report." A Charles F. Kettering Foundation Program, I/D/E/A. Dayton, Ohio.

Wilson, L. Craig. 1971. *The Open-Access Curriculum.* Boston: Allyn-Bacon.

Wolf, R. M. 1979. "Achievement in the United States," in *Educational Environment and Effects.* H. J. Walberg, ed. Berkeley: McCutchan.

Wolpe, J. 1958. *Psychotherapy by Reciprocal Inhibition.* Stanford, Calif.: Stanford University Press.

———. 1969. *The Practice of Behavior Therapy.* Oxford: Pergamon.

Wolpe, J. and Arnold A. Lazarus. 1966. *Behavior Therapy Techniques: A Guide to the Treatment of Neuroses.* Oxford: Pergamon.

Worthen, Blaine R. 1968. "A Study of Discovery and Expository Presentation: Implications for Teaching." *Journal of Teacher Education,* 19:223–242.

Wynn, Edward A. 1980. *Looking at Schools: Good, Bad and Indifferent.* Lexington, Mass.: D. C. Heath.

Yarger, Sam, et al. 1980. Inservice Teacher Education. Palo Alto, Calif.: Booksend Laboratory.

Zaltman, G., R. Duncan, and J. Holbek. 1973. *Innovation and Organizations.* New York: Wiley.

Index